Advanced Pr

"Pay not attention

wrote Napoleon. But how does one conjure up courage without method, inspiration and direction? That's where *Guts, Smarts & Love* leads the charge."

—Mark Will-Weber, author of *Mint Juleps with Teddy Roosevelt*

"Sacchetti is like Ranger Superman, the class guy who never quits & never surrenders."

—Damon Feldman, Founder of Celebrity Boxing

"Ranger school? It's the best life insurance policy in the world: just think of how many soldiers are alive today because they had a Ranger like Joe Sacchetti leading them. Read on and learn!"

—Rick Merritt, 14th Command Sergeant Major of the 75th Ranger Regiment

"Leadership skills that can't be ignored when your teachers are real-life, battle tested heroes!"

—Mark J. Silverman, author of *Only 10s;* and the Mastering Midlife Podcast

"A beautiful tribute to our military! This book has captured in words what gives me the inspiration and admiration I have when writing music!"

—Country Music recording star **Jessie G,** singer of the hit single 'Army Ranger'

"Spending time with these Army Rangers is exciting, instructive and emotional. It's fantastic to have a connection to real people striving to accomplish extraordinary Ranger missions and to see how they bring those leadership lessons home."

—Brace Barber, author of *Ranger School, No Excuse Leadership*

"This book makes us all believers in the Brotherhood of Heroes!"

—**Tony Degliomini,** author of *Believe Like Me*

"At last, a true war-fighter has described how the Ranger Creed assimilates to leadership principles . . . from all ranks and skill sets — makes this work the best of the best."

—**Colonel Dominic J. Caraccilo,** author of books on Military Strategy and History

"Leaders at every level and industry need to read this book to see what true leadership looks like."

—**Andrew Sheehan,** author of *Freedom 1-3: An Army Ranger's Journey to True Freedom*

"Gracious. Long overdue… Not only for the the troops, but for the public."

—**Camille Harper Deal,** Founder of Homegrown Happiness Co.

"Captain Joe Sacchetti 'walks the walk' with heart-moving stories on how to take tactical command of your life."

—**Brian Lahoue,** author of *Deal With It!*

"Joe gets it right from the first page, powerfully teaching with high stress examples of "walking the walk". A must have for every leader's library!"

—**LTC Paul Carroll,** Professor of Military Science, Johns Hopkins University

"This exceptional man endured where so many failed. Great read, perfect!"

—**Daniel Pope,** author of *The Adventures of Dayne Traveler*

GUTS SMARTS & LOVE

GUTS SMARTS & LOVE

LIVE YOUR LIFE THE **ARMY RANGER** WAY

JOE SACCHETTI

DUDLEY COURT PRESS
SONOITA, AZ

Published by Dudley Court Press
www.DudleyCourtPress.com

Publisher's Cataloging-in-Publication Data
Names: Sacchetti, Joe, author.
Title: Guts, smarts & love : live your life the Army Ranger way / Captain Joe Sacchetti.
Description: Sonoita, AZ : Dudley Court Press, [2021] | Includes index.
Identifiers: ISBN: 978-1-940013-83-1 (paper)
978-1-940013-82-4 (ebook)
LCCN: 2020910627

Subjects: LCSH: Leadership. | Success in business. | Conduct of life. | Self-realization.
Self-actualization (Psychology) | Motivation (Psychology) | United States. Army—
Commandotroops—Training of. | Military education.
BISAC: BUSINESS & ECONOMICS /Leadership.
BUSINESS & ECONOMICS / Motivational.
SELF-HELP / Personal Growth/ Success.

Classification: LCC: HD57.7 .S23 2021
DDC: 658.4/092--dc23

Cover and interior design by Dunn+Associates, www.Dunn-Design.com

To connect with Joe Sacchetti, please visit www.ArmyRangeratMIT.com

To three fantastic sons—

Joey, Jake, and Dustin—

my best friends and

fellow world travelers . . .

Life is a storm, my young friend.
Bask in the sunlight one moment,
be shattered on the rocks the next.
What makes you a leader is
what you do when that storm comes.
You must look into that storm and shout,
"Do your worst, for I will do mine!"
Then the fates will know you
as we know you: as a Ranger!

Contents

Foreword: Command Sergeant Major Rick Merritt, Ranger Regiment . . . 1

The Ranger Creed . . . 3

Introduction . . . 5

Prologue: You're Not Big Enough . . . 7

Chapter 1: "R" . . . 9

Walking the Walk *Staff Sergeant (SSG) Jimmy Patton* . . . 11

Relating to Your Peers *Staff Sergeant (SSG) Andrew "Andy" Sheehan* . . . 15

Positioning Your Team for Survival *Staff Sergeant (SSG) Jimmy Patton* . . . 18

Inspiring Grit *Command Sergeant Major (CSM) Rick Merritt* . . . 22

Being "On-Mission" with My Boys *Staff Sergeant (SSG) Jimmy Patton* . . . 28

Honoring the Fallen *Staff Sergeant (SSG) Jimmy Patton* . . . 35

Celebrating Life *Sheila Patton (Gold Star Mom)* . . . 37

Rebuilding What Has Crumbled *Colonel (COL) Dominic Caraccilo* . . . 42

Pressing the Advantage *Colonel (COL) Dominic Caraccilo* . . . 44

Bridging the Gap *Colonel (COL) Dominic Caraccilo* . . . 47

Mentoring from the Middle *Staff Sergeant (SSG) Jim "Bull" Bullock* . . . 50

Prevailing with a Cool Head
Staff Sergeant (SSG) Jim "Bull" Bullock 54

Understanding the Warrior
Staff Sergeant (SSG) Jim "Bull" Bullock 59

Being Happy for Others' Success
Specialist (SPC) Andrew Siemer 61

Answering the Call *Operator Billy Mac* 63

Making Progress Out on the Edges *Operator Billy Mac* 65

Marketing Ourselves for Success
Master Sergeant (MSG) Dave Maestas 67

Chapter 2: "A" 71

Heroes Aren't Born, They're Tabbed *Rangers Lore* 73

Knowing the Only Way to Get There *Rangers in School* 77

Becoming an Army of One *Rangers in School* 83

First Man through the Door *Rangers in the Desert* 87

The Mission's Not Quite Over until the Debriefing
Rangers in the Desert 98

Taking Ten When It's Offered *Rangers in the Desert* 101

Poking a Stick at Yourself *Rangers in the Desert* 105

Promoting Your People to the Universe *Rangers in the Desert* 110

Learning from Experts Who Work for You
Sergeant (SGT) Scott Mandeville 115

Making a Positive First Impression
Master Sergeant (MSG) Ralph "Ike" Jackson 120

Chapter 3: "N" 123

Just Ask Me *Command Sergeant Major (CSM) Donovan Watts* .. 125

Choosing Yard Dog over Porch Dog
Command Sergeant Major (CSM) Donovan Watts 128

Diversifying *Colonel (COL) Christian Karsner* 132

Sending a Cordial Invite of Trust
Colonel (COL) Christian Karsner 134

Contributing to Doctrine *Colonel (COL) Christian Karsner* 136

Applying Wisdom *Colonel (COL) Christian Karsner* 139

Letting People Inspire You
Master Sergeant (MSG) Al "Action" Akers 141

Solving Asymmetric Challenges
Master Sergeant (MSG) Al "Action" Akers 143

Going Where You're Needed
Master Sergeant (MSG) Al "Action" Akers 145

Not Being Shy *Command Sergeant Major (CSM) William "Monty" Montgomery* 150

Building It If It Ain't Built Yet *Command Sergeant Major (CSM) William "Monty" Montgomery* 155

Giving Wise Counsel *Command Sergeant Major (CSM) William "Monty" Montgomery* 159

Fighting as You Train *Sergeant Major (SGM) Jeffrey Koenig* 164

Moving Up and Up *Sergeant Major (SGM) Jeffrey Koenig* 165

Overcoming Limitations *Sergeant Major (SGM) Jeffrey Koenig* .. 168

Walking Among Heroes *Sergeant Major (SGM) Jeffrey Koenig* .. 172

Staying Young Enough for New Tricks
First Sergeant (1SG) John "Roses" Rowe 175

Appreciating a Comeback Story
First Sergeant (1SG) John "Roses" Rowe 178

Being the Hero of Your Own Story
Staff Sergeant (SSG) Chris "Merc" Mercadante 180

Chapter 4: "G" 185

Creating a Persona
Sergeant (SGT) Panagiotis "G-Man" Giannakakos 187

Motivating Outrageously
Sergeant (SGT) Panagiotis "G-Man" Giannakakos 190

Rewarding Those Who Shine
Sergeant (SGT) Panagiotis "G-Man" Giannakakos 195

Having the Brass
Sergeant (SGT) Panagiotis "G-Man" Giannakakos 198

Ushering In Workplace Morale
Sergeant (SGT) Panagiotis "G-Man" Giannakakos 204

Assuming Permission *Colonel (COL) Jim "Mac" McCloskey* 207

(Not) Sneezing in the Ambush
Colonel (COL) Jim "Mac" McCloskey 210

Coming Back to Teach *Colonel (COL) Jim "Mac" McCloskey* ... 213

Protecting the "Flock"
Command Sergeant Major (CSM) Greg Patton 217

Standing Up for What You Believe
Command Sergeant Major (CSM) Greg Patton 220

Rising from the Ashes
Command Sergeant Major (CSM) Greg Patton 223

Being Accountable
Command Sergeant Major (CSM) Greg Patton 225

Connecting *Command Sergeant Major (CSM) Greg Patton* 227

Improvising *Command Sergeant Major (CSM) Greg Patton* 231

Being a Part of Something Big
Staff Sergeant (SSG) Doug Quitmeyer 233

Watching Your Six *Staff Sergeant (SSG) Doug Quitmeyer* 238

Chapter 5: "E" 241

Being Extraordinarily Creative
Master Sergeant (MSG) Dave "The Mexican" Cardenas 243

Evaluating ROI
Master Sergeant (MSG) Dave "The Mexican" Cardenas 246

(Not) Doing It for Money
Master Sergeant (MSG) Dave "The Mexican" Cardenas 248

Waxing Poetic
Master Sergeant (MSG) Dave "The Mexican" Cardenas 250

Choosing ROI over Personal Risk *The Mindset of the Ranger* . . 254

Competing for What You Want *The Mindset of the Ranger* 260

Empowering Teams *The Mindset of the Ranger*
Staff Sergeant (SSG) Noel Cantu 265

Creating Mystique for Your Brand *The Mindset of the Ranger* . . 268

Upholding the Ranger Creed *The Mindset of the Ranger* 275

Keeping Them Safe *The Mindset of the Ranger* 278

Topping the Charts *Corporal (CPL) Todd Williams* 282

Thinking Fast on Your Feet *Corporal (CPL) Todd Williams* 284

Nipping Problems in the Bud *Corporal (CPL) Todd Williams* . . 287

Recognizing Expertise *Corporal (CPL) Dave Lafaver* 290

Accepting That Stuff Happens *Corporal (CPL) Dave Lafaver* . . . 293

Being Authentic *Master Sergeant (MSG) Joe "Trapper" Brewer* . . 295

Bringing Factions Together
Master Sergeant (MSG) Joe "Trapper" Brewer 298

Staying True to the Cause
Master Sergeant (MSG) Joe "Trapper" Brewer 301

Creating a Higher Purpose
Master Sergeant (MSG) Joe "Trapper" Brewer 305

Chapter 6: "R" 307

Punching Above Your Weight *Rangers with Fists*
Command Sergeant Major (CSM) Aubrey Butts 309

Seizing the Chance for Greatness *Rangers with Fists*
Command Sergeant Major (CSM) Aubrey Butts 314

Volunteering for a Galvanizing Event *Rangers with Fists* 316

Getting Up When You Get Knocked Down
Rangers with Fists – Smokin' Joe 319

Praising It Forward *Colonel (COL) Brad Nelson* 322

Highlighting Others' Successes *Colonel (COL) Brad Nelson* 325

Putting Your Money on the Underdog
Master Sergeant (MSG) Arthur "Hard Art" Kakis 327

Protecting and Delivering
Master Sergeant (MSG) Arthur "Hard Art" Kakis 330

But Nothing *Master Sergeant (MSG) Dale "Onion" Roberts* 334

Gathering from Great Sources *Desert Storm Rangers* 339

Guts, Smarts & Love Epilogue 345

Acknowledgments 347

Index 349

Captain Joe Sacchetti 354

Foreword

CSM Rick Merritt, 14th Command Sergeant Major of the 75th Ranger Regiment:

Command Sergeant Major (CSM) Rick Merritt's career totaled 35 years in the military with an unheard-of five total calendar years of combat and over 1500 raids (I love that old-school term for missions). He spent 25 years of his career in the Ranger Regiment and earned the reputation as the most hardcore sergeant ever to wear the Ranger tab. Once as a young leader, he showed up to a 5-mile run barefoot and outpaced nearly everyone in the formation — the hardcore legend was born. He was OK with adding weight too. In the Georgia heat with a forty-five-pound rucksack and boots while joining his Rangers competing for their Expert Infantryman's Badge, he set the 12-mile course record in one hour forty-six minutes (8:52 per mile in full gear). Privates and colonels alike looked up to him as a legend right in their midst.

For seven straight years as senior advisor to the ranger commander on the ground, he powered through an aggressive schedule most COOs would not be able to handle for more than a month. In-country, he rotated with each joint strike force for a week (more than 10 of them) and accompanied them on their missions. Then, he would reverse cycle his sleep to spend some time with the support troops and staff, and he held that Olympic pace for nearly a decade.

CSM Rick Merritt:

The famed US Army Rangers have been on continuous deployment for an incredible nineteen straight years battling the Global War on Terrorism. For that entire time, the Rangers have fought in multiple countries, most heavily in Iraq and Afghanistan. It's a marvel of Ranger leadership to stay as frosty as possible year after year. Rangers are pushed hard from the moment they land, averaging 100 missions via chopper, Stryker, or fast-rope in their 3-5 months, and then each Ranger battalion of the three rotate out while another takes its place. Its success is sure to be marked as legendary in the history of warfare for sustained ability to perform, re-set, and return.

After four decades of serving this grand nation of ours with love, I retired a content servant leader, knowing that we are in good hands, and I'm sure of one thing. The Ranger Regiment is the world's greatest leadership factory. Everyone has to meet the *same standards* and must prove themselves *every day.* And troops see us doing it because we're doing it with them.

If you love the thrill of Ranger training and seek the most exceptional glimpse of all things "Ranger" you will ever find, then read on to Ranger Joe Sacchetti's exquisite, poignant, and insightful profiles of everyday heroes, called US Army Rangers, and the leadership principles they embody. Rangers like Captain Sacchetti lead the way.

Hooh-ah!

CSM Rick Merritt
Former Command Sergeant Major of the 75th Ranger Regiment; 10th Mountain Division; and 8th Army, Korea
Awarded the Distinguished Service Medal, Legion of Merit, and the Bronze Star; veteran of Panama, Somalia, Iraq, and Afghanistan

The Ranger Creed

The Ranger Creed is the iconic six-paragraph mantra conceived in 1974 that all new candidates must memorize. It captures a mental checklist for their success and much, much more. Over the past half century, it has become a professional guidepost for Rangers to lead their lives. It reaches down into the soul and demands superhuman dedication.

The first letter to each of the creed's six paragraphs initiates a pivotal component to the elite mental state required of an Army Ranger. Try reading it now and then make sure to glance back again at the end of the book and see if it still means the same to you. You may find it leaps off the page at you next time around.

R-A-N-G-E-R

Recognizing that I volunteered as a Ranger, fully knowing the hazards of my chosen profession, I will always endeavor to uphold the prestige, honor, and esprit de corps of the Rangers.

Acknowledging the fact that a Ranger is a more elite soldier who arrives at the cutting edge of battle by land, sea, or air, I accept the fact that as a Ranger my country expects me to move farther, faster, and fight harder than any other soldier.

Never shall I fail my comrades. I will always keep myself mentally alert, physically strong, and morally straight, and I will shoulder more than my share of the task, whatever it may be, one hundred percent and then some.

Gallantly will I show the world that I am a specially selected and well trained soldier. My courtesy to superior officers, neatness of dress, and care for equipment shall set the example for others to follow.

Energetically will I meet the enemies of my country. I shall defeat them on the field of battle for I am better trained and will fight with all my might. Surrender is not a Ranger word. I will never leave a fallen comrade to fall into the hands of the enemy and under no circumstances will I ever embarrass my country.

Readily will I display the intestinal fortitude required to fight on to the Ranger objective and complete the mission, though I be the lone survivor.

Rangers Lead the Way!

Introduction

This book openly explores the relationship of the leadership principles that guide both battle and business. The tricky part is simulating the fire needed to forge the selected principles. To that end, most readers won't ever have the opportunity to live through Ranger School and see battle, but they can read this handbook of guiding ideals extracted from both of those agonizing experiences. These ideals, distilled into crisp chapters, are presented here.

Each chapter highlights a leadership principle, illustrated through real-life stories of Army Rangers I had the privilege of serving with over the past few decades. You'll come to know and love those featured here. Some of their stories will make you laugh, and some will make you cry. These Rangers will likely become like family.

Some chapters have colorful titles—perhaps because the nature of the related guiding principle is itself colorful. Life frequently bucks against giving easy answers. They're often complex. Fear not, each chapter begins and ends with a primer and recap of its relevance to the business leader. And as you'd expect, how they relate to the combat leader will leap out at you from the accompanying story.

The title *Guts, Smarts, & Love* plays on the multiple layers of meaning of the words. For the heroes portrayed in the stories you'll read, the nature of Rangerhood starts by leading self beyond the breaking point. It then expands to leading other super-Rangers in the crucible of war. Finally, it sets an example remarkable enough to be revered as "the best of the best." Those with the guts, smarts & love to make a profound difference in the lives of their brothers are the ones you'll read about.

The stories and the people you'll meet are not invented; we lived through it all. Names are real; characters are flesh and blood. Their courage and insight offer a lifetime of leadership lessons. I really didn't want to write about me; I just happen to be the thread of continuity that connects them all.

There are three things you won't see in this book: negativity, off-color situations, or gratuitous blood and guts. These are distracting to the message, so I have plucked them out. It's not that I've sanitized their stories to make them palatable for the fainthearted. Rather, I've chosen to stay on-theme and bring you the Rangers' best leadership principles.

I promise you won't be overwhelmed with any distracting military jargon—no mysterious acronyms. If the story calls for it, I explain it and keep moving. I hope you'll feel like you're serving alongside the outstanding people you're about to meet in the following pages. You'll also net a good primer on what's been happening over the past 50 years from a military insider's point of view.

Today's elite military forces play a prominent role in the power psyche of young America. We want to be like them and admire how they channel their superpowers. The energized demographic at home craves to learn what they learn and know what they know. By reading the experiences of real Rangers, that's now possible—minus the hunger and the gunfire. Along the way, you'll encounter some of America's best. Their counterparts probably live right down the street from you.

The leadership principles these Rangers had to learn through trial and error will make sense to anyone building a foundation as a leader in the business world—or in life. If that is you, welcome to *Guts, Smarts & Love.*

Prologue: You're Not Big Enough

All your life, you might hear, "You and your team aren't strong enough; you're not big or nimble enough." U.S. Army Rangers, especially, hear this all the time. "Boys, we're outnumbered, we're outgunned. We have to hold this piece of ground until reinforcements get here." Or you might hear five words that most humans could never imagine without experiencing meltdown: "Rangers, we're on our own."

Maybe what drives them to such superhuman places is to prove to themselves—and the rest of the world—that a higher level can be reached. It's a plateau that requires relentless dedication and never giving up, as in never-ever-ever giving up. That's one of the many gritty lessons I learned from surrounding myself with United States Army Rangers.

The battlefield is a tough place to be, and kudos to Hollywood film makers for showing the world how our troops perform under conditions of hell. Their heroism and sacrifice are often beautifully expressed on screen. But films need to cram everything into two hours. Unlike the movies, troops pinned down by gunfire, wounded, low on ammo, and out of food and water don't vault ahead to the next scene 24 hours later for the final gut-wrenching attack. Rather, they live every one of those minutes fiercely using their skills to fight the enemy and keep their buddies alive.

Try the following leadership exercise: Close your eyes and imagine a time when you were the thirstiest you have ever been in your life. Your mouth opens and closes to suck in only heated, dusty air. Now, recall a time when you were the most tired you've ever been—pulling an all-nighter for an exam or running an ultramarathon race in the 30th hour. You can barely keep your eyes open, and your head splits with pain at the slightest noise. Almost there.

Keep your eyes closed for just another moment. Look down along your body and relive an ache from a time when you broke an arm, fell down the stairs, or banged your head so hard you got a concussion. Or perhaps when you were stabbed or shot. Finally, add a filthy bandage that doesn't quite stop the bleeding.

Now, wake up to the world spinning fast with explosions in front of and behind you. Wounded men in this calamitous scene are looking to you for calm direction and knowledge about what move to make next to keep everyone alive.

This is the life of a U.S. Army Airborne Ranger.

CHAPTER ONE

Recognizing

that I volunteered

as a Ranger,

fully knowing the

hazards of my

chosen profession,

I will always endeavor

to uphold the prestige,

honor, and

esprit de corps

of the Rangers.

Walking the Walk	SSG Jimmy Patton
Relating to Your Peers	SSG Andrew "Andy" Sheehan
Positioning Your Team for Survival	SSG Jimmy Patton
Inspiring Grit	CSM Rick Merritt
Being "On-Mission" with My Boys	SSG Jimmy Patton
Honoring the Fallen	SSG Jimmy Patton
Celebrating Life	Sheila Patton (Gold Star Mom)
Rebuilding What Has Crumbled	COL Dominic Caraccilo
Pressing the Advantage	COL Dominic Caraccilo
Bridging the Gap	COL Dominic Caraccilo
Mentoring from the Middle	SSG Jim "Bull" Bullock
Prevailing with a Cool Head	SSG Jim "Bull" Bullock
Understanding the Warrior	SSG Jim "Bull" Bullock
Being Happy for Others' Success	SPC Andrew Siemer
Answering the Call	Billy Mac (Operator)
Making Progress Out on the Edges	Billy Mac (Operator)
Marketing Ourselves for Success	MSG Dave Maestas

Walking the Walk

Staff Sergeant (SSG) Jimmy Patton

In today's business, leading by example might be the most genuine way to engender loyalty from the people with whom you work. It certainly provides an easy path to establishing workplace credibility. The tricky part comes from the high level of commitment required to learn all the little tasks, or at least to understand what they are and what order they come in.

Genuine desire to cover all the details gets us 33 percent of the way; mental acuity to learn it all nets the next 33 percent; the guts to put it into practice when it counts take us to 100 percent. Plenty of folks learn to "talk the talk," but that's only a piece of the action. Real leaders "walk the walk."

If Jimmy Patton lived on your street, you would've been friends with him. I first met him when he was a toddler keeping a watchful eye on my infant son crawling around the playpen. He grew up to be five-foot-six inches tall and 135 pounds, and he possessed the unique combination of being both the most fearless and the friendliest kid in the neighborhood. Young Jimmy "talked the talk" with a mischievous smile that his siblings Cliff and Megan idealized. His authentic heart propelled him to believe he was invincible enough to make the world a safer place. And with a legendary sergeant major as his father, Jimmy developed the same protective instincts at a young age. That's about the time he decided to be a U.S. Army Airborne Ranger.

Jimmy did set one condition, though. He needed to prove himself independent of his father and earn his reputation fair and square. So when he entered Basic Training at Fort Benning, he filled in "Puerto Rico" as his home of record. That would throw the cadre off the scent of giving him special treatment connected to CSM Greg Patton, his dad, who at Benning was *Top Dog*. Jimmy spoke Spanish decently and figured the U.S. Army had better things to do than investigate further. He was right.

Private James Patton soared through training and earned follow-on slots to Airborne and Ranger schools. It was *his* merit, not his dad's coattails, doing the talking.

When it came time to prepare for Jump School graduation, a young captain addressed Jimmy and his classmates in the bleachers following their last jump. "Airborne candidates: congratulations, you're graduating tomorrow, so we need to know if any VIPs are coming." Jimmy raised his hand with a mischievous smile and said, "Does the guest speaker of the graduation ceremony count?"

The cat was finally out of the bag. The captain looked at the puzzled instructors who shrugged back. That's when they all made the Patton connection, and they were impressed the kid had never spoken up until that moment. Nobody knew it was CSM Greg Patton's boy who had sailed through training without even a mention of Pop.

Jimmy wasn't the typical young private assigned to a Ranger Battalion, either. He had already set his career course on being a poised leader, and he enjoyed acting the part en route to getting there. His engaging air of confidence breathed life into the workplace while still being able to have fun. People enjoyed being around Jimmy. And he wasn't shy to improvise.

Back at 3rd Batt barracks, he had gotten scolded for some minor thing he forgot to write down, so his sergeant told him he wanted to see the infraction 1,000 times in his handwriting and on his desk by morning. Jimmy made it through two full pages, counted the number of times he had written the phrase, divided it into a thousand, and then photocopied the rest of the pages—all neatly placed on his sergeant's desk by morning. Task completed.

Shortly after he made Private First Class (PFC), Jimmy's dad, the sergeant major, drove to the post to pick him up for the weekend. As Greg pulled up to the curb of the regiment building, Jimmy was hurriedly signing out of the barracks holding a bag of laundry under one arm. Just then, the staff duty sergeant floated a different idea. "Hold on, Patton, get back over here . . ." He was ready to volunteer PFC Jimmy for an impromptu task. But Jimmy was already half the distance from Greg at the curb and the staff duty sergeant at the door. He looked at Greg, then back at the sergeant, then back at Greg, and said in a clear voice to his dad, "Just a minute, Sergeant Major. I'll be right there!" The kid had a set of *cojones*, and he wasn't afraid to use them. When the staff duty sergeant heard the words "sergeant major," he straightened up to look past Jimmy and down the walking path. There stood Greg with the passenger door open and the engine running. He thought about his next career move for a couple of seconds, then said, "Go ahead, Patton, get outta here."

Jimmy loved the Ranger life. He was promoted soon to specialist and then to sergeant. He made lifelong friends and even brought them home to eat Mom's lasagna and do their laundry. He hunted and fished, played Call of Duty videos with the boys, and bought an American muscle car with the money he earned.

Once, while hustling back to the post from Tennessee after spending his coveted vacation time with the family, Jimmy put the pedal down to the floor in his new Mach 1 red Mustang and got pulled over by a state trooper. He turned down the country music on the radio and sincerely apologized, telling the officer not to arrest him—please—because he was an Army Ranger speeding back to Fort Benning and might get deployed. Jimmy knew he deserved to get tossed in jail for going 190 mph, but he didn't want to let down his guys in the unit. He apologized, and the officer let him go.

Part of walking the walk is doing it on our own two feet and not trading on anyone's else reputation. Credibility that's earned independently speaks loudly on our behalf. By comparison, notoriety gained from a higher source in the organization speaks only to theirs. The advantage may not last long when tides change or when a benefactor retires. There is nothing as rock solid as a foundation laid in stone by our own hands. We know where every piece has been carefully placed because we did it ourselves.

Enjoying the ride is part of life. When it's backed up by real achievement, it can be the positive spark it's intended to be. Infectiously good spirit uplifts everyone.

Relating to Your Peers

Staff Sergeant (SSG) Andrew "Andy" Sheehan

Relating to your peers as the boss doesn't just mean being one of the guys. It may not even mean that at all. Sure, it's cool when the crew "gets you," yet there may be a better way to achieve that than through after-work happy hours and funny meme exchanges.

Good leaders realize it's powerful to be able to complement each other's work on a relatable level. Natural-born leaders are even able to achieve it between ranks.

Andy felt like he was a peer to Jimmy Patton. After all, they were both Rangers in the same squad. Jimmy was three years older and a couple of ranks higher—and in army terms, that's a lifetime. The military develops its technicians quickly, so Jimmy had learned a lot in those three years. Similarly, Andy was soaking it all in at a similar pace so he'd be ready for leadership soon enough.

But there was another reason why the two felt like peers. Jimmy's leadership style was "relatable" (Andy's word). For the younger soldier, that meant he could count on his direct boss, his team leader, to share his failures. Together, they would learn from those failures. Andy was able to save a lot of time by avoiding mistakes because of his team leader's wisdom. And Jimmy had always been happy to share previous trials to prevent future errors.

On their first deployment to Afghanistan early in '07, Bravo Company of 3rd Batt had landed ready to rock. Rangers were expected to be squared away in every detail. They had zero tolerance for the slightest mistake because errors can cost lives when you're downrange—as everyone who has ever worn the Ranger tab (the designation that the wearer has completed Ranger School) on their shoulder could freely tell.

As they laid out their gear, young PFC Andy Sheehan realized he had forgotten the swing arm adaptor for his night vision goggles (abbreviated as NVGs). Modern NVGs have improved fantastically since their inception in the '80s. They can literally turn night into day in near- blackout conditions. A further advancement is a sturdy helmet mount that clips the NVGs to a soldier's head for hands-free vision. And the latest progress is the swing arm that allows its operator to angle the light in every direction, as the name suggests—a marvelous boost in night vision technology over the past 30 years.

If you packed the NVG swing arm in your kit, that is. This $29 item might as well be a $1 million item if you didn't have one when you needed it!

Nobody is capable of panic better than a private in the U.S. Army. Andy rushed over to Jimmy, his team leader, to own up to the disastrous situation, and he feared the worst. Jimmy smiled, and the hyperventilation immediately subsided. Jimmy had packed an extra swing arm and handed it over without hesitation. He then told Andy to have a seat on a nearby cot. In a brotherly way, he said reassuringly, "There are going to be times in your life when you make a mistake. I've forgotten things on deployment too, and it's an awful feeling. And that's why I brought extra gear."

Andy had fully expected a different reaction, believing he deserved a scolding. But he didn't get one from his peer-brother-boss, and he never forgot that. Andy had learned a lesson he planned to leverage when he stepped into leadership positions over the next decade. He could hear a voice in his head that sounded like Jimmy saying, "If sharing my failures makes my boys better, then I've done a good job."

The same kind of transparent leadership seems to me like the gold standard for corporate leaders of any age and seniority. A self-effacing approach and willingness to share can brand an indelibly positive mark of integrity. That's what lasts well after the current team disbands for future opportunities.

Today's business environment is seeing a resurgence of peer leadership in which the traditional age differences between mentee and mentor have vanished. Work experience in a high-pressure industry can be condensed such that Haley the 25-year-old team leader who hit the ball off the cover for her first three years is now managing eight 24-year-olds. If a company can land a "relatable" young leader with a great head on her shoulders, the ability to create **relatable leadership** *is staggering.*

Positioning Your Team for Survival

Staff Sergeant (SSG) Jimmy Patton

Name any successful firm, and I'll bet it has a flair for seeing around the bend to what's coming next. If all those companies with long-term profitability have the same gift, it has to be more than luck. Being prepared, doing the research, and brainstorming contingencies help keep the unit in the best position for winning, and in some cases, for survival. Forward-thinking individuals may just be more wired to think this way: where to buy, where to stand, where to lay low.

When the crucial moment comes for us to figure out what position to assume, they're already there waving at us to join them.

Jimmy had a knack for being at the right place at the right moment, something Andy had seen repeatedly. He had the sixth sense to check around a corner over here or sprint to better cover over there.

On a 2009 mission during their third Afghan deployment together, the squad got cut off during a patrol. They were five hours into a foot chase up in the mountains where an ambush awaited them. Jimmy's team was down to just him and Andy; the two had become separated from the rest of the squad. Fire was coming from all sides. Jimmy's instant repositioning to an exposed but effective spot got them out of the jam and allowed the other team to call in an A-10 gun run, which ended the skirmish and saved the squad. How?

Five hours earlier, a squad of seven Rangers from B1/1 in 3rd Batt had come in "hot" on a Black Hawk helicopter 500 meters outside a compound. Their mission: to clear the compound. It was hot enough that their buddy, Thomas, broke his leg on the chopper landing.

One man down.

The squad covered the 500 meters into the compound in a hard sprint and started using clearing techniques to move through the buildings. Reed, from Jimmy's team, who bounded down the steps wearing full gear and moving fast, hit a foreign object in the darkness with his weight going forward and shattered a bone in his ankle.

Two men down.

A gunfight then ensued with the last of the Taliban soldiers at the rear of the compound, but one got away. He ran into the foothills behind the buildings and disappeared. The five remaining members of the squad took off after him, and the chase was on. The mission called for securing the compound and also eliminating communication of its capitulation. The second piece was about to be blown if that Taliban fighter reported back.

For four more hours, the five tracked the lone Taliban soldier into the foothills. They retained radio contact with base camp, reporting that they were still on the trail with sufficient ammo. They had yet to see evidence of any additional enemy. So far so good—until fire opened up on them at a rock outcropping.

Jimmy and Andy took cover behind a boulder with the rest of the squad just out of reach. A combination of machine gun, mortar, and sniper fire poured in on them from three sides. The squad, divided into two distinct pieces, was facing more fire than they could handle. To make matters worse, Jimmy's two-man team was cut off from the other three men who couldn't see where the fire was coming from in the foothills. They were in a predicament.

Within moments, Jimmy viewed the battlefield like a chessboard. Just as Andy was starting to see it too, Jimmy was already gone and on the move. Before things turned severe, he'd figured they needed him to come out from behind the safety of the boulder into the relative open. There, he could eyeball each of the three enemy locations that were pinning down other team members – including the all-important JTAC teammate, who was the one in radio contact with the aircraft that could be called in for help. To make the call, the JTAC needed to be able to lift his head to direct a gunship overhead toward the enemy.

As Jimmy exposed himself so he could engage the enemy in the hills, thoughts ran through Andy's head. *Jimmy is not obligated to do that . . . his instinct to protect the group propels him out there into danger . . . and he's going to help us get outta here.*

The bad thing about Jimmy being in the *right* spot to see the enemy hideouts was that they could also see *him*, so his bold move needed to bear fruit quickly. It's not like the movies when the star yells "cover me" and then does something crazy while the others seamlessly back him up. In real life, Rangers rehearse these kinds of scenarios until they become rote memory in their playbook. Jimmy's move triggered the squad's response to lift up, pour steady fire on the enemy, and call that dang plane in ASAP.

Jimmy's move drew fire from the enemy's Russian-made machine guns, and immediately triggered a sliver of daylight for Andy to fire back on them from the other side of the boulder. This made the Taliban soldiers in the foothills react and keep their own heads down. The gunfire action cued the JTAC, only a few meters away. He stood up high enough to call in an A-10 gunship flying overhead that had been standing by to receive coordinates.

Next, the A-10 Warthog swooped in and lit up the foothills with its 30mm gatling gun. Whoever or whatever enemy soldiers used to be there ceased to exist. On that cue, both teams maneuvered their withdrawals out of the rocky outcropping and hustled back down the mountain to collect Thomas and Reed. They then boarded the chopper back home, mission complete.

Sometimes the lead people need to stick out their necks and position themselves in the line of fire. The goal is to deflect attention from the others so they're able to look up and do their job.

How do we transpose this goal into business strategy? The analogies seem bountiful. Sticking your neck out to protect others places the needs of the many over the needs of the single person. Initiating a well-rehearsed sequence that depends on the first person's boldness takes fortitude. It also takes confidence in knowing the team will be there to "cover you."

What about the knack of the chess player to see two moves ahead and know where to position the next piece? Maybe that skill is learned, or perhaps it's a sixth sense. Aspiring leaders pay attention and tuck away this lesson for the day they will be team leaders.

Inspiring Grit

Command Sergeant Major (CSM) Rick Merritt

Being hardcore from the top inspires mental toughness. It logically follows that it will be contagious throughout the organization, just like the other attributes of impressive leadership trickle down.

Tough, realistic training and fatherly confidence also inspire sky-high esprit de corps and the ability for the team to go farther and faster when they find themselves smack inside the crucible of competition.

Sergeant Major Rick Merritt and the Patton family used to be neighbors in the quiet Fort Benning community where the only weekly concern was to keep the grass mowed. Back in Georgia as a kid, Jimmy had helped the CSM do that yard work when he was overseas. He idolized the future Sergeant Major of the world-famous Ranger Regiment, whose advice to him had been to "stay out of trouble; listen to your parents; and eat up, son… cause you're too skinny." Years later, the sergeant major and grown-up Jimmy were together once again – but now it was in the daily chaos of Afghanistan.

Twenty-two-year old Jimmy Patton was now a Ranger sergeant in 2009 alongside the CSM. They were on an all-night mission with rangers and a 2-man OGA (other government agency) team attached to their strike force in which the company commander and fire support officer had both been shot in action.

When squirters (fleeing Taliban) escaped from the village, the unit chased after them all night long through the mountains and into caves to secure them.

As the sun came up, it was CSM Merritt, Jimmy, and the OGA team pulling security during a short halt when they saw an old man in the valley tracing their movement and possibly "spotting" them for the Taliban. They knew they were about to get hit and immediately formed a "bounding overwatch" to maneuver to a compound in view. There they hoped to re-group and defend the attack until they could exfil out safely. The enemy knew exactly where they were heading and raced toward the same spot. While carrying the detainees with them, the unholy trinity nailed them - PKM machine fire, rocket-propelled grenades, and mortar explosions - hitting all around and kicking up metal, rocks, and dirt in their face. "Here we go, game on," thought the CSM.

With daylight already breaking, they needed to get out of their unenviable position, which was a small compound in an open 500-meter diameter bowl with only small scrub brush for concealment and an irrigation ditch to crawl through. Air support would not be able to get to them for hours more, and groundfire peppered a speeding Cessna's attempt at dropping resupply items that missed the compound. The parachute from the second attempt by a C-130 turboprop found the target and landed close enough to retrieve. It would have to tide them over until air support arrived. Jimmy set to the task of reloading ammo mags and cross-loading gear. Luckily the Rangers found a working well inside and restocked for the continuation of the battle that was coming.

The OGA team had now completed their task with the detainees and rejoined Jimmy and the CSM. Eight hours of fighting had already passed. This was not the normal "grab and go" with their quarry via chopper. Instead, they had dragged them through the mountains on an all-night skirmish.

The team leader asked, "Sergeant Major, how are you planning to get us outta here?"

"Well," the CSM began, "we're outnumbered with 100 hostiles in the area, and sometimes, well, getting off the objective is the toughest part of the job."

He wanted to remind them that it's not like back home where you can snatch up a target and then roll back out in your black SUV's in time to make happy hour. In this case, he didn't have to.

"We're stuck here in the Alamo."

CSM continued, "We've got three choices:

One, we got 'em right where we want 'em, and "higher" will call in reinforcements to join us and finish this thing right here.

Two, we hold on till night and slip out on foot, dragging our casualties with us and trying not to wake up the whole world with these detainees,

or

Three, we execute a hot exfil in a blaze of fire in broad daylight."

"OK Sergeant Major, but what do we do if they overrun us, crashing through the compound entrance in a hail of bullets?"

"Tell them, Jimmy," he said with a point in Jimmy's direction.

"Sergeant Major," Jimmy said, spitting tobacco onto the sand, "we gonna stack 'em up like firewood."

The crazy dichotomy of life and death situations mixed with dark humor in combat has existed throughout the history of warfare. It's a vetted outlet that allows elite soldiers to perform under frightening conditions.

At the moment the Taliban unleashed their fire from elevated hill positions, CSM Merritt had already been on over 1000 missions in his career. With his fire team at full gallop and racing for cover, he yelled over to Jimmy, "It's the cans, it's the cans!" ala Steve Martin in the 1979 movie The Jerk." Jimmy, of course, hadn't been born until the following decade and didn't know the movie line. But he did hear the word "cans" over the explosions and considered two possibilities while at full sprint - one was that the sergeant major wanted a can of tobacco in the middle of battle, so probably not that one. Or, more likely, he wanted him to "pop a can of smoke" - which Jimmy pulled and chucked towards the enemy as he raced to the compound. CSM and the team later had a good laugh about it after they got back home to base.

During the heat of battle in the compound, two donkeys that were tied up both recoiled from the tremendous noise and chaos of explosions and bullets. Thinking this might be the end of their donkey days, they decided to have one last final act at sexual relations right in the courtyard as the battle raged on.

CSM Merritt points out I could add the word laughter to the title of the book, making it *Guts, Smarts, Laughter & Love* as the standout attributes of great leaders. That's 35 years of military career talking, and it makes good sense.

CSM caught the hint of a bulge in their eyes as if to say, "dang we didn't sign up for this," and before the OGA had a chance to process the response any further, the sergeant major let them know, "we'll take option two, slipping out of here after dark.

Daylight had brought the opportunity for the afghans to call more Taliban on their radio frequency to come and kill some Americans, so it was time to leave. Still, they couldn't risk bringing helos during daylight while surrounded by enemy fighters.

Fast movers finally arrived, and lit up the Afghan hills throughout the day and just into nightfall, when exfil choppers screamed in behind them to load up the rangers. CSM Merritt was one of the last men to get on the bird as Jimmy emptied his final mag from the base of the ramp to suppress the Taliban fighters firing at the chopper, and then he jumped aboard. Mission successful: they had secured their detainees, won a decisive action against a significantly superior force, and Jimmy's captain and FSO both recovered from their wounds.

The sergeant major passes along six sweet tidbits for young leaders making their way in the business world.

Be the ***commandant of common sense****, which you can only effectively do by leading from the front. Be there, be seen, be heard.*

Coaching, mentoring & training will cultivate ***individual characters*** *into* ***units with culture****.*

Be ***omnipresent in the battlespace*** *area. It's essential to leading the high performers you intend to ask the most of.*

Swear by the oath like I do, "more sweat in training means less blood in combat."

Train even harder than combat conditions. Shiver now to stay warm later.

Live hard to be hard.

CSM Merritt on retiring for the next wave to take over:
In 2019, after completing a 20-mile "force march" in my final year of service, a young ranger proudly walked up and asked me,

"Sergeant Major, can we take a photo?"

"Certainly."

"I love the rangers…and my grandfather served too."

"That's great, who'd he serve with?"

"You, Sergeant Major!"

I smiled, realizing maybe I was near the age to think about retirement.

Being "On-Mission" with My Boys

Staff Sergeant (SSG) Jimmy Patton

Knowing how to describe tasks is one thing; it provides a start when the business's team is beginning to jell. Then comes the ultimate test of the first-line managers: Are they willing to roll up their sleeves and show everyone how to do that task? For example, Joe, the young sales mentor at Power Home Remodeling, would be the first to teach the reps in the pit how to follow a sales script. He then picks up the phone in front of his eager audience to demonstrate how to nail a "set." Haley, that energetic manager at Insight Global, "Zooms"with her eight reps every morning during COVID-19. She role-plays objections and joins in on client calls. Haley represents the exact kind of manager the CEO would select for a promotion.

In these examples, the leaders love being "on-mission" with their teams, and everyone loves having them firmly in the lead.

On April 18, 2010, intelligence confirmed the presence of two of Osama bin Laden's top lieutenants in the Tikrit vicinity near Lake Thartar and Saddam's hometown in Iraq. The area 80 miles northwest of Baghdad had seen its share of rebel activity. Five years earlier, it had housed an insurgent training camp that had been raided, resulting in 80 rebel deaths. This time, two of the highest-value targets (HVTs) in the entire campaign were reported to be physically together in the same location. Abu

Ayyub al-Masri, who headed Al Qaeda in Iraq (AQI), was said to be Bin Laden's #2 man in the whole organization. With him was Abu Omar al-Baghdadi, an almost mythical character rumored to have already been killed many times. He had become a cult figure among the insurgents for his reputation of staying alive.

Finding al-Masri would be a spectacular win for the nation's morale. And catching al-Baghdadi with him would be an incredible two-for-one coup not to be passed up. (At this time, the worldwide hunt for Bin Laden was still a year away from the event that killed him in Abbottabad, Pakistan, on May 2, 2011.)

Selected for the mission were both Rangers and Delta Force. (Although Delta Force had been renamed CAG followed by ACE in 2010, I still think of this group as Delta Force.) They planned to scream in low using seven choppers—four for the 30 Rangers and three for the 15 Delta operators—then land 600 meters from the six-building compound and get the two high-value targets (HVTs), dead or alive. The Rangers would take responsibility for clearing five of the six structures, and Delta would handle the building marked as the one with *highest probability* of where al-Masri was holding his meeting.

It was a dark night with a light mist in the air and mild temperatures in the 70s. Their objective location was only 15 minutes away from their base by chopper, and they planned to go in around one in the morning. UH-60 Black Hawk helicopters were fitted for combat by removing all the seats and doors on both sides so there would be no impediments in the way of quick infil and exfil. The three Night Stalker choppers for the Delta teams were additionally fitted out with machine gunners to cover the teams with fire upon the landing and extraction phases for the teams if needed.

A lone cargo strap spanned each open chopper doorway where three men sat side by side with their feet dangling outside over the edge. That strap would be removed by the chopper's crew chief at the "one minute out" mark before landing. Plus there was a 36-inch tether with one end anchored to a floor bolt and the other hooked to each man's belt—the only thing holding soldiers inside the bird.

Hot landings—referring to descending at high speed—were inherently dangerous, especially in the darkness. This night was exceptionally dark. The men were sitting in the door, one hand on the rifle trigger and the other holding the D-ring to unhook a split second after landing, and jump out. Survival senses were on full alert.

The men had landed like this more than a hundred times on missions and rehearsal dry-runs, and they had this piece down cold. Two pilots in the seats up front and a crew chief in the far back operated the Black Hawk. In a seven-man squad like SSG Jimmy Patton's, each team of three sat in the open doors. Jimmy, the squad leader, sat in control on the floor in the middle along with any extra specialists, radiomen, or higher command. This night, it was the team's platoon sergeant in the bird with them. As the ranking man, he would take charge of the comm headset to talk with the pilots, allowing Jimmy the freedom of movement to reposition himself where needed.

As the team members were loading into the chopper, Jimmy switched places with his A-team leader, moving into the first location forward on the right side. That put him in the pivotal position to lead the charge into their assigned buildings once they hit the ground. The switch was Jimmy's protective instinct in action—and he always insisted on being the first man. He was small in stature but full in heart and had earned his squad's respect as its ever-present caretaker. The A-team leader moved to the middle with the command element one step behind his doormen, still keeping him in fine position to take up the fight.

The Ranger birds came in together in an *L* formation with two of them heading down to the right edge of the square settlement. Thirty seconds later, the other two, including Jimmy's squad, came heading down to the lower side. At the same time, the three Delta choppers converged on the opposite edge of the settlement to head straight toward the targets. For the pilot to clearly see through the mist and virtual darkness was nearly impossible, even wearing night vision goggles. And turning on the chopper's lights was not an option. Doing that would jeopardize the security of the landing and could potentially blind everyone in the mission wearing goggles, too. Hence, the chopper pilot had to rely on the radar altimeter—and experience.

The bird came in hot for the final 100 feet. Once on the ground, low-light conditions would provide a substantial advantage to seven choppers that were full of operators crossing open land. None of the pilots wanted to turn on their spotlights and endanger the men. It was the right call.

At "one minute out," the crew chief pulled off the cargo strap across the door. The doormen checked their grips on the floor D-ring holding them in. Jimmy, like the doormen, had a choice of floor anchors to hook onto with some back a few feet and others positioned right at the doorway. To have the best field of vision, Jimmy clicked his 30-inch tether to an anchor close to the opening as he had done countless times before. He knew it would give him the extra edge to control the squad in the final moments of flight.

Descending in the pitch black to the landing zone, the pilot saw the ground come up too fast and flared hard to pull up the chopper's nose. But by that time, the Black Hawk was already too close to the ground, and the flaring hard caused the back end and its rear rotor to slam onto the ground. The rotor broke off just as the back end hit hard, and then it counter-lurched forward. It was a disaster happening in real time. Centrifugal force from the lost rear rotor sent the chopper to the right, causing the right wheel to stick as a pivot point. It broke off. The forward momentum created a roll hard to the right, throwing whomever would be sitting in the most forward right spot out of the helicopter—Jimmy. His tether couldn't hold him in, and he shot out from the helo like a cannonball, while still attached. The helo crushed him as it flipped over and landed full force on top of his body, killing him instantly.

Just like that, the spectacular young life of Jimmy Patton was over.

Incontestably, the Ranger mission he prepared his men for had to continue. Andy was a team leader on one of the first two birds that had landed 30 seconds previously. As his own two helos "flushed" the area and left, he looked back to see that only one bird was flushing from its landing zone behind them. Then he saw the wreck and felt the sharp stab of worry for his buddies on board. He could only pray for the best.

The other six sticks disgorged their passengers, who charged toward the objective. The six remaining choppers hit the ground with varying degrees of hard landings, and they dusted right off again. Although Jimmy's chopper lay flipped on its side and mangled, miraculously the other ten troops inside were alive. Seven of the remaining Rangers crawled out. Those well enough to join the fight reassembled and raced across the open ground to catch up to the platoon.

As the teams cleared the buildings, Andy didn't know the extent of casualties, but the possibility of brothers being hurt back at the landing zone ate at him from the inside. Hopefully, the helo crew could tend to those who were wounded. And hopefully, medical help was on the way.

The Ranger platoon cleared the first four houses with ease and encountered a couple of noncombatants living in house number five. They brought the people outside and sat them down while the rest of the platoon provided cover for the Delta team that had stormed into building six.

Both al-Masri and al-Baghdadi had been inside the buildings just moments before, along with a jackpot of documents and laptops. Actual communications from Osama bin Laden were found onsite. They certainly couldn't get far out there, and Delta knew that a favorite choice of hiding spots for Al Qaeda was a big hole they had dug to crawl into.

It didn't take the teams long to find the two who had fled with no intention of being captured alive. Both were killed and carried back to the helicopters for ID. Al-Baghdadi's identity could be confirmed locally, but al-Masri was such a catch, he'd have to be flown back to the U.S. for identification.

The mission had struck gold. Intel was good, and execution had been heroic, stellar even, given the conditions. But although the U.S. military scored a huge win at Lake Thartar, it cost Jimmy

Patton his life. My buddy's firstborn son. He had always stressed to his men the concept of *surviving at all costs*. With sad irony, he was the only one lost in the battle that day.

In his little *blue book*, which each Ranger in B Co kept as a memoir of thoughts and final wishes, he wrote about hopeful conditions if he left this world early.

"How do you want to go out?" it asked.

"On-mission with my boys," Jimmy had answered.

When leaders have prepared their people well to know the project's intricacies, they'll be capable of closing ranks and seeing it through to conclusion, no matter what obstacles arise. The shepherd's stewardship organically passes down to the subordinate leaders who will seek to protect the flanks, just as the shepherd taught them to do.

Thankfully, when it comes to caring for its heroes, there are few civilian equivalents to the extreme lessons we learn in the military.

Big organizations that devote quality time and resources to caring deeply for their people attract loyal employees. They look after more than basic needs; they're aware of the nuances; they go the extra mile for the long-term welfare of the group.

Tending to thoughtful little details can be long remembered by your people. What tops my list for essential people-to-people skills? Timely communications and personal caring that can't be faked. Working with a company whose leadership go out of their way to take care of its people helps us survive times of hardship.

Honoring the Fallen

Staff Sergeant (SSG) Jimmy Patton

Big wins rarely come without a cost. Along the way, hard work is bound to take its toll on some members of the team while the rest are left wondering if the trade-off was worthwhile. It's important to catch your breath after a landmark victory to recognize how people's sacrifices contributed to everyone's enrichment. And it's important to pay the dedication forward as freely as it flowed.

Gifted leaders acknowledge that their people may need downtime to process, rejuvenate, and retool for the next campaign.

As the Delta team carried the remains of al-Masri back to the exfil point, Jimmy's body was recovered from the wreckage. The global significance of the mission notwithstanding, it was still a terrible exchange—that is, Jimmy's life in exchange for Al-Qaeda's #2 man. It penetrated deep and damaged the souls of 1st Squad B Company.

The Al-Qaeda man had ordered car bombs and destruction for a decade. Our man, Jimmy, had trained young troops through everything an infantry squad can experience—from early days at Fort Benning through combat missions in Afghanistan and then in Iraq. The troops thrived because they did everything together. Their leader never missed the opportunity to compliment them for all the wins and to take the blame for any failures. In fact, they loved him for it, and the feeling was mutual.

On this night, the team had survived a crash and expertly executed the greatest mission of their careers, thanks to Jimmy's meticulous regimen. They deserved to feel the jubilation of claiming the war's top prize to date. Instead, they loaded back silently into a fresh chopper and took one final ride with their leader back to base. Jimmy would forever be 23, just a month shy of his 24th birthday, and make the journey home to family and Arlington National Cemetery. The boys on the team would soldier on as Jimmy had trained them to do.

For civilian leaders emulating the best practices of the Rangers, here are three of SSG Patton's core principles that will stand up in any setting, whether bullets are flying or not.

The first is the ability to ***create a team identity****. Jimmy accomplished it by doing everything together. In and out of work, he created an environment by spending time with his people at weekend home barbeques, candidly sharing work lessons, or staking out a dining table at the Iraqi base where teams ate every meal as a family.*

Jimmy's second principle is ***accountability****. Success always belonged to the team, but failure belonged to him alone. He passed on all kudos to the group, praising the cohesiveness of the unit as a factor of its success, which is a brilliant double down.*

His third principle is ***reflecting the best practices of the executive team enthusiastically****. Jimmy's B Company first sergeant had been on Task Force Ranger in Somalia in '93 and passed along ideals that Jimmy embraced: taking the role of mentor seriously, loving your guys, and preparing them to the fullest with extra water, ammo, bullets, and body armor! The boundless enthusiasm of the boss, which bubbled down to the leader, kept on bubbling all the way down to the individual contributors.*

Celebrating Life

Sheila Patton (Gold Star Mom)

> *I think it's wise to assume that the rank-and-file members of any organization look to the executive team to see how they react to crises. They likely respect their leaders enough to take cues from their reactions and emulate them. It becomes a hefty responsibility for leaders to be in the spotlight. But they have the potential to be more influential than ever in times like these.*

Back in Indiana, Sheila Patton had received a phone call from her husband Greg in Afghanistan before he took off for the long haul.

"Sheila, you can't cry now, you have to stay strong."

Greg had just arrived in Bagram, and word had preceded him that a sergeant major with a KIA (killed in action) son in Iraq was choppering in through a storm. People were poised to help him. The sergeant major needed to get to Kuwait to complete the triangle and board the plane coming home to the U.S. At the time, Admiral McRaven's personal C-130 turboprop was the only bird on the tarmac ready to go. With a heartfelt note from the admiral himself, the base's sergeant major welcomed Greg and took him out to the blacked-out plane, then off he flew 2,000 miles to meet up with his son's casket for the final flight home. Sheila would take care of the rest.

And that became her mantra. It carried Sheila toward closure. She drew Jimmy's young wife and infant daughter close to her, and together they planned a "celebration of life" ceremony for Jimmy a week later. Beatriz was just 21 with their 16-month-old baby girl Ceci, and Sheila helped the adoring young mother and child find their way in the post-husband-and-daddy world that awaited them.

It was also the start of helping grieving soldiers and their family members over the next 10 years.

Complying with Jimmy's blue book wishes, Sheila made sure from 800 miles away that his body was fitted in his dress uniform with meticulous detail by the experts at Dover Air Base. She also made sure a bottle of Wild Turkey was tucked at his side. Andy checked his best buddy's uniform one last time at Arlington and placed the Ranger coin Jimmy had asked for inside the casket. Then Jimmy was interred with full military honors amid 10,000 other American fallen heroes in the solemn environs of Arlington Cemetery.

Sheila took people back to Indiana to share stories of their "brother" and find sunshine behind the clouds. Because of her, her son's death evolved well beyond a single family's loss. Their poignant memories of going to mass with Mama at Fort Benning and cooking turkeys side by side over the phone while miles apart continue to be cherished.

The leadership lessons I learned from this powerhouse lady were transformative. She's a Ranger mom and wife who has chosen inspiration over sorrow. She adopted the uplifting nickname "Sonshine" for her departed son and told friends not to feel sadness for young people who leave us too soon. Rather, she asked them to pause momentarily, find ways to build the fallen into their lives, and then go on living. She also knew the surviving siblings and friends would "feel it double," so she has continued to focus on survivor guilt through an ongoing involvement in the survivor outreach program. Today, she's steady as a rock when helping grieving families.

Sheila starts by sharing a few dos and don'ts:

Do – ask to be notified by someone you know, use the deceased's name in conversations, and laugh at funny stories about them.

Don't – say "I'm sorry" (a human reaction), stop living your good life, get depressed from nonaction, or accept being told, "It's time to move on." And if you've put together a healthy

Jimmy's blue book requested two father figures to deliver his eulogy. The first was his dad Greg, the 101st sergeant major who'd escorted his son's flag-draped casket home from Iraq. And the second was Rick Merritt, command sergeant major of the Ranger Regiment who he looked up to as the hardest-core ranger that ever lived.

"Jimmy was a young schoolboy in my neighborhood who told me he wanted to be a ranger," eulogized CSM Merritt among family at Arlington National Cemetery. A few years later, we jumped together, trained together, and fought together. In 25 years in the Ranger Regiment through 59 months of combat and 1500 missions, I've spent a lifetime surrounding myself with people better than me, and I know what a warrior looks like. If I had to give that warrior a name and a face, it would be SSG Jimmy Patton."

remembrance model for the departed loved one, you don't have to take down all your photos.

Sheila says, "I welcome all types of grievers." In a time when military suicide is at a crisis level, surviving families need the military community for support. Sheila knows the military can't officially recognize the dependents of suicide as a Gold Star family.

When Andy Sheehan left the army in 2017, he wrote down his memoirs from his 11-year career and eight deployments in the Middle East. It began as a voice to exorcise demons and turn dark times into light. It ended up as a book[1] called ***Freedom 1-3,*** his Ranger call sign.

In the book, Andy wrote about his journey to true freedom. He described the pain of losing his best friend Jimmy and told stories about their Ranger buddies—and about coming home to search for the sense of it all in smoky bars and mental wards. At one point driven to the edge of sanity, he finally discovered the reason for each of us to live. That was to celebrate the life we are living—at this moment in time—specifically with the people we are living it with. With that discovery, he forgave himself. Having a supportive wife with a second baby on the way helped him avoid falling over the edge.

Andy has something to say that's worth the read if you're not afraid to stare into the abyss. This young author might have more in common with the rest of us than you think.

---

[1] Andrew Sheehan, *Freedom 1-3: An Army Ranger's Journey to True Freedom* (2019). Available on Amazon.com.

But she says she had a dream that Jimmy came and asked her to honor all the deceased, whether they died by suicide or as a hero. It has emboldened her to stay in constant contact with young wives, survivors, wounded vets, and retirees to assist in their grief.

Leaders of every kind can take note from Mama Patton, the lady Andy thought of as the mother he never had, and the granny rock for baby Ceci. And because Mama asked, Admiral McRaven came to Ranger Battalion to celebrate her son's life with a heroes' toast.

Jimmy's spirit stays alive because of her actions.

Rebuilding What Has Crumbled

Colonel (COL) Dominic Caraccilo

Many new business leaders inherit an organization that needs reframing, relaunching, resizing, or even a completely new focus, form, or fit. It's a brave new world for those tasked with a rebuild. Hard decisions are on the menu for managers who need to think like nimble entrepreneurs.

Wartime dictates a lot of destruction, but when it calls for rebuilding, specialized know-how is required. A touch of independence and a flair for organization are musts; a CEO's knack for people skills and a background in policy would round out the qualities of a perfect commander.

Colonel Dom Caraccilo, in a role akin to a CEO, found himself in the Triangle of Death south of Baghdad, Iraq, in September of '07. As a brigade commander over an area the size of West Virginia, he got this terse directive from the commanding general: *Turn it around.*

With the authority to get the job done, he weighed the choice to either drop bombs or empower people. Dropping bombs could undoubtedly send a message aimed at the Iraqis' sense of fear. On the other hand, empowering the people would be a more circuitous journey, but it had the potential to send a message appealing more broadly to their sense of progress and trust.

Colonel C chose development. On the resource side, he made sure chicken hatcheries and fish farms to bolster the food supply were put back into place. On the infrastructure side, he had police academies reconstituted to backfill the void of law enforcement.

The colonel breathed full life into the Sons of Iraq initiative, which empowered previously known "bad guys" to become "good guys." They hired former terrorists, idle discontents, and those with no means of support to assist in the rebuilding effort by guarding over their own people and keeping the peace. This psychological technique sought to fill the need of the reformed terrorists for empowerment by putting them in charge of something—in this case, the orderly rebuilding of their homeland. That gave them jobs, with the U.S. military as their employer working beside them in the new collective effort. This program alone was aiding the country's economic development. At its height, the rolls of the Sons of Iraq numbered 109,000, and the colonel's staff was deployed to oversee its success. It existed from '05 to '13—until its disband due to Sunni vs. Shia ideological turmoil.

"Turn it around" is a tall order for a newly arrived boss. The decisions made immediately divide people into one camp or the other. For example, it might mean either stacking the lumber inherited into neat piles for safekeeping or rebuilding with what's left. The first is a safe choice; the second is risky.

Armed with a fresh way of thinking, the new boss knows resources and personnel can be repurposed to rebuild what had been—or create something entirely new.

Pressing the Advantage

Colonel (COL) Dominic Caraccilo

In the sixth century BCE, Sun Tsu suggested "pressing the advantage," and industry has been fond of applying his principle ever since.

When your company finds itself with an unexpected advantage, continue to press it. If your chief marketing officer has hit paydirt with a campaign that requires allocating additional funds, then extend it for as long as it flourishes. Product managers who realize that adding a feature grabs market attention and places favorable eyes on the product are smart to add another. They can gain a reputation as market innovators.

However, being smart enough to identify an advantage is only the first key to pressing it.

Four years earlier, in March of '03 over northern Iraq, Lieutenant Colonel (LTC) Dominic Caraccilo stood in the rushing air of a C-17 aircraft's open door. It was the morning of Operation Northern Delay, and he was jumper #1 in the left door of plane #4. His 900 men in the 173rd Airborne Brigade had loaded into 15 birds and prepared to jump out of the sky.

As the battalion commander of 2/503rd Sky Soldiers, Dom had orders to secure the Bashur airstrip, 150 kilometers north of Kirkuk, where a downtown riot was in process. Over the previous months, his executive team had trained the unit in taking the initiative, confidence, and responsibility for turning tasks into rote memory. They had already completed 12 training jumps in 11 countries and had done their due diligence to make a combat jump when it counted. This would be the first-ever combat jump in C-17s and the largest of the war.

By midmorning after the jump, the battalion had confidently secured its assigned piece of the airstrip with brigade command securely in place. LTC Caraccilo looked to press the initiative onward to Kirkuk. At the same time, a sister unit broke off to deal with securing the nearby gas-oil separation plant. Six Iraqi divisions were lingering in the area north of Baghdad and south of Kirkuk. They needed to be "delayed" by the threat of a second front, so Dom's 2/503rd headed south to grab their attention. Securing a city of 1.5 million with 900 men wouldn't be a cake-walk under normal circumstances, and with chaos in the streets, it would be even more dangerous.

As the convoy pulled up, the colonel drew up a play like Villanova's basketball coach during a timeout. It called for one of his companies to go left, the other right, and the other center with mortars in support. From there, it called for a basic *react to contact* right into the heart of town.

Before long, they quelled the riot and kept the city calm, establishing seven central locations downtown for effective command and control. Meanwhile, over the next two weeks, friendly tanks, supplies, and troops flooded into the airstrip. This created the delaying action that stopped Iraqi President Saddam's six divisions from marching into Baghdad—all thanks to the initiative of the 173rd.

Keep an eye on the success of the initial advantage and the coach's call to press on by observing the effect it produces over the coming weeks. Pay attention to the times it worked, and any times it didn't. In the game of finite resources, recognizing the same advantage in the future will lead to a no-brainer decision to keep your foot on the gas—or not.

Bridging the Gap

Colonel (COL) Dominic Caraccilo

> *Unless young go-getters plan to stay in the same line of business for an entire career, they should prepare to take what they've learned in one job and carry it over into the next. Culling ubiquitous lessons learned that you can easily apply to your future endeavors helps you mind the gap and then jump over it.*

As a young captain at Fort Bragg, Colonel Dom Caraccilo began forming a command climate that featured respect and flexibility. At that time, he'd always been adamant that soldiers needed to wear helmets, for example. After all, it was the regulation, and it was for their protection. Then after one particularly grueling field exercise came to a close, he left to find cases of beer for his men along with a well-deserved swim in the lake as a reward for a great job. He returned to find 200 completely naked paratroopers frolicking in the water, wearing nothing except their Kevlar helmets strapped on. Grinning like clowns, they were sending a funny message to a commander they respected and would willingly follow into combat. He received the message well, going on to build a 20-year command climate of respect and flexibility that he took with him to the boardroom.

Over the past 10 years, Dom has leveraged his CEO-type experience into the corporate world with senior positions at Amazon and Facebook. Back at West Point in 1984, he had initially set his sights on being a Ranger because *Rangers were the best infantry in the world.* As he moved on in his commercial career, he reinforced the goal of being "best in the world" through every other organization he led.

Most critical to him was capturing lessons learned—that is, assessing what you have acquired *here* and taking it with you *there.* The diversity of skills he garnered as a senior leader in the military's elite forces provided his entrée into two diverse senior corporate roles.

In 2012, Amazon coaxed him into his first post after retirement to run its fledgling West Coast distribution division. You know that crazy idea Amazon had to deliver products overnight? With Dom at the helm, the west division grew to 15,000 people across nine centers and 35 million square feet of product.

A year later, Facebook came looking for a rock star to take over as its new IT director. When he walked into his first meeting, he found he was the oldest guy in the room by a decade, and that cans of Monster Java outnumbered mugs of coffee at the table of smart techies. They were measurably scared of him; the closest they had ever been to a Ranger had been playing Call of Duty. Dom addressed the gap and bridged the past to the present. He knew the lessons he learned in the military could now guide his team to be the "best of the best" in the corporate world.

Governments seek the same kind of talent that Fortune 100 companies do. The United Arab Emirates recognized a "slam dunk" résumé and tapped him to head a transformation project for the entire UAE army of 20,000, bringing troops up to speed in training and readiness. That paved the way to step in as a principal and COO at Parsons Corporation, consulting directly with allied governments on their missile defense and security plans.

A success story like Dom Caraccilo's truly embodies the theme of leading Rangers. The Ranger mentality led him to an early string of career wins as a young officer. Mentoring by Generals Petraeus, Odierno, and McChrystal while Dom was a senior commander refined skills on a more global level. That eventually caught the eye of corporate and consulting players.

Over the years, Dom has authored 10 books on victory and strategy, including *Beyond Guns and Steel: A War Termination Strategy*. He has also become a loyal friend.

Mentoring from the Middle

Staff Sergeant (SSG) Jim "Bull" Bullock

Those who have had mentors in their careers can count themselves lucky. One doesn't always materialize in the right place at the right time. The benefit of a mentor's maturity and experience is worth millions to someone who is trying to figure it all out.

Less familiar than the benefits is knowing where to find a good mentor. That person needn't come from the tippy top. "Mentoring from the middle" can work well if he or she has been in our shoes. And every once in a while, we even find that extraordinary personality who "mentors from below." A smart leader pays attention to both directions.

And don't forget to flip the script. The fast mover on the climb up the organizational ladder should be looking to mentor both up and down. The ability to do both gets someone noticed faster than you can say R-a-n-g-e-r.

When SSG Jim Bullock was a Ranger instructor in Florida, a youngster named David signed into the Ranger Support Element comprising the opposing forces (OPFOR) for the Jungle Phase of the Ranger School. David was a private who had washed out of pre-Ranger training and got reassigned to Ranger Support to assist with the candidates earning their tabs. With this assignment, David would have to content himself with role-playing the enemy during Ranger School patrols as well as doing menial support jobs for the actual Rangers.

David was assigned to SSG Jim "Bull" Bullock, who immediately saw something bright in the young private. He began mentoring him, showing him best practices on getting signed in, finding quarters and equipment, and more. David did these smartly with time to spare. That left time for Staff Sergeant Bull to assist him in getting a bank account, doing paperwork, and finishing the transition in record time.

Over the next few months, the private emerged as such a reliable soldier that Bull thought he would do well in college and could even apply for Officer Candidate School (OCS). Bull enjoyed working with him and seeing the spark of intellect. In a more relaxed environment, David now capitalized on the time to get in shape and learn Ranger skills more thoroughly. He especially valued his direct supervisor's endorsement. David knew the college and OCS track was a tough road, and he needed realistic guidance. Bull wholeheartedly supported the idea and offered his help. David went on to finish college, receive his commission as an officer, and finally graduate from Ranger School. Years later, he retired as a major with an MBA. Humble Bull takes no credit for David's success—not a surprise—but he does take great pride in the achievements of his favorite private who benefitted from his mentoring.

• • •

Sometimes it can be the private who extends his friendship up the chain of command, and that's how I met Bull 10 years earlier in the Italian Alps. Thirty days after taking command of my first platoon in the 82nd, we shipped out to winter survival training in Italy. At the conclusion of a land navigation exercise high up in the Alps, Private (PV2) Bullock and I popped off our snowshoes and rested on a rock that was nearly as high as the clouds. We could gaze down onto a village below, its lights peeking out into the twilight. For half an hour, it was just two guys talking about life and how fate had landed us on this scenic overlook in the Italian mountains. Not bad.

At the time, I was a 26-year-old lieutenant, and Bull was a 26-year-old private, probably the oldest in the 82nd Airborne Division. I was certain he was the more mature one between us. He had already seen more of life, and it was indispensable to have a friend and sounding board, all due respect given to rank.

Parallel to mentoring up and down, a profound respect for rank exists in the military, both upward and downward. Conversations like ours happened precisely because of the respect for each other's position. Being a new commander, I specifically appreciated the junior soldier's perspective and ear to the ground, and conversely he valued my perspective and command view of the unit. This combination helped us both. We maintained a respectful friendship through the rest of our service and then through life. His son was born on the July 4th weekend of our 10-year Desert Storm reunion, and we all busted into his wife Elizabeth's hospital room to celebrate. She's a gem too. Fun times.

After we first identify a trusted person who has good advice —a prospective mentor—carving out time for mentoring is critical to reaping its benefits. It seems obvious to say, but we need to be in the right place to spawn frequent comfortable conversations, and we also need to make it easy for our mentors to be involved. When shared activities provide a natural environment to relax and chat about life, the wisdom can flow.

The ability to mentor in both directions is a gift—one that's treated that way by the folks who are able to help and especially by those close to the top of the organizational ladder.

Prevailing with a Cool Head

Staff Sergeant (SSG) Jim "Bull" Bullock

Bold personalities are a signature quality of the heads of big businesses. Often, it's their brash and immediate movement that propels an organization into action—and profitability.

A company's success is built on a reputation that precedes its leaders before they even enter the room. In the game of chicken often playing out in the boardroom, that bold envoy who doesn't flinch is the one left standing in the end. The codicil that ought to be written into the leaders' manual is that each organization needs a rational-thinking executive to know when today's game of chicken might lead to a crash. That's when cooler heads need to prevail.

The Ziggurat of Ur is an ancient pyramid-shaped temple in southern Iraq on the edge of the desert. It was built in 2000 BCE, making it one of the oldest temples (some say the oldest) in the world. Everyone has heard of the nearby Tower of Babel, which was also a Mesopotamian Ziggurat temple but nearly a thousand years younger. The Tower of Babel attracted a lot of attention in its day. And then in 331 BC, it was destroyed by Alexander the Great. Meanwhile, the quiet Ur Ziggurat has survived the past 4,000 years almost wholly intact.

Staying humbly under the radar can be a valuable trait for survival, as Staff Sergeant Jim Bullock knew when he stood in awe at the base of the Ziggurat in 2010. The quiet power of the structure inspired him, and he felt lucky he could view this ancient wonder that few Westerners ever will.

Eighty-five miles north up the dusty road from the Ziggurat, Bull led a security convoy to escort a high-ranking U.S. State Department official who was meeting with the Iraqi provincial governor in Rumaytha. At this time in 2010, open hostilities had ceased, and the U.S. and Iraq were working to establish a coalition that would stabilize the country and neutralize the reckless insurgency. Because the balance was delicate, cool heads in all phases of the new peace were needed. As the vehicle commander, Bull had to safely negotiate the trip along the road, followed by rolling into the fortified compound and keeping visitors or trespassers away while this meeting took place.

Two drop arms and Iraqi guards secured the entrance to the compound. The VIP's lead vehicle, an armored Suburban and a security detail, passed through both arms. When the vehicle stopped, the official was efficiently whisked inside to meet the waiting governor. That armored Suburban stayed in the compound courtyard by the door facing outward. Bull kept his vehicle in between the two drop arms as a further blockade that he could control rather than leave security up to the Iraqi guards alone. His and the Suburban were the only vehicles in the courtyard as the meeting was in progress. Smooth so far.

Then a recent-model Toyota Corolla came racing up to the compound. It was skidding in and kicking up dust, as witnessed by Bull's two security men in the Suburban who turned at full alert. The Corolla came to a stop at the first drop arm, followed by an animated discussion between the driver and the Iraqi guard. Clearly, the driver and passenger were in a hurry and wanted to enter the compound.

Bull jumped out of the safety of the six-ton, steel-plated Chevy blocking the way into the compound. He put a pair of eyes on the situation and saw the traditional brown cloak called a *bisht* on a distinguished-looking passenger in the front seat. The local sheik! Apparently, he had been invited to the meeting but was late to arrive, so he wanted to get inside as quickly as possible. Bull confirmed what was said with the interpreter and let him pass.

That took just over two minutes of fresh thinking. Breathe. Stay cool.

Not 90 seconds later, with the second drop arm still up and the Chevy out of position, another vehicle blazed in from the main road. This time, the driver drove a large Land Cruiser SUV and wore an Iraqi uniform. The timing was bad. Across the courtyard, the U.S. official was just coming out of the building at the most vulnerable moment in the transport sequence. Not thinking, the guard lifted the first arm, allowing the Land Cruiser and its driver inside. That's when Bull stepped out in front of the vehicle to block its path. The driver was telling the interpreter he was a part of the sheik's entourage and demanded to be let through. But the timing was too coincidental. Bull knew the security detail inside the courtyard needed another 60 seconds to load up the VIP. His 190-pound body covered in armor was the only thing standing in the way of the Land Cruiser driver hitting the gas and getting inside the compound.

Maybe the driver was legit. Bull had to consider this. So he cupped his hands with fingers joined together and then bobbed them slowly up and down in the Iraqi gesture that means "have some patience." The driver wildly responded with the universal gestures of "why are you stopping me?" and "move out of the way." Bull's calm demeanor prevailed as he gently repeated the "have some patience" gesture.

Meanwhile, everyone on the U.S. security team jumped out of their vehicles. The Land Cruiser driver inched forward and bumped Bull, which elicited his calm repetition of the hand gesture. A second bump into his thigh invoked a firm facial rejoinder and stern fist from Bull landing on the vehicle's hood. Its third lurch jostled Bull back a step, and he knew it was time to bring his slung M4 rifle to the position of low-ready. The rest of the security team took the cue from their vehicle commander and raised their weapons too. This then caused the Iraqi guards to point their weapons at the Americans, causing the Americans to respond similarly toward the guards. Time froze.

Cool heads need to prevail, said the voice in Bull's head. Breathe.

Then he thought, *If I shoot the driver, it will end the threat right now. But the guards and security detail standing twenty feet apart will then open fire on each other, and there will be a bloodbath. Or I could try one last time.* So Bull looked calmly at the driver through the windshield, and this time slowly motioned to him to back away. Even the interpreter stopped yelling for a minute.

Pause.

The driver looked down defeated, put the stick shift into reverse, and backed up 30 feet until he was entirely outside the compound. At that point, all weapons were lowered.

Maybe the driver really was with the local sheik and had momentarily lost his head. Perhaps their culture is inherently an impatient culture and actors fly off the handle with little regard for consequences. In this case, though, everyone involved lived to tell the story because a patient American took a breath and enabled cooler heads to prevail.

Humble professionals in the workplace should have a sign above their desks that says, "Cooler heads prevail here" with an arrow pointing down at them. That way, we'd know to bring along these people during negotiations and contentious meetings.

What happens when there are no signs to tell us? Here's the shortcut: We can align ourselves with a humble, cool-headed professional or give a whirl at being one ourselves.

Understanding the Warrior

Staff Sergeant (SSG) Jim "Bull" Bullock

Smart managers destined for becoming CEOs will steadily learn just how far to push the competition in negotiations. Likewise, they will learn the limits of their own folks when placed in pressure situations. Sensing the reactions of both the foe across the table and the team members on the same side gives the point person the ability to make instant calculations when things get hot.

In the moment of "do or die," smart negotiators anticipate their opponent's next action, and they base their next steps on it. The challenge for the rest of us is not to escalate to the point of taking attention away from our leader. We might confuse the issue. Rather, understanding the warfighter mindset is a key to either competing with our own company strategy or complementing it.

Technology and weaponry notwithstanding, the concept of understanding the warrior's mentality for advantage still stands. While on a security mission for a copper and gold mine in the mountains at 14,000 feet, Bull had the chance to observe Melanesian indigenous tribes in Papua, Indonesia. He had once seen two rival tribes at a standoff in ankle-deep water down in the river. Clad in animal skins and homemade weapons, neither would budge out of each other's way. The situation escalated into a splashy impasse with shouts and threats for the other to step aside. The warriors pulled out pointy sticks and bows and arrows, which they fired haphazardly at each other.

From the road above, Bull and his security detail could hardly believe what they were witnessing in the year 2012. But the human warrior mindset seems omnipresent. One tribesman appeared to have made a more sophisticated bow than the others and launched an arrow that landed in the stomach of one of the combatants. That's when everyone in that tribe stopped the aggression, turned, and walked away. Understanding they were outmatched and would probably suffer more arrow shots, they moved on.

Company leaders today who understand the needs of the warrior are likely to be smashing their competition. Today's tech campuses that make the work environment a collegial, competitive place entice workers to devote their best talents and mental energy. Giving them a place to build their architecture and weaponry to face competitors is smart. And enlightened boards of directors in today's successful startups have looked down from the mountain road at those tribes duking it out below with bow and arrows. "That's not for us," they declare. They understand what the corporate warrior needs, and they set out to provide it.

Being Happy for Others' Success

Specialist (SPC) Andrew Siemer

Have you ever noticed when you start a new job that it's easy to spot the team players? They come and find you to offer helpful startup advice. They go out of their way to do it, and you always remember them. This activity is highly noticeable to the management team, so it makes good sense to become one of them. These are the folks who want their teammates to win, and when it happens, they're happy for their success.

Andrew Siemer spent time from '94 to '98 in the Ranger Regiment's 2nd Battalion during years that, thankfully for him, didn't involve combat. With the Rangers' heavy focus on filtering out low-performing personnel, Andrew stayed on top of the game by embracing self-improvement. Specifically, the M240 machine gunner concurrently learned computer architecture and taught himself CAD programming. And he also loved the physical rigor required to nail a 30-mile training road march complete with airfield seizure.

One night, Andrew made a deal with himself that he'd package his skills to help fellow vets in the civilian world. So after his enlistment ended, he worked his way up in the tech industry to became a chief architect in the consumer division of Dell.com. Today, he runs his own company called Inventive Group that helps veterans incubate fresh business ideas.

I like that Andrew has six kids and raises pigs and chickens. Ranger hooah to that. He also has a couple of cool business mantras I like. The first is to *emulate folks who have started with nothing and worked their way to success*, such as Kevin Hart and Dwayne "The Rock" Johnson. Great start. The second is to *be happy for others' successes.* We don't hear about this concept nearly often enough. As Andrew points out, there may not even be a well-accepted English word for it.

Remember the German word *schadenfreude* from psychology class? It means to revel in the misfortune of others—and then think the exact opposite. The ancient Sanskrit language offers the term *mudita* for "vicarious happiness," and modern Norwegian offers *unne* to "be glad on behalf of another." Andrew settles on the quasi-English term *compersion*—"joy that comes from witnessing another's enjoyment of something."

In business, your own brand of compersion can refer to orienting your behaviors toward achieving personal success that will complement the success of colleagues.

Great perspective.

Answering the Call

Operator Billy Mac

Want to get noticed at work in a positive way? Then volunteer when asked or do it even without needing to be asked.

Want to be remembered as a captain of industry? Then step up when everyone else is afraid to jump into the fray seeking solutions.

There never seems to be a shortage of folks who gather people near them to say how they "thought" about doing this or fixing that. Happy hours are full of guys telling stories of how they "almost joined the airborne" or were "this close to becoming a Navy SEAL." Yet there are precious few gems who step forward quietly and raise their hands without saying a word.

My good friend, whom we will call Billy Mac, is currently serving overseas in classified missions.

Ten years after separating from the U.S. Army as a Ranger in '92, he jumped back in to answer the call after the 911 attacks on the World Trade Center. I admired that about Billy, considering the rest of us were content in corporate America or back on the farm by then, growing fat and lazy. Here he was launching himself into the call of duty for a second bite of the apple. A piece of my heart lifted and grew fuller.

At the time, he was running a successful high-rise window glazing company in Vancouver. But this horrific assault on America called to him. He felt he had to slip his uniform back on to join the fight against terrorism. After signing up, he met five new brothers from the West Coast, all of whom had reached the same conclusion. These prior-service vets—a marine gunnery sergeant, a navy man, a couple of Rangers, and an army infantryman—made a pact to train and pass the Special Forces Selection Course (SFAS) at Fort Bragg. Why? They wanted to become *Green Berets.*

These six called themselves the Buckley Boys, since they had all converged on the Special Forces training center in Buckley, Washington. Symbiotically, they benefited from their separate strengths plus the electricity of the group to ready themselves for the army's premier "small unit operators" training. Command HQ in Buckley applauded the anything-but-traditional "old-guy" group of candidates and stood ready to welcome those who completed the course into the 19th SF Group. Billy and four out of the five old-timers passed. SF Group let them stay together, and over time formed a crucial A-Team that was deployed throughout the world. They have since gone on to log 16 successful years of missions overseas.

Billy Mac and his fellow operators provide wonderful role models for fellow seasoned professionals in the corporate sector. A hiatus or shift in industry needn't ever stand in the way of changing gears to commit to a new endeavor. The five mates—all aged more than 50—are living examples that we're never too old to serve.

Making Progress Out on the Edges

Operator Billy Mac

> *Business teams are fond of using descriptive terms like "frontal assault" and attacking at the "core and edge." When the preferred frontal access is not available (e.g., you can't contact an owner), then finding a way to nibble at the edge is the next best option. At these times, having an expanded set of skills on the part of the worker is helpful. It affords the Renaissance man a comprehensive set of talents, thus providing the best chance of success.*

When our mission is to teach, it's only natural to grade ourselves on how well the students have learned. Our operators deployed in western Afghanistan have the dual mission to protect the western flank and also teach the Afghan forces to step into the role when the time comes for American servicemen to leave.

In the Herat Province, Billy's team has been actively training one unit called the National Mission Brigade, who are reportedly taking the task more seriously than the other groups making up the ANSF Afghan National Security Forces. This brigade is proving to be a success story. Together they've made baseline wins that bolstered security near the Iranian border and southern trade routes. Using U.S. techniques and shadowing our teams, for example, they've gathered intel that Iranians are teaching Taliban forces near the border how to operate surveillance drones and, in some cases, how to engineer weaponized drone strikes.

Even in Afghanistan's tough political climate, these kinds of wins are possible with the right teachers and willing students. For those facing change in similarly tough business climates, the approach that Billy's teams use may be useful—that is, to find a small but motivated segment within the larger organization that can learn the technique at hand. After a few wins where they receive accolades, the rest of the climate is likely to improve.

As a leader of men, Billy is personable and talented—one of the few Renaissance men I know. Due to his vastly different jobs, he can hold a conversation on any topic I can drum up. I've known him as a volleyball player, restaurateur, retailer, and small businessman. He's a lover of art and travel, can "Inspector Gadget" anything that needs a solution, and is the first human I ever knew to have a bag phone in 1990. While we were on top of Grouse Mountain in British Columbia, Billy introduced me to Canadian ice wine and then taught me how to dig a volleyball spike by tucking my knuckles under and absorbing the velocity.

After Billy graduated Ranger School, we all lined up and pounded a blood tab (hitting his newly earned pin) into his chest, which he said was the sweetest pain he ever felt. Quite a turnaround from a warrior who once changed my son's diaper that, he said with a laugh, was the worst thing he had ever smelled.

Young leaders who desire to be incredibly diverse in their talents or may not have fully decided their career path yet are smart to emulate the way of the Renaissance man. It's all about being intellectually curious and multifaceted—and being able to attend court (and someday perhaps even hold it) on a diverse range of interests.

Marketing Ourselves for Success

Master Sergeant (MSG) Dave Maestas

Brand-new companies need an extra boost to lift their business off the page. With a keen focus only on the core product or service —where it ought to be for the new business owner—those little boosts might get forgotten.

Marketing your business to let consumers know you are up and running seems like the first best boost for investment. Following that is enlisting the proper marketing resource—someone who knows the market or the geography or both.

Dave Maestas made the jump from helping warfighters and indigenous peoples in the Middle East to assisting businesses to market themselves for success. A 20-year career took him through 2nd Ranger Battalion, 10th Mountain, and 5th Special Forces, with four deployments overseas. But for Dave, nothing was as hard as Ranger School or his early days as a lowly private in Ranger Batt. There, getting "smoked" for every little mistake made him desperate to strive for perfection. Enduring an hour-long smoke session of pushups and flutter kicks for not having his bootlaces tied in a prescribed square knot at a surprise inspection taught him always to be ready. His motto: *Just be prepared and anticipate whatever might come next.*

In the zero-tolerance world of combat preparation, he learned from Battalion Commander LTC Stanley McChrystal that the young troops would always remember two things: honesty, and leading from the front. They met again in Afghanistan, 15 years later, after General McChrystal had earned his fourth star. The general recognized Dave at a base in the Balkh Province during a mission briefing, and expressed genuine excitement for Dave's promotion to Green Beret team sergeant.

McChrystal, the commanding general of all the Afghan forces in 2010, told Dave it made him proud to see great young soldiers who had once been his. Now, they were taking leadership in the global war on terrorism where they were most needed. Facing overwhelming obstacles can make a soldier want to quit. Dave had plenty of chances to do so while in the field, but he didn't. Perseverance became his best attribute.

Transitioning from field leader to business leader, Dave saw too many vendors selling services that don't positively affect the customer's bottom line. As one example, marketing a fledgling business is a core function that needs to be high on the priority stack—or no one may ever hear about the business's excellent new product. Some entrepreneurs attempt to perform the marketing function themselves, or they engage a marketing company that doesn't have a local viewpoint of the business. Either choice can spell risk, which is why Dave created a company that manages marketing for new companies. And Dave believes no one can be successful on just eight hours of work a day. That's why his company aims to provide extra hours of sweat to help new businesses.

In today's business world, Ranger leaders might compare the concept of quitting to "shifting priorities to less essential or just more comfortable tasks." They regard this as the civilian version of giving up. The challenging jobs are the ones that should really be attacked full frontal, especially since they're often the ones that make money.

Just as an A-Team employs the latest technology to succeed on the battlefield, savvy companies use up-to-date technology to drive business to the client. Employing email software to conduct drip campaigns and maximize open rates are the kinds of items seen on marketing radar screens, and these tactics are paying off for new businesses.

CHAPTER TWO

Acknowledging the fact that a Ranger is a more elite soldier who arrives at the cutting edge of battle by land, sea, or air, I accept the fact that as a Ranger my country expects me to move farther, faster, and fight harder than any other soldier.

Heroes Aren't Born, They're Tabbed	Rangers Lore
Knowing the Only Way to Get There	Rangers in School
Becoming an Army of One	Rangers in School
First Man through the Door	Rangers in the Desert
The Mission's Not Quite Over until the Debriefing	Rangers in the Desert
Taking Ten When It's Offered	Rangers in the Desert
Poking a Stick at Yourself	Rangers in the Desert
Promoting Your People to the Universe	Rangers in the Desert
Learning from Experts who Work for You	SGT Scott Mandeville
Making a Positive First Impression	MSG Ralph "Ike" Jackson

Heroes Aren't Born, They're Tabbed

Rangers Lore

> *Most multilayered companies have vaunted positions that require advanced credentials. Many C-Staff officers have earned their PhDs or MBAs, and project managers their PMPs. Solution architects may have an alphabet soup of certifications such as CISM, MCSE, or CCSE. The payoff for these credentials is excellent, especially since the road to getting there ain't easy. Folks with the right stuff set their sights on achieving them. They deserve all the praise they receive, as the company relies on them in the toughest situations.*

When you hear the term Army Ranger, a mystic image of heroes bounding out of the smoke under heavy fire to rain hell upon the enemy comes to mind.

And it should. Tabbed warriors—those who've earned a special "tab" to wear on their uniforms—are the closest thing we have to superheroes today.

The Ranger mission requires heavy combat. Force on force, it involves our best-trained and best-armed troops massing against the enemy's best. Enemy combatants would be smart to realize they have no chance; they're already defeated before the first shot is fired.

Why? Because the Airborne Ranger is simply the most highly skilled, ruthlessly tested combat soldier in the free world.

> The U.S. Army authorizes only two unique two-inch tabs (with the words RANGER or SPECIAL FORCES) to be worn on the left shoulder of any soldier's uniform who completes the required course. The distinctively placed tab can be easily seen by anyone approaching. It identifies the soldier as elite. It's coveted enough that some Rangers tattoo the image of the RANGER tab directly onto their shoulder, and whether they go on to serve in the Ranger Regiment or Airborne/combat infantry—or just serve their careers in a noncombat role—they are always considered Rangers till the day they die.

Rangers often operate without food, without sleep, without shelter, without creature comforts or communication with the outside world. They carry on their backs the water and ammo they need and then carry out the wounded the same way. They know they will be handed the most perilous jobs that no one else wants, and they expect to be the last ones standing regardless of the odds.

No Ranger brother I know would allow himself to be called a hero—and that's precisely part of the selfless persona. A better question to ask them is whether they have served with many heroes over the years. You'll most likely get a thoughtful or teary, "Hell, yes."

What motivates a Ranger to sacrifice all if necessary?

Brotherhood.

This concept known as brotherhood is powerful. Shakespeare wrote about it 500 years ago, and warriors had already been forging the same bonds 2,000 years before that. Men who would sacrifice and bleed together form a union as strong as steel—a bond that fills their hearts, too.

Experiencing a rare type of love such as that reserved for brothers in arms is beautiful.

Disaster survivors and championship teammates feel a similar version of brotherhood. It's the sense of love that can keep them alive on the battlefield and then sustain them as life-long friends when they "get back to the world."

Yesterday's threat from communism has been replaced by threats from extremist religious-based countries in the Middle East. Through the decades of these various oppressive regimes, the good old U.S. continues to forge ahead. She stands up for democracy again and again. Distilled into military terms, this translates into maintaining an elite force ready to deploy wheels-up anywhere in the world within 18 hours.

As long as there is turbulence threatening to disrupt peaceful people living in freedom, the world will always need Navy SEALs, Green Berets, Delta Force, Marine MarSoc, and our Rangers.

The fundamental culture of Ranger brotherhood exceeds what exists in the corporate world, but its similarities still outweigh its differences. Humanity breeds camaraderie no matter the environment. It blossoms whether colleagues are charging across a compound with grenades or welding shoulder to shoulder on an assembly line.

Brotherhood is like a lemon tree that grows to different heights in different places. For example, the six-foot Meyer tree gives us a sweet lemon with thin skin that bruises easily, while the 20-foot Sicilian produces thick-skinned lemons that can ship out in sturdy crates worldwide and last a long time. Like the limits of brotherhood, the tree's growing environment determines the heights and lengths they both might grow. They're sweetly similar but tartly different.

With that filter in mind, we can understand that the corporate equivalent of brotherhood offers us special teams, user groups, conferences, and industry-specific awards to keep the advanced-degree professionals up to date on the latest trends. It also fills that niche of keeping those in the brotherhood in touch with each other. The chance to have a room full of general counsels would be rare but invaluable when found. Gathering as a herd helps fill a professional need—and also the human need for nurturing.

Knowing the Only Way to Get There

Rangers in School

Sometimes in corporate America, we hear a rags-to-riches story of an entrepreneur who hits it big overnight. Great stories like these fuel the sales world and keep new ideas flowing. Yet on the certification/advanced degree side of the business, there aren't any shortcuts to the path set by the granting institutions. Get ready for the CPA–MBA–PhD grind if you want to bask in the adulation that might follow.

There is only one way to become a Ranger, and that is to graduate Ranger School. There is no executive session for senior officers; no short course for qualified NCOs; no honorary tab, no grandfathering in, no online portion, no unit designation, nor any other shortcut you can conceive. The only way to get there is through the gates of Ranger School at Fort Benning for 61 days of hell on earth.

If you plan to become a Ranger, just accept that the course will be the worst two months of your life. You'll endure starvation and sleep deprivation right up to the limit of human endurance. You'll be on the move for 20-hour days with two hours of sleep a night and one meal a day. Attrition is designed into the program. Typically, Ranger candidates lose 20 percent of their day-one bodyweight. Having trained like a maniac through five previous

The length of Ranger School is a fun topic among Rangers of different generations, which is why you'll see it listed at varying durations by old-timers versus current Rangers. They're all correct. The course lasted 59 days up until the 90s, then expanded to as much as 68 days to build in extra sleep after the unfortunate swamp-phase deaths in 1995. Oh, and for exactly a dozen years from '83–'95 (I got to enjoy it in '89) there was a fourth phase called "desert phase." It's now settled back into 61 days of 19.6 hours of daily training (not counting two hours of logistic time, leaving 2.4 hours of sleep per day), or 62 if you count the in-processing day. So, everyone's right, and the discussion is normally just a good reason for Rangers at the bar to order another round of tequila.

months of Infantry Basic followed by Jump School, I came in on day one of Benning Phase at a studly five-foot-nine inches and 173 pounds of solid rock, only to whittle down to 142 pounds of skin and bones at graduation eight weeks later.

A typical class starts with 400 candidates, of which only 125 graduate. About 36 percent of the cohort flushes in the first four days of the Benning Phase, which is chock full of immediate pass/fail events that weed out the unprepared. When the Benning phase concludes, roughly 60 percent of those who will eventually fail are already gone. Not surprising. Any candidates who fail the PT test or the obstacle course on day one are out. If they're injured at any point for any reason, they're out. If they get sick, gone. If they fail the Ranger assessment overall score in the first five days, adios. If they fail two missions in a row, they're axed. And if they receive a "bad" peer review at the end of any phase for not being a team player (based on Ranger teammates seeing something the instructors cannot), that's it.

The staff in charge, called Ranger instructors (RIs), are the toughest, meanest, and most unforgiving crew of supersoldiers the military has ever assembled. They only care that their students reach the standard; anything else is a FAIL. Absolutely no excuses are accepted in Ranger School. If candidates can't hit the measure on a task, they get a "minus." Two minuses in any phase, and they get recycled. Two recycles, and they go home.

Of course, you can always accelerate the go-home process via injury, sickness, or quitting and then go home directly. But assuming you have the indomitable grit it takes to gut out each new day of Ranger School, you'll be continually required to accomplish near-impossible team tasks that are, in fact, physically unfeasible to achieve alone. And that's the whole idea.

To succeed, a 10-man Ranger squad must work together and split up all the tasks to complete the mission to earn a PASS. Everyone rotates skill positions, such as squad leader or machine gunner, so no one can game the system. All Ranger candidates need to perform their assigned skills on the current mission—no slack given.

A typical graded mission is a platoon-sized (40-man) raid to be completed 12 hours after a warning order is given. The first hours require a few kilometers of ground movement to a specific meeting spot for intense planning, gathering of supplies, and preparing equipment. Next, they require more progress on foot to a place a few kilometers closer, then they conduct a live rehearsal of the mission. At the same time, a small recon element moves out to lay eyes on the actual raid site. A final briefing follows, and then the entire unit moves out at last light.

Already starving and exhausted as the mission begins, members of the platoon set out on any variety of treacherous terrains for five to eight more kilometers until they link up with the recon element. (That's the group who left earlier to get eyes on the target.) They await outside the raid site as a whole unit poised to attack. Specifics and critical timing are confirmed one last time before the platoon of 40 breaks off into four squads of 10 each. Then they set a time within the next hour to rain down coordinated hell onto the raid site that's full of enemy soldiers.

The grading instructors (RIs) have already been watching every move since the prep location. By now, they have undoubtedly handed out several minuses during the daylight hours. Next comes the crucial time when the platoon leadership will pass or fail.

Intense scrutiny falls upon them all to succeed. If any small piece of their task fails or one of the assigned troops falters, then the leader fails the mission. However, if the mission goes off like clockwork, even through the fog of fatigue and starvation, the task will be graded a success. Then every Ranger candidate gets to live for another day.

And next comes the clever trick of the RIs. They allow everyone to relax at the end of the mission while collecting their gear and moving away from the objective back to camp. On the one hand, the march back to the patrol base is no longer filled with pre-mission tensions. Each Ranger candidate can breathe a small sigh of relief. But the night march back is guaranteed to be eight to 10 more kilometers—starting about three in the morning.

The Ranger School activities that led to a lot of adrenaline pumping through the Ranger candidates' veins have ended, allowing their anxiety to subside. But that relief gives way to realizing their starved bodies must endure an unthinkable two-hour march with heavy packs and gear. What cruelty!

Within minutes after the excitement of the shooting and prisoner-capture finishes, the platoon starts back through the pitch dark in silence. At this point, their bodies realize they have no adrenaline left for bursts of energy. Instead, the voices in their heads are begging them to stop and sleep. They scream to address the scrapes and scratches, and for God's sake, find some food. It becomes a struggle for survival just to make it until sunrise while the voices in their heads keep begging.

> One of Ranger School's most effective cruelties turns out to be unleashing your mind against your body to see which will prevail. When there's no glory on the line and no juice left, no one to talk to, and miles to go before you sleep, can your mind beat your body?

What happens when the Ranger candidates honestly can't imagine taking more than the next few steps before quitting? Grit will have to get them through. And soon it gradually flows into their consciousness to survive. How? By staying in back of the man in front and leading the man behind. Inexorably, the interior voice changes and repeats, "Okay. I'm gonna make it home safely."

For the corporate warriors pulling double duty, working a full-time job and going to school on nights and weekends, how often does it occur to them that not many could handle this load? What percentage of the workforce even realizes the level of dedication needed to earn that extra credential?

The mind plays similar cruel tricks to pull a student off course —all the more reason to applaud the ones who remain diligent and complete the requirements.

Becoming an Army of One

Rangers in School

Have you ever found yourself in a class where you feel like you're the only underprepared one, or you're at a new job where you feel like you're in over your head? Why does this feeling come in the first place? After all, you can't expect to be an expert on day one or know the course material before it's even taught. What's happening here?

If you're game, try the Ranger method to overcome that feeling. There are a pair of realizations/reactions that surface, which are useful to the newly promoted or newly enrolled professional. The first realization is having so much to learn that it feels impossible to do it alone. The accurate reaction ought to be "yes." The second realization is that, under the present conditions, it feels like "I can't do it."

What's the response of Ranger candidates? It's to "group up" for survival. We see smart alliances spring up in the form of study groups at grad school or as cohorts coming out of sales training. For a new employee, the trick of merging into an established cohort is to quickly identify a workgroup(s) with a similar scope of duties, then join via its email distribution list, meetings, etc. Connecting with people who can help will accelerate the learning curve in any environment.

The Rangers help candidates ditch their fears by being part of a group that's doing fantastic feats together. After all, there's less chance of being fearful when everyone is doing the same thing. I think back to a Ranger instructor in the swamp phase of

Ranger School who barked, "Let's go, Rangers. Get in the water." We single-filed in the pitch black of the Florida swamps, entering chest-high water for a mission requiring us to slog three hours to get to the other side. It sounds scary, but with 100 other people doing it, I told myself, "I guess I can do it too."

Imagine this. It's just after midnight, and no one has slept more than 90 minutes at a time in the past three days. No one has eaten a significant amount since yesterday's daily MRE. Even packaged army rations taste like four-star dining when you're starving.

The army's famous Meal Ready to Eat (MRE) is a brown plastic packaged sack with 3,500 calories worth of food. It features main meals like "spaghetti and meatballs" helpfully written in large letters as a notification of what's inside. Sometimes that's needed to remind us of what we're halfway through eating in case we fail to recognize the taste.

The freshness date is stamped on the bag. Because the army likes to stockpile items for future readiness, the preservatives in the meals soldiers are eating today could maintain the food's freshness until 2045. Each main meal is located inside in a sealed foil pouch, most conveniently eaten by ripping the top and sucking the contents while simultaneously squeezing the bottom.

Soldiers who prefer a heated meal can do so by pulling the foil pouch out of the big bag and sticking it between their boxers and their groin for an hour. That way, it warms up as they walk. I refer to this method as the microwave, which is only slightly funny. Seriously, a Ranger doesn't let anything go to waste—not even the heat generated between his legs.

However, on this mission to make it back to camp, no one is thinking about warming up an MRE. They're thinking about surviving the trek back. Ranger School methodology pushes these candidates swiftly toward survival mode. It then evaluates their ability to hold on and function from there: starving, sleepless, wet, and carrying a full ruck with rifle overhead in water in the dark. Anyone would be justified to feel afraid and, if left alone, fear the variables of alligators, snakes, mud, vines, extreme fatigue, starvation, and drowning. Sane humans might even be driven to a state of blind fear.

But when the Ranger team of 30 is united in the effort, they just believe. Everyone does their part—that is, rely on bodies directly in front to keep in contact with those farther in front. They also rely on the patrol leader's sketch, which was vetted by everyone in the chain during the planning process. If everyone does their job, they win. And as for dangers like alligators and ambushes—or IEDs (improvised explosive devices) later when it becomes real combat—we're not focusing on the distractions. Even a green soldier learns to keep his mouth shut about the perils of war, knowing his number can quickly be up. Best plan is to be with the herd.

The elite soldier quickly figures out there's simply no point in devoting mental energy to danger. It can be paralyzing and infectious. The focus is on the night's goal. "Brothers, the team's mission is to traverse the swamp and fight a battle on the other side." That alone provides plenty to think about. The goal is to leverage the kinetic energy of the group into a mind-clearing tool.

Coalescing into a unit at the outset allows for the group to divide up the routine tasks at work they know should run smoothly. Once the team is functioning like a well-oiled machine with 20 arms and legs, they'll be ready to handle new projects that one person couldn't possibly handle alone. They'll organically do what they always do, which is to attack the problem together.

First Man through the Door

Rangers in the Desert

There's a term in business called "blazing the trail" from the settler days when the first folks to enter burnt a path through the forest via little notches that everyone could follow. Due to the immense danger involved, their effort was hailed as authentic leadership.

I genuinely love the pure guts of my beloved Airborne and Army Rangers. The brotherhood among men who bleed for each other on the battlefield is a phenomenon that only a minuscule portion of the population ever gets to experience. And I would find out that MIT (Massachusetts Institute of Technology) loves them too.

Nearly three decades later, the tech mecca and business school would carve a niche for Special Operations–qualified officers in the hopes that combat-experienced leaders might lend a perspective that helps the classically trained business mind. That was my entrée to the school and the best academic decision I ever made.

Once again, I loved identifying with the best of the best and hustling to be worthy of these great new academic alumni. On my first day of class, the professor asked me to describe a prominent lesson emblazoned in my mind from the military. I immediately thought of my first patrol into Iraq even before the ground war had started. My response to the professor? To be the first man through the door.

On a moonlit night in Iraq in January of 1991, our Red Falcon Recon platoon (also called the Scouts) was on the Saudi Arabian side of the Iraqi/Saudi border at Phase Line Razor. Razor was the several-hundred-mile-long line of disembarkation stretching west to east along the border that would mark our advance into Iraq. We assumed that advance would happen in the coming month, but it was still top secret to us grunts at the front.

Our 30-man unit was the tip of the spear for the entire 82nd Airborne Division of 10,000. The Falcon Brigade of 3,000 men was at the tip of the other two brigades in a triangle formation spanning 40 miles across at the rear. Just 300 meters in front at the sharp tip were my Scouts, pointed toward the enemy at the border. We buried everything we needed for our patrols right beside us, as we'd been dropped off days earlier with enough provisions and ammo to last a month.

After digging in to become invisible, we were self-sufficient enough to conduct nightly small unit operations. We'd do that for as long as General Schwarzkopf needed us to gather intel before the allied advance into Iraq. The ground invasion, which came to be known as G-Day, depended on intel from little sections of the border like ours to see what awaited us. Until then, we were entirely on our own.

To visualize the 10,000-man 82nd Airborne Division in your mind, you can draw a picture of a 40-mile equilateral triangle with three smaller triangles of combat units inside.

It was formed by the 6,700 men of the 505th "Panther" and 504th "Devil" (now called "Strike Hold") brigades that were 40 miles across the south edge and parallel to the border. The 3,300 men of the "Falcon" brigade were in front of them to the north. They formed the shape of a smaller triangle one-third the size of the whole to complete the 40-mile equilateral triangle shape.

Further, the front brigade-sized triangle broke into the same proportion of 2,200 men of the Blue Falcon and Gold Falcon Battalions to the south and the 1,100-man Red Falcons to the north—closest to the border. For the Red Falcons, it was Charlie company in front of Alpha and Bravo. As per doctrine, the Battalion Scout platoon was placed 10 miles in front of the lead unit to act as the recon element for the entire division. Doing this formed quite a sharp tip of the spear.

For four days straight, we hustled to get ready for our first patrol. An objective had been set to reconnoiter a few "clicks" (kilometers) out across the border. Because that night would be the division's initial mission into enemy territory, both the Battalion S3 major and brigade colonel personally handed out the order in the brigade HQ. They warned us to not get captured and show up on TV. The fate of one unlucky American captain who had been taken was currently all over the news. In the world of the military, that type of warning is standard fare and not nearly as dark as I recalled years later. "Stay frosty and don't get captured" was an entirely salient admonition.

Our Red Falcon Battalion had just arrived up at the border via a short flight from Al Jubail to King Khalid Military Center. Then we trucked all the way up to Phase Line Razor courtesy of a four-truck convoy—two to carry the men and two to haul our building equipment (tin sheets, stakes, and empty sandbags) plus 30 days of provisions. We worked like dervishes to dig suitable two-man and three-man holes and hide everything so we could be mission ready. Now we were. Brigade wasted no time getting us out into the unknown either. A giant blank grid was drawn and hung at HQ for the Scouts to fill in potential hot spots. On day three, headquarters prioritized the targets. On day four, we were ready to rock and roll at sunset.

Our 10-man patrol began to assemble right at the last light of day (standard procedure). This gave the chosen squad of that evening the maximum time to prepare to launch across the border into Iraq as soon as darkness came. This night was the first mission, which meant it would be 1st Squad. That honor belonged to SSG Akers, the squad leader known as the best NCO in the platoon. We would be limited only by the number of dark hours and the amount of distance we could cover on foot before sunrise. So if we could make 11 kilometers out and 11 back plus the 60 minutes we needed on the objective—all in darkness—and then climb back into our holes before daylight, we would have a viable plan. We did the math, and it worked. In truth, even if the math had not worked, we would still have planned to launch the patrol. Five months of anticipation through Operation Desert Shield had built up to this night, and we were stoked like hot coals!

With sunset approaching at Phase Line Razor, we emerged out of our foxholes to prepare for the night's mission. SSG Aker's squad tightened their gear and dropped the heavy stuff they wouldn't need. To have extra firepower, we added a three-man element from SGT Mandeville's squad at the last minute. It made good sense to bring a second seasoned squad leader with us, and SGT Mandeville was eager to jump in. Dunbar and Thompson lent extra skill in setting up a release point when we got near the objective—that is, if we found more than we bargained for and needed reinforcement. Since the outpost was 11 clicks away, 10 of them over the border, we planned to trek to the farthest safe point and drop gear. There, we could break down to a smaller probing element of three and check it all out.

Last light of the day was upon us. We were double-checked to Ranger standards. Then we launched out on foot "on azimuth" —following the magnetic direction on the compass—across the border toward the night's objective: a single one-story structure in the middle of nowhere.

Over the next three hours, the moon came out in full force, producing 87 percent illumination. I had never seen a moon this bright back in the States. Or more accurately, I hadn't ever seen such strong effects of its illumination. In the open desert, the moonlight is free to bathe the ground unobstructed, and when it does land, it gleams off the sand to produce a significant amount of light. An illumination factor of 30 percent allows you to see all around you even at midnight. At 60 percent, the visibility is bright enough to operate without night vision goggles. At 87 percent, it was nearly daylight. I was thankful for my own team's ease of navigating the desert night toward the objective. But at the same time, I became keenly aware of the same advantage in the enemy's favor.

At three hours in, our patrol halted 800 meters short of the target. By the book, we formed a small defensive perimeter to see out in all directions, letting us gain visibility of anyone approaching while at the objective. We dropped our big packs and broke down our group to only three of us—me, Sergeant Akers, and Sergeant Mandeville. We shed all the unnecessary equipment that might make noise or slow us down; then we proceeded in total silence for the final half mile across the open desert floor.

We approached the long, low building described on the intel report. From 100 meters out, we could make out three doorways

> If you're walking across the desert floor with only camo and your stealth to protect you, you are exposed and vulnerable—like sitting ducks. Each kind of terrain carries its vulnerable moments. In the desert on a moonlit night with no hills or trees for cover, you are like a carpenter ant making its way across a concrete patio, totally exposed on the way to the job. You're hoping not to be seen nor to be casually flicked away before arriving at your destination.

spaced evenly about 10 meters apart. The building seemed quiet as if abandoned long ago. I wondered what life would be like for an Iraqi outpost soldier stationed in a building like this just five miles from the Saudi border at the extreme southern edge of the homeland. The building clearly didn't have running water or electricity.

Whatever planning went into this outpost had been perfunctory. That is to say, some Iraqi general likely told Saddam Hussein his government needed to establish outposts covering a 300-mile stretch of open desert border. Hence, the Iraqis erected this concrete building with a corrugated tin roof in the middle of nowhere and 50 miles from any paved road. They probably plotted its location via the 1980s-generation GPS and sent two or three unlucky soldiers there with a week's worth of water and supplies at a time to guard the frontier.

Silly, really. If any soldiers were even manning the outpost, it would be unlucky for them to be there. Our troops and vehicles would easily maneuver around them and put a TOW missile round through the building on G-Day when they came rolling through. Yet that just might not be in time to stop them from sending off an emergency message that Allied forces were heading for Baghdad. That's why we scouted there that night and for the next month of nights—to recon just who might threaten to ruin our element of surprise come G-Day. The Iraqi soldiers out on the frontier would need to disappear.

At 75 meters out, we slowed our pace, looking for signs of life coming from the building or behind it. We had muted our radios all the way so they wouldn't squawk at the wrong moment, plus those in the main squad force knew to stay off the channel unless they spotted contact heading our way. In that case, we'd hear the soft squelches of the push-to-talk button to alert us. If anyone broke radio silence, they'd have SSG Akers to deal with. That was a punishment worse than kicking a bear cub inside its den and finding Mama suddenly standing there, snorting, mad, and blocking the entrance. It was safe to assume the radios would stay quiet.

At 50 meters, we could estimate more accurately that the doors were about seven meters apart and symmetrically spaced across the front. We spitballed the hut to be 30 meters wide by four meters high and maybe five to eight meters deep—long, low, and difficult to cover from inside. As a soldier, I would never plant myself in a building like that and defend it entirely from the inside. I'd want eyes outside it and would post exterior guards on shifts to watch in all directions.

But with only a handful of soldiers and no one to check on them for 100 miles, chances are they would get lazy and dull over the months of quiet, especially in the middle of the night, even knowing the Americans were just a few hundred miles away. They'd have no idea that, on this particular night, we were quietly stalking our way toward their location to recon any activity and eliminate them stealthily if possible.

Easy math: 3 Rangers x 3 doors = 1 man on each door . . . me in the middle as the patrol leader and two fellow Rangers on each side waiting for the signal to move. We had been walking in a small triangular wedge formation to get this far. At 25 meters and seeing the lanes we needed to cover, we fanned out in a straight line directly in front of each door to close the final distance. If we could cover down on each entry at the same moment and then sweep left to right like the rifle team in a high school marching band at halftime—just adding coordinated M16 fire—we'd be inside and clear the building in a few seconds.

The first small tricky part, though, was the multiple entrances, so we'd all have to be tight on getting inside our doors one after the other—boom, boom, and boom. There could also be a considerable amount of scattering inside. Last, there might be a back door, but we'd worry about that after we got inside. I wasn't worried about Iraqis running away and escaping with their backs to us, especially scurrying half awake into the desert with nowhere to go.

At 10 meters, quiet still prevailed. We halted as the three of us stood online like gunslingers in an Old West movie. It was as if we had posed directly in front of each of our entry points in the windless, noiseless desert night. At the pause, I looked left at SSG Akers and right at SGT Mandeville to get a thumbs up from each. Still quiet. No one else in sight. No alarm warning from the main element overwatching from a safe distance away. All checks were complete and ready to proceed forward to breach the building.

My mind involuntarily completed one final test—my own heartbeat. The desert floor had been so warmly tranquil that on any other night, we would have marveled at how peaceful it made us feel inside. Maybe that's why I noted my heartbeat at that moment. It was pretty calm and under control. *Good*, I thought, happy that autonomic functions were running smoothly.

Then I saw that my assigned middle doorway was blocked with rubble and concertina wire four feet high. Unlike the other two doors on the ends, there was no actual door in the doorway, just a waist-high heap of blockage that I was not about to breach silently. If I went in first as planned, it would cause a helluva lot more racket than a swift door kick. It would also be an enormous challenge to get up and over the debris to get inside the structure, ready to spray fire in one fluid movement. Thus, our plan of preserving the element of surprise had just nosedived.

Thinking tactically, I eyeballed SSG Akers and hand signaled, "My entrance blocked . . . you enter first . . . spray fire right to left . . . we'll follow." It was a logical call based on the situation, but boy was I wrong. It was our first mission of the war, and emergent leadership probably needed to trump tactics on this maiden patrol. Thankfully, my NCO respectfully steered me to the right course.

I trusted my spectacular Ranger NCO. He had guided me respectfully since I had taken command 90 days earlier after sizing me up as a leader who placed the men's welfare equal in importance to the success of the mission. He also knew we had the potential to achieve that textbook symbiosis between officer and NCO team that is vaunted among field combatants, and he relished going into the fray as a real leadership duo.

He calmly signaled back, "Sir, you're leading the patrol . . . YOU go right up the gut . . . WE follow."

The revelation hit me—right there in the suck, 8,000 miles away from home. I *knew* the leader should always be the first man through the door. When you're the one in charge, barbed wire, rubble, or waiting enemy inside don't matter. Given this patrol was the first of the campaign, the patrol leader who expects others to follow him into the breach for weeks to follow has to establish that he dives into hell before anyone else. Only then will others reflexively follow without hesitation. Tactics may solve the immediate problem, but pure guts can baptize an entire army.

SSG Akers also realized this patrol would set the tone for the rest of our battalion—and beyond. The moment was more than my baptism into Desert Storm; it was a plunge into the water as a leader. SSG Akers was signaling the way for me. *School's over; here we go.*

I covered the final 10 meters. Then I busted into the heap of rubble blocking the door, and tumbled inside with a thud. I came up, pointing my rifle left, and then cleared from left to right. No one was shooting back at me when I paused. Then SSG Akers came into the cleared left door, followed by SGT Mandeville in through the right. Threat neutralized, building cleared, patrol completed, and with the help of my senior NCO, my first test of leadership passed.

Leadership at that moment was crystal clear: *Be the first in, blaze the trail without fear, and set the example.* Word will get out, make no mistake, of who leads and who hesitates. Be the *leader*, and that reputation will stay with you forever. That's what I learned that night in Iraq, and I thank Sergeant Akers for it.

Young leaders profit from this particular combat lesson. What student or new sales exec doesn't benefit from raising a hand in class when the teacher asks, "Who wants to go first?" The pure guts it takes to go first is always rewarded. I might go a step further and advise any young leader who wants to impress to always "go first." It's such an easy life hack.

Being first in a race means you have to be speedy fast and train for years.

Being first in a karaoke contest means you probably need silky pipes.

But going first when asked for volunteers is as simple as raising your hand. Why ever waste the opportunity to take that initiative? You'll be noticed and rewarded for it.

For emerging managers making their way up the corporate ladder, being first through the door might mean taking preemptive actions such as volunteering to model the new sales presentation for the rest of the team as soon as it comes out.

Anticipating the need to show everyone "how it works" and getting things standardized early might pay big dividends against the competition. Leadership like this can answer the tough questions from the crowd. A great young manager who's not scared to go first can be quietly galvanizing the team and anticipating obstacles before they even arise.

The Mission's Not Quite Over until the Debriefing

Rangers in the Desert

In today's business environment, we often see a remarkable win wrapped up by a quick congratulatory "way to go" email sent to the team. Then it's back to the phones instead of a quality wrap-up with best practices written down for future campaigns to model. Why is that? Is it because a debrief ***requires time****, or is it because it* ***requires thought****?*

After we returned from the all-night patrol, we devised a working routine for the next 32 patrols to follow. The men would hunker back into their foxholes in morning's light to crack open an MRE for breakfast and then get some sleep. I would walk to the rendezvous point 500 meters to the rear to be picked up by a Humvee and then take the 10-mile ride back to brief the staff and fill in the blank wall-sized grid hanging at brigade headquarters. That way, as each night's mission covered a different sector that I could fill in, the brigade's intel officer would get a clear idea of what might lay ahead for our upcoming invasion across the border.

We rinsed and repeated this process for a month straight in whirlwind fashion. It was exciting to be contributing hard G2 (military intelligence gathered for use in the field) to the division's effort every night. The adrenaline rush kept me going all the way—sort of.

When the task was over and we were heading back to HQ, the hot sun beat down on the Hummer's hood while I'd be switching mental gears into talk mode. Fatigue rushed in hard like a charging bull. I prepared for the energy letdown by stowing a dehydrated pork patty in my ammo pouch to munch on during the ride back. I also slept for most of the 25 minutes, which wasn't all that easy. We bounced up the swales and down the wadis (dry ravines) of the unpaved Arabian desert.

Another impediment to getting a decent catnap was the young driver sent to get me. He would invariably want to know what we had found out in the desert during the night's recon. For the first five minutes, he'd make excited chatter until I could wedge my Kevlar helmet between the seat back and the door to

How does U.S. Army field-expedient coffee brew? By tossing the grounds, water, and a little salt into a pot over a flame that never quite makes it to a boil. However, it does manage to get hot enough to release the grounds' flavor into the water. All you have to do is dip your canteen cup in the pot and scoop out some of that black gold. Then you try to ditch the grounds floating on top inside your canteen cup with something clean—certainly not filthy hands.

My brother Ed had taught me the trick of dropping a single ice cube into hot coffee, which would make all the grounds gather round for removal. But we didn't have any ice cubes in the desert. I just drank around the grounds. I knew they wouldn't kill me.

lean in for a quick snooze. I'd bounce awake soon enough so I'd be fit to debrief the brigade staff—including the colonel himself if the night had produced significant contact.

There wasn't any steaming hot food waiting in the HQ tent. No helpful corporal handing over a mess tin of chow like in the movies. But there was always a welcome pot of hot coffee, which tasted great since we were out in the field underground with no refinements at all. And by "pot," I mean it was an actual cast-iron three-gallon pot with metal handles and a lid keeping the sand and flies away. *Just fine.*

"Team, we don't get paid to sit around and dwell on our old wins. It's about what have you done for me lately." Well, boss, maybe we really ought to get paid to sit around for a few minutes to capture the brilliance of the strategy that the team employed to nail the win. To that same Neanderthal boss asking, "What have you done for me lately," I might reply with something like, "Do you really want to reinvent the wheel every time?"

Good teams model the behavior they want to repeat. With a strong debrief that stays as "frosty" (clear and crisp as winter ice) as the mission itself, future campaigns can reflect on the notes you made and emulate the strategy. It's a win-win.

Taking Ten When It's Offered

Rangers in the Desert

We're always on the lookout for a word of wisdom from the experts who pop into our careers. What if it comes in the heat of the moment or from a casual source? Will we recognize it?

If we are always ready to receive the pearl of advice we seek, we'll be able to heed the offering and act while the moment is at hand.

It was an exhilarating month of missions with a few chunks of revelation thrown into three of the patrols. That is to say 29 of the patrols went quietly, allowing us to map the terrain and mark it unoccupied. But we got our hands dirty a couple of times on the recons, starting with a patrol that took us out to the limit of our 15-kilometer nightly walking range—that's as far as we could walk out & back and still make it back before daylight.

At about 14K along our azimuth, we pulled up 250 meters short of a hut to see what was going on. It turned out to be 22 Iraqi soldiers standing around outside the hut. Quite a few stood surrounding an industrial-sized trash can with a fire inside. They were warming their hands over it like a scene out of a *Rocky* movie in South Philly.

We also saw a Dodge Ram truck fitted out with a .50-caliber machine gun mounted in the truck bed. It was parked just off to the right of the trash can, not more than 15 meters from the hut. The Iraqi soldiers were making far too much noise and creating too much light from the fire to be aware of us creeping up on them.

Our state-of-the-art 1991-era GPS dish was a nine-by-nine-by-one-inch square green plate with rounded corners. It weighed about two pounds and gathered satellite info from above, then spit out a 10-digit grid coordinate about two minutes after it powered on. We needed to get closer and grab the reading, so I handed the plate to Dunbar with a caution about no need being a cowboy and getting too close. Off he went crawling to get the coordinates about 75 meters away from the target. When he returned 15 minutes later, the plate had indeed acquired a 10-digit reading we could use to target the gaggle of Iraqis below.

A quick ping of excitement coursed through my bones. I realized we had a B-52 aircraft on station a few thousand feet above to call in an airstrike! Then the other quick ping of realization also hit me. Those enemy soldiers had no idea they were yacking and laughing down there for the last few minutes of their lives.

I took the handset tuned to the aircraft frequency. Then I pulled out the CEOI booklet I carried in my breast pocket. The CEOI held the day's call signs and authentication codes we had been trained to use. I began, "Victor 22, this is Uniform 56, I authenticate JJD20DHS . . ."

A crackle of air sounded, and then the pilot's voice came over. "Dude, you can talk in the clear. They can't hear us . . ."

Onion, my radioman, looked at me as if to say, "You gotta love those U.S. Air Force pilots." I continued, "Grid coordinates PJ 1204521487 [or whatever they were]; twenty-two enemy personnel on foot, one single improved building, and one vehicle."

The pilot processed it for a few seconds and responded with a question I wasn't expecting. He asked, "I've got five-hundred pounders and thousand pounders. Which do you want?" The pilot was referring to the size of bombs he had on board.

Knowing we had air supremacy and he'd get off an uncontested clean drop, but not knowing if he was just having fun with me, I answered, "Five-hundred pounders ought to do the trick, right?"

"Roger that; two on the way." The flamboyant pilot keyed the radio once more. "How many mikes do you need to un-ass the AO?" In English, that meant how many minutes do you need to get away from the immediate area?

I answered, "Give us five mikes."

The voice over the radio turned suddenly paternal. "Better make it ten mikes."

We hauled out of there, backtracking the way we had come, and paused when the distant drone of the bomber entered into audible range. The plane seemed so incredibly far away and high in the sky. It was amazing to think that it could release a pair of bombs through its bay doors and hit the target we had called in.

By now, we were at a pretty safe (we hoped) distance looking back when it detonated. The sky turned bright as an earth dart plunged on top of the men standing by the trash can. Then it bounced back up and shot out white light in every direction, even over and past our heads nearly a mile away. A moment later, the night returned to dead silence. The B-52 faded away, and we all took a breath. It had been a direct hit, well-executed on the ground and in the air. What struck me was nothing was left except a crater. No sign of anything existing five minutes prior to that—no hut, no truck, and no bodies.

Our Scout mission was to recon forward areas, eliminating threats in advance if possible, and only if we could do so entirely undetected. We had no charter to take prisoners or expose our presence in the area. If we couldn't eliminate the enemy without detection, our mission would have to settle for reporting location and strength, and then return home. It just so happened that, at night during Desert Storm, we owned the skies. We had been able to surgically strike the enemy's forward element without anyone knowing we had ever been there.

That night left an impression on me about how to operate with diverse groups. My team could only run with the ball so far. After we had acquired the coordinates of the enemy location, it was up to our air force counterparts to deliver the punch. But that organization brought with it an entirely different set of focuses from ours, along with an entirely different skill set. Their casual way of doing business took me by surprise and some amusement at first. Yet, I later reflected on the pilot's complete grasp of the situation. That's when he turned off his cavalier attitude for a moment to tell me I should take sufficient time to get out of the blast radius.

I realized that sister groups in business may not always work the same way we do in our department. Their focus and skills require them to approach work differently. The value comes when groups mesh to create a win.

Poking a Stick at Yourself

Rangers in the Desert

Good leaders need to have a human side they're willing to show. Since nobody's perfect, bosses who vainly try to maintain a façade of infallibility or who are unwilling to laugh at themselves probably won't connect with the rest of the team. Everyone in charge is bound to make mistakes or look silly at times. I'd wager that people are less likely to poke fun at bosses who already poke fun at themselves.

The MLRS patrol is my son Jake's favorite recollection of Desert Storm because he is the toughest kid I know and enjoys knowing Dad isn't afraid to poke an embarrassing finger at himself. Here's what happened.

We had a relatively easy mission to take a squad to an overwatch location and confirm the accuracy of a rocket strike. The MLRS was the multiple launch rocket system that fired two six-packs of missiles from an armored Bradley vehicle that tilted its canister to fire. Our job was to quietly crawl to a position, verify the strike, and deal with any survivors.

Our squad moved through the night desert and reached the location in time to assume a good viewing position—that is, six of us lying straight across a berm in a perfect spot to see the missile strike. The place I chose was a little too close, though, being only 700 meters from the target. That near half mile originally seemed like plenty of distance since we were tucked behind a berm for protection.

The 3/27th MLRS battery out of Fort Bragg was stationed several miles behind us and had set the coordinates for the airstrike. I hadn't stopped to think what the trajectory would look like from missiles traveling four miles in the air and then descending to strike just in front of us—that was until we heard the supersonic crash of the projectiles breaking the sound barrier high above.

We all stared into the night sky. Darned if it didn't look like they were coming straight down on top of us! As they were racing down to destroy whatever they hit, the fiery trail in the sky still made it look as if they were coming right for us. Gulp—a rush. In a few more seconds, the projectiles screamed in to hit the target squarely. Boom. Again, night turned into white daylight for a couple of moments. It was the loudest earth-moving sensation I had ever experienced—one that rattled my organs from the inside.

"Whoa! Holy sh*t, that was insane," I said, but no one could hear me since our ears were all ringing. When the quiet returned, I repeated to the man next to me, "That was truly insane. What a rush." It felt like I had given up all control of my own body, and for a few moments, some earth-moving force had taken charge. Seeing the rockets destroy the target left us with a feeling of euphoria.

It was then I noticed a warm feeling between my legs and realized that, in the crazy moment of jubilation, I had peed myself. It struck me as funny, and when I shared it with the scout next to me, he thought it was more hilarious that I said it so earnestly. We both laughed.

Some events may take over our bodies spiritually, physically, or both. For Jake, who was an elite wrestler with mad moves, yet also a pole vaulter and hurdler who had *majorly* wiped out many times and laughed it off en route to becoming proficient, it was good to know that Dad could laugh about peeing himself. Recounting the story in a "no big deal" manner also helped demystify the aura of what happens out there in the dark doing dangerous business. On the enterprise side, it can let new team members know that everybody's human, especially the boss.

Hands down, my favorite soldier who ever poked a stick at our surroundings was a young specialist named Mike Land. Skinny at six foot four, he was one of the smartest troops I had in my first Charlie Company platoon in the 82nd. NCOs kidded him that he was "bilingual"; he could connect with enlisted folks on their level in one conversation and then talk to officers in the next. He joked about the social etiquette we had been advised to follow in the Middle East—an etiquette that deprived us of any gestures we might like to make with our left hands. "Never," he pointed out, "should we show the soles of our feet in polite conversation." We happily tucked this tidbit of manners away in case we ever had the opportunity to take tea or do something pleasant with the population.

Land hilariously accepted the presence of flies in the desert, all tens of thousands of them. As the rest of us futilely swatted them like we were doing a bizarre tai chi dance, he reached a Zen understanding that, since they enjoyed landing on him, he needn't bother with any acrobatics to shoo them away.

I respected Land for two reasons. Number one, he had been my best SAW gunner before I moved up to the Scouts. The

M249 SAW (Squad Automatic Weapon) was a light machine gun that provided substantial firepower when we had to hump a long distance on foot, and the Scouts were taking a patrol across the border into Iraq.

Since we didn't have any SAWs, I got permission to ask him if he wanted to saddle up for the mission. I knew he'd say yes. He actually had more creative ways to put the word m**fker in a sentence than anyone I knew, and I think he used a couple in his response. I told him we were headed out for a long night walk to a target but with questionable intel as to what we might be facing. As Mike remembers it, the report said, "You could be facing a battalion of resistance, or they might have left!" But he didn't care which one.

The second thing I admired about Mike was his faith. The only Jewish soldier in the platoon, he was quietly committed to his cause—a conflict that was religiously based by Iraqis who publicly said they were taking the fight straight to Israel after they dealt with the U.S. forces. I admired him for that as well, besides knowing he was a SAW gunner I could rely on.

After a long walk across the border, sure enough, we found the objective. It was a small round shed, ostensibly still in use. Land set in with the overwatch team to cover us as the assault team approached. The shed was full of gear, but no people. Quiet. Nobody. With a whistle, Mike came up to join the action and have a quick look-see inside before we called in artillery to blow it up. By the book? Not exactly, but after six months in the desert, I thought our trusty SAW gunner was entitled to tell the boys back in Charlie Company what he'd seen in Iraq with the Scouts.

Ten minutes later, the site was gone, and we were heading home.

A couple of times while we were in camp before moving to the border, a Humvee from Camp Red had picked up our task force's five Jewish soldiers for Synagogue services. They'd drive an hour to where we had quietly escorted a chaplain rabbi into the country. At the time in 1990, the Saudis waved enthusiastically at their U.S. heroes passing by on the highway. Mike wondered with irony as he waved back if the roadside Arabs would have been surprised to know they were cheering on Jewish soldiers heading to Synagogue. The boys in camp loved that one.

For being only 19 years old, Mike had a lot of chutzpah. I couldn't help but admire his endearing approach to keeping the faith.

Team members who are smart enough to poke fun at themselves help us stay relaxed during tense times. And the credible ones committed to keeping the faith are those you want on your side when the unexpected happens. Leaders remember the sparkling personalities they've worked with and will call for an encore to achieve bigger and better things.

Promoting Your People to the Universe

Rangers in the Desert

Old way of thinking: Find talented staff to work for you and keep them happy in their jobs forever.

New way of thinking: Excellent personnel will never be satisfied doing the same job forever. The advice is to promote them and attract a steady stream of new personnel who recognize your reputation as a mentor and promoter, and they will want to excel.

Some forward-thinking firms are grading their execs on how many people they promote. That's brilliant! Who wouldn't want to work hard to prove themselves when they genuinely believe they work in the land of opportunity?

It's fun to "talk your people up" and get them some PR, which builds the reputation of the whole department, too. Business leaders can start by getting their junior leaders' names out into the ether with positive press.

It was easy to get caught up in the missions and block out peripheral objectives like publicizing my team members' well-done work. So when our battalion operations officer came rolling out to Phase Line Razor to ask me about a CNN crew going with us on that night's mission, I knew it could be a morale builder.

"Lieutenant Sacchetti, how about taking out a news crew with you tonight?"

I already knew the answer would be yes, but I figured I should ask some type of cerebral question to show I was a thinker.

"How many of them are there, sir?"

"Three."

"Good with me."

By nightfall, a Hummer delivered the news crew to us. The three got squared away and brought only light equipment, so we could tell this wasn't their first rodeo. It was newsworthy for them that since we hadn't yet declared G-Day into Iraq, they'd be among the first reporters to venture over the border. Maybe the first for all we knew. That could be a big win for CNN.

It was up to me to ask the crew for something in return, so I told the reporter my boys hadn't had any contact with their loved ones back home for over a month. For effect, I added that they hadn't been all that keen on carting three civilians around in the desert tonight, so maybe the crew could help? "Sure," he said. "What can we do?"

The boys had written messages on scraps of paper with phone numbers at the top that they handed over to the cameraman and his assistant. The crew hadn't associated living in a desert foxhole to being isolated from the world until that moment. Still, to their credit, they picked up on this request immediately. In fact, one of them came from New York, like Hiram, or maybe Richmond, where Eggy was from. All good.

The CNN guys loaded the crumpled messages into their courier bags as we bumped our way east a couple clicks along Phase Line Razor. Then they promised to call the numbers and read the notes out loud when they got to a phone. I felt like Andy in *Shawshank Redemption* when he sat on the roof, satisfied to have helped his guys feel like men and enjoy a little slice of home.

Plus, the reporters got the story they wanted. Two hours later, in a hushed voice, as we walked, the stringer asked me for a quote as we approached the release point where they were supposed to stay behind with our rear security. So I made him a deal. If he added a quote from each man in the squad into his article, then his crew could come along for the rest of the mission.

Deal. The night ended safely for us, and the CNN guys had gotten their story from inside Iraq. It aired at 2:17 a.m. East Coast time. Coincidentally, my family at home—starved for any kind of update—had become CNN news junkies. They were always up watching the news anchor, Wolf Blitzer, late into the night. So while they were making a pot of tea, the piece aired, and they heard *my voice* coming from the TV.

Bedlam broke out in Springfield, Pennsylvania, as everyone in the house was awakened. Our extended family members were called, in case the news segment came on TV again an hour later. CNN did rerun it at 4:17 a.m., which prompted tears of joy from Mom and Aunt Lucille on the phone with each other while they watched and probably shed more tears, knowing them.

CNN's written article featured a quote or two from all six men in the squad. It was picked up by local papers around the U.S., especially in the states where the boys lived. A few kindly old ladies who read it in their hometown gazettes and free presses went to the trouble of clipping the article and mailed it to us with a note and smiley face. Using only the address info in the headline, they trusted it would find its way to us out in the desert. That was pretty good. What a morale boost.

Eggy is SPC Ryan Eggleston, a ranger whose superpower was reliability. He was quiet, determined, and not flashy. Meaning he was a valued role model by being a follower. Sadly, he experienced what it's like to lose a brother, a real brother. Of all ironies, his older brother Lieutenant Ross Eggleston, a wrestler from VMI attending Chemical Officer school back in Alabama, was killed by a drunk driver on New Year's Eve 1990 while returning home from his Sergeant's house. We were in the Saudi Arabian desert, preparing to invade Iraq.

When the news reached us, Eggy and I were standing together, and I could only watch as he dropped to his knees and asked if it was real – over and over, stunned and motionless in the sand for five endless minutes. The moment haunted me for 30 years, wishing I could have made the pain go away.

Back in Richmond, Virginia, as Mrs. Eggleston looked out her window to see two officers in dress uniforms pull up to her house, her heart sank, knowing she had two sons in the Army with Ryan 8000 miles away in the Middle East. When she found out it was her firstborn that had died, the Army arranged a phone call for her out to the desert to tell Ryan he could come home for his brother's funeral.*

After the funeral was over, Eggy found himself without orders to return to Desert Shield and Fort Bragg wanting him to stick around stateside. Like the episode of Band of Brothers where Popeye broke loose from the hospital to rejoin his brothers, Eggy, without any return orders, retraced his flights from Virginia to Philadelphia to Dover, Delaware. And then he got himself to England, Frankford, and finally Saudi Arabia, where he hopped in a deuce-and-a-half truck for four hours bound for King Fahd airbase, and finally three more hours in a Hummer back to the Iraqi border. How he found us buried in the ground at Phase Line Razor is a blur, but he joined the boys in Scout platoon two days before G-Day, back where he belonged.

*Consumed with grief over her older son's death in a senseless drunk driving accident, Mrs. Eggleston dedicated the next decade of her life to the *Mothers Against Drunk Driving* organization. She and Eggy stay close, keeping Ross's memory alive.

Remember this: If you don't ask, the answer is already no. Good things happen when you ask for what you want, especially when it's for a good cause like promoting your people. Most leaders find it's easy to ask for favors and make deals when the purpose affirms the need.

Learning from Experts Who Work for You

Sergeant (SGT) Scott Mandeville

> *Remember the one about the boss who thinks he knows everything? Someone always has a version of that cringe story, so how about if we flipped it around? It's not enough that good bosses should be open to learning just from the exec team. That's expected. How about if they identify and gain relevant skills from team members who work for them?*
>
> *Now, that would make a good story.*

On our second patrol in Iraq, I had noticed one of my squad leaders had an M203 rifle/grenade launcher as his weapon of choice. SGT Scott Mandeville was a young sergeant E-5 on the fast track to E-6. A model Ranger leader with imposing size and physique, he was extremely well-liked by his men and his superiors. As the leader in charge of a six-man squad, Scott's style complemented the two other recon squad leaders, both of whom outranked him as staff sergeants. Also note that squad leaders don't usually carry an M203.

A rifle/grenade launcher looks exactly as it sounds: It's a seven-pound M4 rifle (or an eight-pound M16) with a three-pound grenade launcher mounted to the underside of the barrel. Besides being used as a standard rifle, it also launches a 40mm (size of a Twinkie) grenade out to 350 meters. It had come straight out of a video game and became one of the most ingenious and versatile weapons in the inventory. Caveat #1: Becoming accurate enough to plunk a projectile 150 meters on-target requires serious skill. Caveat #2: Trying to run while carrying 48 rounds (half a pound per grenade) in a custom vest (that's an extra 24 pounds) ain't no joke. And there's a further issue to deal with: getting the enemy's full attention as the guy who's lobbing in explosive grenades on top of their heads.

Talent moves me. I could have been impressed in a different setting from watching a grade-schooler playing Mozart, but in this case, I watched a bomblet-thunking marksman. The 82nd had previously set up a hasty city-training area (MOUT site for Ranger junkies). I watched SGT Mandeville putting 40mm grenade rounds through a second-floor window from 120 meters out and then onto a rooftop 200 meters over to the left. Boom. High explosive round in one window. Scatter. Buckshot round in the other. Glow. Red flare round on the rooftop to mark it for inbound Cobra gunships. Dang, he was tight! I remember Scott shrugging it off as "what he was supposed to do." But I stood there chilled.

The addition of a grenade launcher was practical, too. For a self-reliant recon unit of 30 in the desert far away from fire support, an additional M203 on patrol could be a big plus. So I decided to get proficient at shooting it as well and to carry it as my weapon of choice. It felt good, and its parabolic aiming made sense to me.

The next morning, we were back at HQ. After the battalion commander's debrief, I got the Humvee driver to make a detour. "Blasch, can you run me over to the armorer's tent?" I asked, hopping in. I liked Private Blasch. He was over in Charlie company, not HQ company. I knew him from his can-do attitude and figured he'd wind up being pretty successful in life.

"Roger that, sir," he replied, and we rolled over to the GP Medium tent that housed extra weapons for the battalion. The armorer and his assistant also had their bunks in there along with the soldiers who guarded the tent.

The armorer was a friendly enough sergeant who had an assistant to help him keep track of the 1,000-man battalion's rifles, heavy weapons, and ammunition. Neither of them saw the light of day much, as they were stuck 24/7 in a dark tent. He reminded me of the pale old fuel guy in the movie *Waterworld*, cloistered in the hold of the smoker's tanker ship and in charge of the fuel level. That guy was half blind and crazy from the fuel fumes. Knowing I could never be happy stuck in a small space, I counted my blessings to be able to be in and the heck out of the "cage" (the armory's nickname) in a couple of minutes.

Blasch and I walked in together—right through the open canvas flap to a makeshift counter in front of the fenced-off weapons. I greeted the armory sergeant warmly. It's my nature to do that anyway, and it always eases any conversation bound for the unusual. Then I requested an M203, a few dummy rounds, and a full vest of grenades to pick up before the next patrol. The armory sergeant took it all in for a moment and then came out from inside the cage. Next, he closed the door behind him and said, "Sir, lieutenants don't carry those."

My smiling response was, "Well, I hope this one does."

For some reason, both of them thought my response was good enough for a laugh, and then I was glad I had Blasch with me. His first name was Clifford, which was unique as a first name. Officers and NCOs don't often use a private's first name when addressing one another, so it's not unusual to *not* know a soldier's first name. But Clifford and his big personality stood out. He was quick with a snarky comment and had a round face that opened with a ridiculously giant smile. No one could resist loosening up and smiling back, and that's pretty much what happened next.

The sergeant glanced at the equipment chart of who was assigned what gear per company. He noted out loud that HQ company still had four extra M203s in the cage, and he saw no reason why the Scouts couldn't have one of them.

"Great!" That was easy, I thought.

I flashed back to my old colonel's Vietnam story of brandishing his .45 pistol on the armory clerk to hijack needed ammo to save his soldiers from heading into a patrol underequipped. The story grabbed attention for sure. And I had no doubt there were exigent circumstances at the time. I didn't intend to go into battle underequipped either, but I certainly didn't mean to pull a pistol in the modern army.

Times had changed, so I had started with a softer approach to see if it would work. The sergeant even sent me out of the tent with the vest plus an extra case of high-explosive (HE) rounds. Success. Blasch threw the Humvee into gear, and we headed north.

A few hours later back at the Iraqi border while checking gear for that night's patrol, I donned my new vest before last light of the day, better equipped to lead my guys. And mostly, I appreciated having experts all around me who could help improve my game.

When subject matter experts want to share their talent, everyone benefits regardless of rank. Know-how shouldn't be hoarded like an unopened box of ammo. It yearns to break out free and equip all unit members (like me) who want to lift their game.

On the flip side of the equation, smart leaders try to improve by learning from the guys with the skills. I had gotten lucky and found a direct report who was glad to share the fine points, and we both benefitted.

When young leaders pay close attention to the executive team to absorb their best practices, it's anticipated, but still a good trait. On the flip side, when seasoned leaders realize there's an untapped treasure to be gained from the subject matter experts who work for them, that's even better. It speaks to coworkers at large that the manager is approachable and grounded enough to see that some of their best learning resources are already in place.

Making a Positive First Impression

Master Sergeant (MSG) Ralph "Ike" Jackson

Making a great first impression is a coin with two shiny sides. Don't forget who makes a great first impression on you, either. There's a reason why, and these folks are worthy of getting to know and collaborate with during your career. It's magical for a business to have the ability to convey a weighty imprint within seconds.

When I reported in to my first command as a new lieutenant in the mighty 82nd Airborne, I was whisked through the halls to quickly meet the key players in Charlie Company for a cursory "here's the new 2nd Platoon leader who just arrived." Aside from striving to make an engaging impression on the 250 troops I'd work with over the next year, I also took note, in parallel, of who stuck out in my mind—and why.

At the same time I was trying to make a positive first impression, I found myself impressively enchanted with three of the senior NCOs. Given the parade of young officers who cycled through the unit, I'm certain they made a far more powerful impression on me than I on them. Each radiated an instantaneous intensity when I entered their personal space. They seemed larger than life. I knew immediately they had their laser-focused attention on me, eyeballing me head to toe without ever changing their expression. Yet, it was the type of spotlight that made me want to earn superstardom so I could be worthy of serving alongside them in their domain.

This aura, I learned, is the magic of the non-commissioned officers—the sergeants who know everything and have seen it all. They have the absolute gift of the tongue. One moment, they could fire off a colorful redress to a private to improve his chances for survival. The next, they could respond with a quip to a general that would have him laughing.

SSG Ike Jackson was an 11-Charlie mortarman, a big man with a sweeping Georgia accent and a smile to go with a permanently can-do attitude. He was never telling you what was broken with the situation—only how he reckoned we could get our tails out of it.

"Sir, I'll bet you never knew the mortarman was your best friend on the battlefield, but my boys and I are gonna get you right up to speed, don't you worry. We're here to do a job together." His greeting was welcoming, reassuring, and valuable—unerringly what a newcomer needed coming into an elite unit.

Ike had been the distinguished honor grad of his Ranger class a decade before, and now he ran the company's artillery. He knew that a young platoon leader had to master the use of indirect fire, and he made it seem like we would actually have fun getting there. Ike never missed an opportunity to train soldiers, and he also loved to joke around. But he told me that game time is always game time.

"We're here to do a job" was a phrase we heard again later in the year after we shipped out to Saudi Arabia for Desert Storm. Katie Couric from NBC's *Today Show* wanted to interview a soldier out in the field, so the army representative pointed to SSG Jackson as the face of the U.S. troops.

Everybody loved Katie, and the excitement of seeing a star journalist from back home buzzed through the camp. Having been given access to millions of viewers, Ike had succeeded in presenting a favorable position they could get behind.

On camera, Katie smiled and asked, "What do you miss from back in the U.S.?"

Ike was honest. "Hell, I miss everything."

"Do you want to go home?"

"No, ma'am. Sure, I miss everything at home, but we've started a job here, and we gotta be here until we finish."

After 240 jumps and retiring as a master sergeant, Ike couldn't stay idle. He was heading back to Iraq as an advisor to help train the new Iraqi army. Later in Kandahar, Afghanistan, he deployed to assist the Guardian Angel initiative in 2013. He helped them understand and curb the tide of green-on-blue incidents—that was the name given to Afghans turning on coalition forces.

I like Ike.

Ike passes his leadership philosophy on to today's leaders. It's centered around two core principles:

1) Training your second-in-command to be able to step in and know your job, and

2) Telling those in higher command the exact career path you want. For Ike, that meant everyone in the organization knew what direction he was pointed. If he (or anyone) was suddenly plucked out, then the unit could continue to function without a hiccup.

CHAPTER THREE

N

Never shall I fail my comrades. I will always keep myself mentally alert, physically strong, and morally straight, and I will shoulder more than my share of the task, whatever it may be, one hundred percent and then some.

Just Ask Me	CSM Donovan Watts
Choosing Yard Dog over Porch Dog	CSM Donovan Watts
Diversifying	COL Christian Karsner
Sending a Cordial Invite of Trust	COL Christian Karsner
Contributing to Doctrine	COL Christian Karsner
Applying Wisdom	COL Christian Karsner
Letting People Inspire You	MSG Al "Action" Akers
Solving Asymmetric Challenges	MSG Al "Action" Akers
Going Where You're Needed	MSG Al "Action" Akers
Not Being Shy	CSM William "Monty" Montgomery
Building It If It Ain't Built Yet	CSM William "Monty" Montgomery
Giving Wise Counsel	CSM William "Monty" Montgomery
Fighting as You Train	SGM Jeff Koenig
Moving Up and Up	SGM Jeff Koenig
Overcoming Limitations	SGM Jeff Koenig
Walking Among Heroes	SGM Jeff Koenig
Staying Young Enough for New Tricks	1SG John "Roses" Rowe
Appreciating a Comeback Story	1SG John "Roses" Rowe
Being the Hero of Your Own Story	SSG Chris "Merc" Mercadante

Just Ask Me

Command Sergeant Major (CSM) Donovan Watts

Many of the principles highlighted in this book differentiate the great leader from the good one. It's always wise to master the role we commit to and become a reliable source for colleagues. What elevates "good" a notch to "greatness" is actively seeking to share with others. Probing younger colleagues to see who needs assistance and then backing them up by delivering what's needed is the stuff of greatness.

CSM Donovan Watts blended being strict, exacting, fair, fun, and fatherly all together in one personality. He loved God, and he loved soldiering. As a lifelong infantryman, he held every position in the book and could coach them all—and was happy to talk to you all about it. He especially loved to tell outlandish stories that captivated the imaginations of young soldiers. They didn't know if the stories were real, but they did understand the point that was being proven or the question being solved. For example, he once asked a young candidate presenting himself to the sergeant's board, "So, specialist, besides being promoted to sergeant, what do you want to do in the army?"

The specialist's snappy answer was, "I want to fill your shoes someday, Sergeant Major."

The CSM paused amid laughter from the other board members who thought it was a pretty darn good response. Then Donovan replied, "That's one of the dumbest things I ever heard

. . . there's only one me." Then he continued softly, "You need to be you and choose your own path and excel." CSM Watts was smiling. That little moment of frank motivation became part of NCO corps' teaching lore at Fort Bragg.

"Just ask me" was something Donovan had genuinely told colleagues from early in his career. Because of it, he garnered a reputation as a go-to guy for collegial support and advice. He possessed that golden resource every organization covets—a sincere desire to help. Like forward-thinking business leaders, the sergeant major anticipated events on the horizon. He wanted to be ready for them, and he usually illustrated them in a colorful and memorable way. He gave advice for young leaders to achieve as many qualifications as they could if they wanted to climb the ladder. He said, "When they come looking to pick a new chief, they're going to look for the Indian with the most feathers on his head. They'll see this one has six feathers, and this other one has two feathers. Well, let me tell you, they'll pick the one with six feathers."

SFC Watts also advised his young troops to present themselves as well-spoken ambassadors of the Airborne, the Rangers, and the U.S. As he said, "If someone thrusts a camera in your face, have your sound bite ready to say why you're here. Tell them how you love America and know your job, and how you're ready to do the right thing.

"I know *I am*," he added.

A couple of weeks after arriving in the desert in 1990 to start Operation Desert Shield, we were still acclimating to the host of suggested etiquette rules as guests of Saudi Arabia. That included showing no outward signs of Christianity while in a Muslim country.

SFC Watts was checking on troops at the same moment our paths crossed in the Charlie company area. He was the platoon sergeant for 3rd and I was the platoon leader for 2nd. I had always enjoyed how SFC Watts could brighten a random task in any environment just by being positive.

As we met and chatted, he caught a glint of metal shining around my neck. With an amused smile, he reached over to discover a cross sitting on a gold chain under my dog tags. He grinned widely and chastised me. "You know, sir, we're not supposed to be displaying those religious adornments." With an equal smile, I told him he was downright correct, but also, that I felt torn. See, my good buddy back home had presented it to me at his wedding to give me strength and resolve. By now, the good SFC knew quite a few impressionable young troops were listening in to our conversation. After a moment's pause, he nodded, "Well, hell, sir. You know, if I had a good friend who thought enough to want me to have Jesus around my neck, I'd wear it too."

And then he reached over with care and tucked Jesus back underneath my T-shirt.

CSM Watts's business manual of success would read like this:

- *Engage colleagues in the workplace.*
- *Listen and react with paternal care.*
- *Give advice publicly or privately as appropriate.*

And about being a 40-year-old dad, he said, "If I would have known it was this good, I woulda done it a long time ago."

Choosing Yard Dog over Porch Dog

Command Sergeant Major (CSM) Donovan Watts

Walk onto any worksite that has clerks, and you can tell those who are active "hunters" versus passive "farmers" in minutes. The hunters proactively come toward you and reach for your business; the farmers follow the guidelines and passively wait for customers to find them. Knowing you'll be viewed as one of these two, which one should you choose?

Sergeant Major Donovan Watts had always been a dog enthusiast. He divided the world into two: the porch dogs who sat around and talked all day, and the yard dogs (like us Rangers) who got things done. Over his 27 years in the military, he has told countless waves of recruits to go out and be yard dogs. And when it came time for a mission, he demanded "*they move out like a Doberman, ears up*."

In Iraq, CSM Watts once eased the fear of a young machine gunner who had just arrived in Iraq and was talking to himself out loud. The gunner tried to sort out the rules of engagement about when to fire or when to wait in a given situation. He feared he wouldn't act correctly in time. CSM Watts looked up at him from the passenger's seat of the Humvee and reassuringly told him, "Just do what you gotta do." The subtle message to the gunner was that he trusted him to handle his own business. For Donovan, it boiled down to being natural. He wanted to pass on the calm notion that any properly trained infantrymen would do the right thing at the exact moment it was needed.

CSM Watts had arrived back in Iraq in mid '06 as the battalion sergeant major of the 1/505th Panthers of the 82nd Airborne. As the senior enlisted advisor to the commander (SEAC), he was the #1 man in charge of the welfare of 1,000 troops. More importantly, he was the #1 role model of how *1Panthers* should conduct themselves in a combat zone. Instead of commanding a desk from HQ, he joined the rotation of patrols out on the roads alongside the troops. At 46 years of age and 27 years of army experience, he was glue for the unit. The battalion commander praised him as the most exceptional soldier he had ever served with.

Four months into the deployment, CSM Watts saddled up with the night crew to patrol the road between Baghdad and Tikrit. His dedication had become infectious throughout 1Panther, and because of their yard dog training, the troops didn't shy away from dangerous duty. Eager young PFC Matt Whipple—always a yard dog—caught up to the CSM in the staging area and volunteered to man the patrol with him. Donovan noted the private's can-do spirit, but told him, in a paternal tone, "We've got it covered tonight."

The convoy launched out of camp. Army vehicles rolled through the Salah ad Din Province and entered the city limits of Bayji, an unremarkable town. But this night, a roadside IED (improvised explosive device) had been planted off to the right side of the road. As the convoy started to pass, someone on the other side of a wire or cell phone detonated the bomb. It exploded the moment the yard dog's vehicle passed. CSM Watts was in the commander's seat in the front right. The blast rocked the Humvee and everything in its radius. When the smoke cleared, Donovan had been killed.

The patrol quickly recovered from the damage, the blast still ringing in their ears. Luckily, they were able to gather personnel and prevent any further hostile contact or injuries. Although they had lost only one man, Donovan was arguably the battalion's beating heart. The loss hurt.

Back at camp, it didn't seem possible to the rest of the men that their father figure could be gone. The unforgiving inequity of war had taken him. The only thing the troops could resolve to do was *know their job* and *do the right things*, the creeds the sergeant major had taught them.

The outpouring of devotion from those who had served with Sergeant Major Watts was overwhelming. He had left his legacy as an inspirational leader at his various units over three decades. And his effectiveness as a role model was echoed nearly a hundred times in the memorials that followed his death.

Mrs. Whipple, the young private's mom, wrote this to Donovan's family:

"We received an e-mail from our son in Iraq, PFC Matthew Whipple, on Friday, telling us of the death of Sergeant Major Watts. He shared deep sadness at the loss and told us of the fine example CSM Watts set for him, and the leadership and high standards he represented to our son. Matt asked to go on patrol that night, but CSM Watts said he did not need to come. We feel that the hand of God—through CSM Watts—saved our son. We will forever be grateful and pray that you will know those lives that were touched by CSM Watts."

CSM Watts had walked the walk for 27 years rolling. The day that was his last turned out to be the final page in an unflawed script. His lesson to young pups rising through the system seems clear to me: *If you choose to be the yard dog with the genuine offer to "just ask me" as you advance through the ranks, you'll leave behind a legacy like Donovan's as an ideal colleague and leader.*

Our legacy in any organization begins the moment we depart, and the only sure way to guarantee its prestige is to genuinely embody the ideal the entire time. I don't think we can ever rig the system and discover heroic integrity at the last minute because we never know when that last minute will be.

Diversifying

Colonel (COL) Christian Karsner

The landscape of business in America allows us to pursue our dreams without limiting our choices. We can establish longevity in one place or perhaps pivot midcareer. With the proper prerequisites, anything is possible. New strata can be reached, and current records can be broken.

The career of COL Christian Karsner uniquely traversed senior levels of both the enlisted ranks and the officer ranks. Why so rare? For one thing, it takes extraordinary longevity—in the colonel's case, 37 years. And second, it requires mastery of different types of proficiencies—time and skill.

Colonel K desired to excel at both. He would say that America is the land of opportunity, that a kid fresh out of high school can rise through the enlisted ranks, give outstanding service, become a sergeant first class E-7 within 10 years, and then earn a college degree.

With the help of Uncle Sam, Colonel K seized the opportunity to pursue his dream at Officer Candidate School (OCS) so he could become an officer and command troops. Then Christian set out to influence troops and be in the middle of the action first as a Green Beret and then as a Ranger.

The ability to diversify job roles and achieve mastery in each is a real accomplishment. Time and skills are two of the factors in question. If professionals enjoy their functions enough to commit to both worlds and do what they love to do, then a fulfilling career can follow.

Sending a Cordial Invite of Trust

Colonel (COL) Christian Karsner

> *It seems like the best work comes from vested individuals who are trusted to carry out a task with independence. They feel the responsibility to produce a valued product. Without anyone hovering over them to give instructions, it's on them to shine.*

COL Christian Karsner has always been a big believer in trust. "Hey, boss, we have a plan and can execute the mission" is the brand of trust he requested as an enlisted man at every rank—low to high. "Gentlemen, you now know the intent, so go form your teams for success" is the brand he granted as commander.

Having faith that those who have been trained can carry out their tasks independently is the opposite of micromanaging. Chris didn't want to micromanage, and for the most part, never needed to. Rather, he leaned on the trust he'd built from high to low and back up to high. As he used to tell his subordinate commanders, "I only micromanage those who send me a cordial invite." This was his semi-humorous way of saying that those who take initiative under his command would always be rewarded. The opposite would be answered begrudgingly with supervisory guidance.

Overall, Chris lived by this belief: "The army is people, and taking care of them means trusting them." So he did.

People who work on a team that requires risk-taking feel the safest and perform their best when they are trusted. Add good training and a clear sense of the mission from the leader, and it equals a winning leadership philosophy—with no micromanaging!

Contributing to Doctrine

Colonel (COL) Christian Karsner

The ability to document best practices is one of the best ways to leave your positive mark on an organization while helping future waves of executives in the same position overcome similar obstacles.

For senior officers graduating war college, the ability to contribute to doctrine and TTPs (tactics, techniques, and procedures) is a military version of 360-degree feedback. The colonel took the opportunity to write articles on leadership topics he'd learned from a valuable 17 years of field time, and he made the following insightful observations.

Asymmetrical warfare – Future enemies will find out what we're not good at, and that's where the next battles will take place. The units that need to polish up on easily lost arts such as close-in patrolling and who even query if something like this is still needed, know that the enemy will be looking for weak spots to exploit. This is the case, for example, where we may never be willing to declare urban areas as war zones where civilians would be affected. Instead, we would find a way to eliminate the need to be in those zones in the first place.

Teams working in concert – Leadership should happen at the lowest level possible, allowing success to rise from the squad on up through the company. While different teams have a variety of missions, they're part of the whole and can more easily complement each other by applying cross-cooperation. That could simply take the form of a courtesy call before heading out in another commander's zone or a reminder of a time and place. That can also apply to the Navy SEAL units interfacing with air force and marine units.

In other operations, smooth communication helps units stay in their lanes to ensure maximum coverage. Chris always reminded his young commanders that if they decided to change targets and engage someone else's, they'd most likely be shirking the ones they were assigned.

Dichotomy between professional development versus victory in the field – This issue arises when the army needs to keep NCOs in place overseas in times of workforce shortage. Rather than pulling NCOs off the line to attend professional development in stateside army schools, the proposed answer is to delay the schooling until the unit finishes the tour. It makes sense to the current mission, but the fallout is that these NCOs may have reached their terms of enlistment. They might then depart the army before attending the professional development school that first attracted them to stay. Others may get wounded and cannot enroll. In both situations, the mechanism of a continual training system for our non-coms based on tenure gets interrupted. If that happens, the long-term efficacy of the enlisted corps suffers.

NCO resurgence – From a colonel who has watched leaders over the past six decades, Chris postulates that the best NCOs the military has ever seen in this time arose out of the Vietnam War. Because of their combat experience, they became the best class of instructors to the next wave of students in the '70s and

’80s. Likewise, the past 15 years have produced a similar class of battle-hardened midlevel leaders coming back from Iraq and Afghanistan. They now flourish in the army as trusted instructors and mentors.

Chris believes the core of credibility for NCOs flows from the tactical grounding they gain in the field that, at senior levels, allows the SEAC to be the mighty “whisper” in the commander’s ear.

Many good leaders have probably experienced similar “aha” conclusions after a successful project. At that point, it doesn’t take much extra effort to outline the steps for posterity. Taking another 5 percent more time to craft a template leaves behind a plan that lives on for the next crew.

Applying Wisdom

Colonel (COL) Christian Karsner

> *Occam's razor is the principle (attributed to William of Occam) that, in explaining a "thing," no more assumptions should be made than are necessary—that "the simplest solution is most likely the right one."*[2]
>
> *My corollary to Occam's razor is this: The easiest* **decision** *is not always the best. Even when a short-term solution can defensibly solve a short-term problem, the larger picture may uncover undesirable effects. Taking into account collateral damage issues to ensure the moral defensibility of our actions often requires a coating of wisdom applied to current events. That wisdom comes from a leader's ability to visualize the ancillary effects.*

Colonel Karsner knows war is not for the faint of the heart. There are darn few warriors who have the dedication to give up chunks of their lives and their souls to protect our free way of life by fighting 8,000 miles from home. He praises the integrity of those who successfully apply wisdom in the most extreme situations.

In the bleak moments of Operation Enduring Freedom in Afghanistan, Colonel K's units had to rebound from losing more good men than they thought bearable. In the brotherhood of Special Forces, no man is expendable. The gifted soldier-statesmen

---

2 "Occam's Razor," Wikipedia, https://en.wikipedia.org/wiki/Occam%27s_razor.

under his command never lose sight of the value of life, be it ours or theirs.

Pursuing a concentration of enemy soldiers into a small village in the Helmand Province, Chris's men knew no adult-aged males had been previously inside. Rather than place civilians at risk and cause undue damage, they put themselves in the line of fire by taking time to enter the village and find its elder. They allowed the elder to exit with all the women, children, and seniors first before embarking on the brutal business of clearing the bad actors out of their hiding spots. This meant 400 innocent civilians were able to get out of harm's way before our men faced off with an enemy who had been willing to hide among peaceful noncombatants. The wise elder reciprocated the thoughtfulness and moved out his folks as orderly and quickly as possible.

When faced with situations that will have dire consequences, we rely on wise leaders to make the smartest decisions—those decisions that can do the most good and cause the least damage.

Letting People Inspire You

Master Sergeant (MSG) Al "Action" Akers

You're doing something right if your colleagues are asked to capture your essence in one word and choose the word "dynamic." It opens the door to create identity and cohesion, and it invites inspiration to enter from every angle.

Al Akers enlisted in 1983 and is still going strong. Twenty years as a Ranger and Green Beret warmed him up to 16 more years as an operational advisor making advances in asymmetric warfare for the active army. Availing himself of nearly every high-risk school the army offers, Al became one the most well-rounded non-coms in the U.S. arsenal. His first mantra was to be dynamic with the goal of creating an identity for the unit. He knew a group with identity can jell. At the upper echelons of cohesiveness, soldiers will perform more confidently knowing they are covered on exposed flanks. Al sought this kind of solidity for each of his teams.

Al's second mantra was to accept inspiration from people around you. As he reasoned, someone else's concern for your welfare—such as from the operator below you and the operator above you—affects your performance. Likewise, your interaction to take care of guys up and down the chain of command improves performance in both directions.

Al built a career of taking care of his direct reports, and it has paid gigantic dividends. For me, working Jumpmaster duty together with Al as a two-man team on sticks of jumpers in the early '90s taught me to have the same level of caring for the rank and file, especially when life and death depended on watchful eyes.

I watched many times as soldiers who were fully geared up and deemed ready to jump waddled over to Al to say, "Hey, Sarge, will you JMPI (jumpmaster personal inspection) me?" They were most comfortable knowing Sergeant Aker's eagle eyes and hands on their rigging provided the final check before they exited an aircraft at 1,000 feet.

Having inspiration to move in two directions is a fascinating concept for you as a leader. It allows you to echo the inspiration you pluck from those who surround you and then radiate it out to the community. When concepts such as caring and performance travel up and down the chain of command, they benefit the whole group.

Solving Asymmetric Challenges

Master Sergeant (MSG) Al "Action" Akers

> *It's easy to learn where people stand on the subject of thinking outside the box. Just ask them. If their answers are lukewarm—like "I think there are times when it's okay"—then you've found a dinosaur and should react accordingly.*
>
> *But imagine the response is, "I EXPECT you to think outside the box. Heck, I would love you to LIVE outside the box. We're facing challenges today that no one even conceived of a decade ago." That's the exec I want to work for!*

The Asymmetric Warfare Group (AWG) is a special mission unit of the U.S. Army dedicated to staying one step ahead of the morphing way an enemy might choose to engage. Its goal is to accurately see battlefield nuances from a high level—above the tactical (company) level and strategic (battalion) level up to the operational (brigade level) and above. It acts as an unconventional set of eyes and ears for the commander seeking trends and anomalies.

With Al's guidance to embed with the unit and do things differently when needed, good commanders were able to make workarounds to solve problems. As an example, the 3rd Brigade/1st Cavalry took Al's advice and used dispersed infantry as hasty artillerymen to own and retain ground in contested areas of Mosul.

Even MSG Aker's approach for collecting and synthesizing data was asymmetric. Although his end game would be to advise the highest-ranking officer in the command center, he gathered his data from the lowest-ranking "joes" far out in the field.

AWG also proposes new methodologies to help ground commanders gain the advantage. One method Al assisted on is *personality targeting* to replace traditional geographic and unit targeting. Today's new type of warfare has decentralized terrorist cells, so time-sensitive human targets of high value might be identified in a commander's area of operation and quickly added to his target package.

This new battle plan of counterinsurgency signals a change in traditional thinking. In past battles, a grassy hill full of troops with weapons might be earmarked and then planned as a target. Now targets include networks of insurgents and high-value individuals' last known locations.

Embracing this shift in strategy nets significant successes with modern thinkers. In warfare or in business, the head who seeks trends and anomalies can stay a step ahead of the competition.

Being unconventional may have the added benefit of solving issues in realms where reasonable minds have been stuck and need a push. When no idea is considered crazy under the blue sky, strategies can freely shift so they can be viable under new conditions.

The more accepted unconventional solutions become, the faster the workplace can react to the next change coming.

Going Where You're Needed

Master Sergeant (MSG) Al "Action" Akers

There's no better position to be in than the go-to person. When the top brass calls with something big to accomplish, they summon the specialist who not only can handle the job, but he's the one they know will say, "Heck, yes, where do I need to be and when can I get started?"

Ever notice a character trait portrayed in the movies that's common across elite soldiers? It happens when the phone call comes in and soldiers spring into action. You see it in the scene where Dad jumps up to answer the phone late at night. He goes to quietly tell his kids he's gotta leave, and they understand. Then he goes into the bedroom to give Momma a hug and tells her what she already knows—because the same call has come before.

Like operators over the past 60 years, Al has answered that phone every time it's rung.

In Desert Storm, Al was with me as a Scout squad leader liberating Kuwait from Saddam Hussein. He galvanized the team spirit of his eight-man team. Watching that happen was a beautiful thing, and it marked him as a great future leader to watch.

In Bosnia, Al was with 3rd Special Forces Group to help stabilize the country's military and population in the aftermath of the Homeland War between the Balkan states. While there, Al's personality became immensely popular among the Bosnians in their assigned patch.

In Central Africa, his A-team deployed to stem the tide of corruption and deal with the leadership gap. An unenviable task, Al worked to facilitate the three-way coordinated effort with the U.S. military, the local army, and the U.S. State Department.

And in Uganda, Al arrived to assist the government trying to resist Joseph Kony, the brutal warlord who had proclaimed himself the "Savior." Camping near the old Entebbe airport that stood fallow next to a newly built terminal and runways reminded him of how fragilely close the poisoned past and the new present were to each other.

During Al's final tour as ODA (Green Beret) team sergeant, the team deployed to Afghanistan in the early days of '02. His team was handed the near-impossible charge of slowing the mounting lawlessness of the Taliban and Al Qaeda. With limited

> Anecdotal reports suggest that the theme of trading Ranger stories in combat to lift feelings of misery happens remarkably often in extreme conditions among Rangers. They recount tales of the mountain and swamp phases that represent "as bad as it can get" in their minds. The idea is to take the focus off of the current misery, even though it would seem that their present suffering would far exceed any in the reasonably controlled environment of Ranger School. Yet that is common ground in the recesses of the elite soldier's minds, which helps them find comfort. Brace Barber profiles many such Ranger School experiences and their lasting impact in his book *No Excuse Leadership.*[3]
>
> ---
>
> [3] Brace Barber, *No Excuse Leadership: Lessons from the U.S Army's Elite Rangers* (Hoboken, NJ: John Wiley & Sons, Inc., 2004).

support and austere conditions not often publicly reported back home, Al faced the worst conditions of his career. On one particular frozen mission, the situation was so bad that the Green Berets resorted to trading Ranger School stories between enemy contact—just to get by.

Lessons learned from a soldier of Master Sergeant Akers' caliber are worth a few moments of reflection for young leaders building their book of knowledge. They can craft their *virtual* environment even if they can't influence their *physical* one. Think of his Special Forces team high up in frigid mountains with little food, operating alone, and Al brings up a shared experience filled with humor.

Imagine. Even though the physical present was harsh, he helped re-create a virtual past that they could manage and eventually laugh about.

Al is a believer in mastering the basics—a mantra that screams "simplicity." During the tight turns, his Ranger and Special Forces teams found that having a reflex action for the basics they had mastered kept them alive. Yet 90 percent of the time, a fault in the basics tends to get folks in trouble. Likewise, doing what teams do best when they feel tired, miserable, and hungry (like in Ranger School) keeps the gang alive.

Al knew the value of having outlets for blowing off steam. He had an epiphany—that "letting loose" by playing football in the dunes was a way to break the tension for his groups of elite performers in the Gulf. And he never forgot it. Over his career, he always built outlets for teams to break loose and rejuvenate between missions virtually. His team's best moments had come from successful missions after 911 in Gardez, Afghanistan, when the U.S. needed to score wins. They had rooted out and killed several truly evil actors who were making the world a worse place—people who were helping fellow countrymen feel vindicated for the unprovoked attacks on U.S. soil. The team needed to process the actions they were forced to take, so Al made an effort to talk about it. That way, they could gain closure and understanding.

From studying WWII, Al knew that the men "returning home from war" back then came with shared experiences. Fortunately, they could walk down the street to a VFW or Legion Hall to drink a beer and talk with a buddy—or just sit and listen. Sharing their stories was therapeutic.

But the nature of warfare today doesn't involve mass numbers of troops. Instead, there are small groups of grievously wounded men and women returning home with not enough colleagues nearby to help them work through the pain.

Like each of us, Al hates the high suicide rate among veterans and appreciates the army's effort to assist, but he knows it will take a groundswell from the rest of the folks at home to keep our warriors safe. He has always valued the creed not to leave any Ranger behind, whether it's over here or there. Transitioning to business and mastering new skills is the most effective way for our young troops to continue winning the fight.

Creating a virtual world of success regardless of the physical environment can transform the ordinary into the extraordinary. For example, a young manager who hangs her college banners above workers' cubicles creates the luster of great college rivalries to encourage the team's competitive spirit.

Emphasizing the principle of mastering the basics and providing the outlet to blow off steam creates more and more cohesion within an already high-functioning group.

Not Being Shy

Command Sergeant Major
(CSM) William "Monty" Montgomery

We'd like to think the quiet professionals at work will always be recognized and receive their due. The reality is they still need to advocate for themselves, to project magnetism and confidence, or else these great folks in industry may not be adequately noticed. For many, self-advocacy comes naturally or can be coached. For others, it becomes a challenge they conquer with introspection, a well-planned strategy, and practice.

Command Sergeant Major William Montgomery (Monty) is one of the most impressive men you will ever meet. He stands a hulking six foot one and 230 pounds of battle-hardened muscle from five campaigns over 25 years. In 2020, he still remains engaged, assisting the U.S. security effort in Baghdad. Over his career, he has helped build the blueprint for the U.S. Army's Stryker Force. He has also guided wartime commanders to battlefield success and achieved a championship athletic victory.

But Monty never envisioned himself becoming a public figure in front of hundreds.

By the age of 25, he had completed Airborne, Ranger, Long Range Reconnaissance, and Water Infiltration courses. He had personally humped the army's bulkiest personal weapon, the M60 machine gun, and was three-time light-heavyweight boxing champion in the 82nd Airborne, which is when I first met him. If I could have snapped a Polaroid shot in 1990, I would have chosen quiet young PFC Monty to one day become a super*soldier*. I was right, but even I didn't realize he could become a super*leader* who'd develop a programmatic stewardship in combat that would save young lives.

Monty left his home state of Idaho right after high school and entered the U.S. Army, quietly determined to seek out the most challenging path offered. He knew that humbly building his skill set in the military would be his foundation.

As he moved swiftly through the junior ranks, senior commanders valued his excellence at the team and squad level. This part is what the army calls the "hands-on" echelon, because it's crucial to have subject matter experts who know their craft blindfolded and can impart it to the young soldiers. Monty became known as the quiet NCO who would comfortably stand in the middle of five guys and demonstrate from memory things like the details for "pushing a hard duck out of a CH47 chopper." (In plain English, that refers to the airborne/seaborne operation where a team of soldiers and a fully inflated rubber boat cast out of a hovering helicopter into the water.)

After eight years of building a textbook-type foundation, Monty reflected on what hurt the worst and required the most self-improvement. For this gentle boxing champ, it was getting out in front of large groups to speak publicly or, heaven help him, having to sing. Yes. Remember the military values leaders who can corral men with the powerful sound of their voice that complements a fearsome demeanor.

The U.S. Army was ready to offer Monty, recently promoted to staff sergeant, any assignment he wanted. With trepidation, he chose a classic posting he knew would force him to conquer his discomfort zone—becoming a drill sergeant.

Fort Benning, Georgia welcomed their young Ranger back to the home of the infantry and justifiably placed him in the limelight for being such a qualified NCO. He had more badges than the other drill sergeants, but he couldn't sing or project a lick. He realized he needed to come out of his shell, and he planned to force his way out.

Especially terrifying was the thought of calling cadence songs to new recruits. Monty was ultraconfident in his mil-skills of shooting and maneuvering but wasn't a loud, outgoing personality. He knew that to achieve greatness, he'd have to conquer operating in front of large audiences. So on his drive from Fort Lewis, Washington, to Fort Benning, Georgia, he unwrapped a CD he bought at the PX called Army's Best Cadences. He played the CD over and over for 2,752 miles and focused on his memorization skills. Somewhere between Salt Lake and Denver, he had the epiphany that memorized material burned into his left brain could be easily accessed when the right brain (responsible for arts and creativity) needed it. A breakthrough. His left brain had long since resigned itself to the belief that articulating things of meaning to audiences was reserved for gifted speakers. Finally, he figured out a trick for his right brain to deliver it—preparation via arduous memorization—and he still had 1,500 miles to practice.

Monty had one more epiphany before hitting the Tennessee-Georgia state line. With the sun rising and "There's a Drill

Sergeant There" playing on the stereo, he made a vow to be overprepared for all public matters—teaching classes, running ranges, speaking at formations, anything. Before he knew it, he had loosened up and even added humor into his instruction. Soon, Monty found he could get up and speak spontaneously on any military topic. A welcome revelation found junior soldiers start to gravitate to him and find comfort in his counsel.

Public speaking and performing can be a showstopper. *The Book of Lists 2019* still ranks it as the #1 fear. No matter if it's business, entertainment, or coaching, this skill cuts across nearly every endeavor that requires a display of human intelligence and movement.

What's the first step in mastering the skill? Memorize your material cold—deep-freeze cold—so you have no doubt it will be on cue when the spotlights turn on and your name is called. For example in my own life, I remember playing the piano in college for a talent show, and I prayed that playing Chopin in front of co-eds wouldn't be a disaster. So I practiced the piece until I didn't need the music, and then I practiced it more until I didn't need to look at the piano. That's when I knew I was ready.

In fact, I had made the same discovery as Monty—that with full command of the material, I could be relaxed and let my personality shine through. First, I sat down on the bench, then I stood up with a glance at the crowd to remove my sport jacket, and then I smiled as if to say, "Get ready for something that's so fast, I can't even wear a jacket." And it worked. They all tuned in and gave me their full minute of attention while I whizzed through the Minute Waltz and received a thunder-sized rush of applause in return.

In business, we marvel at why workers are attracted to confident leaders and the gravitas they project. If we reduced it to a math equation, it could be argued that "credibility" on the part of the speaker + a natural (even humorous) "manner" = the magical combination of "great communicator." Some people possess plenty of one element and just need to beef up a little on the other.

It seems so simple, but think of times you've sat in an audience and had reaction #1 to a speaker: Who is this guy to tell us how to coach when he hasn't won any championships? Or reaction #2: Jeez, this guy is killing us with boredom. Why does management bring in a dull expert and think we even understand what he's saying? Receiving either reaction will hold you back from attaining a "great communicator" status.

To perfect your game, start by self-diagnosing your area of need and, like Monty did, check your gut to determine what to do next.

Building It If It Ain't Built Yet

Command Sergeant Major (CSM) William "Monty" Montgomery

The chance to architect a new organization is the opportunity to build from the founder's point of view. It requires incorporating each element that perfectly aligns to make a team capable of winning over the long haul. It's a dream chance whenever we get it. And it's a crucial step in the maturity of leaders who have the opportunity to craft their strategy, prove it out, and demonstrate they have the energy to roll it out for success.

In the early 2000s, the U.S. Army was forming a new kind of lethal, quick-reaction force known as the Stryker Brigade. Good men were needed from other infantry units to fill the Brigade's rosters. Monty wanted to be where the best warfighters were heading, so he went there to take over a platoon. That gave him the groundbreaking responsibility to vet the army's new doctrine and form it into tactical procedures that would work on the modern battlefield.

Monty's platoon would be comprised of four Stryker teams, each one with nine infantrymen in a vehicle plus a crew of two. The U.S.'s brand-new Stryker was a versatile high-speed attack transport with the firepower of a Mark 19 missile and a .50 cal machine gun perched on top. It made the combat troops on the ground highly mobile, able to shorten the distance to interdict the enemy or rapidly support friendly elements in a fight.

Monty arrived to a platoon that needed work and a system that was untested—a total rebuild job any mechanic would salivate over. He cultivated a three-tiered strategy as he realized he'd no longer be able to build, execute, and improve every single procedure. Nor did the army want him to. Rather, it was time to mature as a leader and grow his subordinates in the process.

Monty's three initiatives were exactly on point: 1) put time and energy into preparation, 2) develop junior leaders, and 3) diagram components of combat operations down to the minutest detail.

At first, men questioned why the training environment at Fort Lewis in early 2001 was so strict—until 911 happened. Suddenly, the extended time spent in the field to get things right made sense. Stryker standard operating procedures were put in place and rehearsed, and junior leaders were independently coordinating their moving parts. In the process, the deployability percentage that had started dismally low from medical profiles and all manner of nonmilitary issues were resolved organically as competence leveled. And if that failed to raise the standard adequately, Monty put in the paperwork time to get rid of the bad apples.

The three tiers of execution Monty employed benefitted the end-user workers in a way that the **beefy middle of the organization was carrying the weight** *of the work. The critical piece for a big organization's architect is to craft the big-picture process and metrics. After that, it's the responsibility of the directors and managers to complete the hands-on execution.*

The architect personality truly craves starting from scratch. Given the inflection point of a new sales organization that has launched its sales force successfully for a year, the time to launch its channel organization to amplify revenue may be at hand. Sales channel leaders will have the opportunity to create the program according to their pillars of success that include margins, tiering, and contracting particulars. Some leaders prefer to enter an organization that is up and running so they can "fix what's wrong." In contrast, other leaders relish the opportunity to lay the entire foundation according to a pristine checklist.

Recognizing preferences helps people steer toward the desirable jobs and avoid the others. From a hiring perspective, asking exploratory interview questions regarding processes and 12-month plans with analytics quickly weeds out the builders from the maintainers.

NFL football coach Vince Lombardi was famous for the motto "Let's go forward to the basics" because any organization that has lost mastery of the basics needs a reboot. Just the simple act of getting everyone on the same page with the little things puts the organization in a superior position over its competitors.

Delegating is what you learn to do when you bump up to the next level of management. Fast movers are comfortable with it if the folks they're delegating to can effectively take the reins. That's the key to the military's success, but we don't always see it (or need to see it) in business.

On the flip side is my buddy Joe Pinto, CEO of Tri-Deca, committed to maintaining the highest echelon of product offering he could and its accompanying white-glove service. This approach tended to keep the rolls trim with only the best technicians. In his case, the aim of the top-shelf brand governed unchecked organic growth. As such, the company remained on top by staying specialized.

Giving Wise Counsel

Command Sergeant Major (CSM) William "Monty" Montgomery

In business, the job description of the lower echelon of roles focuses mostly on tasks and production. Then at a certain point—quite often when reaching the #2 spot on the team—the job description includes advising the boss. Decision power may lie at the top, but that chairperson or department lead needs to rely on the advice of his or her trusted advisors—roles that are time honored for their value to the organization.

The military has a unique and ancient command structure. For several thousand years, every victorious army in history from the Romans to the Rangers has used the separate dual rank structure of both officers and enlisted. This approach, which is not replicated in business, could probably provide a lively discussion in an MBA class. Perhaps it's centered around the reality that soldiers' and sailors' lives are at stake in zero-tolerance environments where turning left instead of right at the precise moment can get them killed.

Since imminent threats are always a possibility, the senior enlisted advisor is charged with the welfare of the troops. As such, he advises the commander with that perspective in mind. He knows how much the troops have slept and how much they have eaten. He knows how full the vehicles are with fuel &

ammo and when the next supply is due. Clearly, his advice is critical to the commander before he decides to fight. The senior enlisted advisor reports directly to the senior officer, who decides where, when, and how the unit will proceed and is ultimately responsible for everything.

However, the senior NCO is not technically the second in command, a situation that confuses civilians. For that job, there is an executive officer whose actual role is "second in command" because of the need to take over if the commander gets killed. As it relates to command decisions, the role of the top NCO is akin to the wise counselor. And all good commanders listen to their wise counselor.

For example, on my first day in ROTC in 1982, my military science instructor gave me advice I never forgot. Major Burke told the class, "Ladies and gentlemen, when your training is complete here, you will be commissioned as officers in the U.S. Army and be responsible for the lives of 40 soldiers and two million dollars of equipment [triple that number in 2020]. It is a mighty responsibility, so the most important thing you can do is listen to your senior NCO." Thank you, Major Burke, I could hug you, because that advice set me on the right path from day one.

By 2006, Monty had become company first sergeant in the Stryker Brigade, returning for a second deployment to a far more dangerous Iraq than its first in 2003. After Saddam's regime dismantled in late 2003, Al Qaeda in Iraq sprung up in the ensuing power vacuum under the control of Jordanian-born Al Qaeda leader Al-Zarqawi.

The insurgency was at its highest point of the conflict, with the U.S. suffering casualties every week. Monty and his company commander had worked perfectly in sync over the past year to drive the troops hard. They were determined proficient enough to direct all their assets toward eliminating risks.

Accordingly, they had put procedures in place before taking the Stryker vehicles out in nonpermissive (suspected hostile) environments. They marked every route "black" until it had been cleared by one of the three primary assets they had. The units followed Monty's procedure to employ either a UAV (unmanned aerial vehicle), a route clearance team, or thermals. They would get the route marked "green" before rolling. This was the kind of methodical process that had sprung from the command teams working in unison, and it also spoke to Monty's ability to influence others.

Unless an urgent mission to save American lives took precedent, Monty's number-one concern was the safety of his men. For all other capture/kill missions, they had set conditions to win while still prioritizing safety needs. It was a wise algorithm.

In early 2007, they were embroiled in the Battle of Baqubah. Al Zarqawi, who had eluded our forces for two years, had finally been killed. After cutting off the head of the leader of the insurgency, they faced an immediate military problem: yet another power vacuum. They knew the leaderless regional insurgents would respond unpredictably. Factions within the main group had flexed a desire to take over, and U.S. forces were forced to deal with multiple kinetic (daily contact) environments.

At this time, 3rd Brigade/1st Cavalry came under heavy fire from all directions, so elements of the Stryker Brigade were called in to assist. The 82nd and Special Forces elements operated on both flanks. Monty's Stryker company faced its fiercest combat during this period as Operation Arrowhead Ripper raged into full gear. Together, they were able to remove the remaining elements of Al Qaeda and put a local Baqubah government element in place.

Shortly after that, Al Qaeda would become ISIL and then ISIS, growing a new head with slightly different venom each time the old one was chopped off. Fortunately, order was restored in Baqubah, where the populace had previously been intimidated.

The company continued to slug it out admirably, suffering its only loss late in the deployment when a Stryker was hit on an uncleared route. That was just three days after Monty was selected for promotion to sergeant major and moved up to HQ.

Nine out of 10 warfighters died in the convoy, seemingly moments after Monty had passed on the reigns.

Monty took these deaths hard. As all great leaders do, he wondered, "What if I had still been there?" But the nature of war is a nasty business, and to Monty's credit, over the eight months he had cared for the men's welfare in the hot war zone, the company only lost a handful. It might easily have been five times that number.

Reflecting back, Monty had co-architected a working system and provided wise counsel for his company commander. Looking ahead, he would serve as sergeant major for two more battalions and mentor hundreds of young NCOs.

In a commercial setting, there comes a time in your progress when you may assume the role of the chief advisor or actually be the #2 person in charge, which means you're now the #1 supporter. Your job is to lend never-ending assistance to the boss to make the company run flawlessly while taking on the role of private counsel to the CEO—like the role of consigliere in The Godfather *movies.*

It's a two-way street, of course. A great boss has the ultimate responsibility of making the hard decisions, but along the way, he has the counsel of his #2 to guide him. It's important to note it's a symbiotic relationship for both of them since the counselor's daily tasks may include personnel and product concerns that complement the CEO's pure fiscal and marketing drivers. Collectively considered actions benefit both of their domains and achieve the right balance. It confirms that, in business, two heads are better than one.

Fighting as You Train

Sergeant Major (SGM) Jeffrey Koenig

A leader's first test is deciding what type of command climate to set. The easiest is to throw down a set of rules and enforce it from the corner office—by far the worst choice. The hardest thing to set into motion is the one that first takes a studied look at the situation and then crafts the right balance of mission readiness with developing a new sense of team spirit. This would be a much better choice.

After retiring from a Ranger career lasting 20 years and four combat tours, Sergeant Major Jeff Koenig took over as Navy Installation Commander in a quiet Maine community. He inherited a crew of 100 people charged with maintaining submarines and equipment. The equipment and facilities needed updating, and so did the morale. Here's how Jeff addressed the 50/50 mix of civilian and military folks he knew would understand this message for them: "For us to be high performing, we have to train as we fight, and fight as we train. We also plan to be realistic, and we want to have fun."

Within a short period, the installation returned to smooth function and a new lease on morale because he had created a command climate that resonated—the right balance of "hooah" and "I care about you." The most recent command climate survey reported a real lovefest for their environment and their leader.

Moving Up and Up

Sergeant Major (SGM) Jeffrey Koenig

Just when you have your job perfected and the team is humming on all cylinders, what happens? As a mover and shaker, the executive team may have other plans for you. It will always be tough to leave a group you've worked diligently to perfect. But likely you'll find a superstar in the group who's ready to move up, and the organization as a whole will get stronger.

Jeff Koenig had always been a fast-mover and shaker. I first met him as he had just been promoted to sergeant and was one of my team leaders in the Red Falcon Scouts. I knew he'd prove to be a rock star in Desert Storm. A can-do attitude and care for his men wound up being a trademark of his leadership, along with his All-American looks and 16-inch biceps. He always did the work to stay chiseled and maintain an immensely fit presentation.

Jeff was off and running toward a great career and was selected for the division commander's staff—a real honor. Major General Henry Shelton, who would go on to earn four stars and serve as Chairman of the Joint Chiefs of Staff, had a personal team. It consisted of a "chief of staff" colonel, a "secretary to the general staff" captain, an "aide" lieutenant, a couple of others, and one E-5 sergeant of outstanding character, all of whom represented the general and accompanied him in the field. And out of all the E-5s in the division, the general picked young Jeff Koenig. His star power had been recognized.

SGM Koenig's most rewarding assignment came as company first sergeant in the 1/32nd Infantry Battalion in the 10th Mountain Division. He had his Rifle company humming to perfection and the ability to mentor dozens of young soldiers every day. After nurturing the subordinate NCOs in the company, the unit reaped the benefits of a finely tuned infantry company ready for combat. They deployed to Iraq for the initial fight in Fallujah in 2003–4.

The 1/32nd had "set the conditions for success" and handled the counterinsurgency mission in bulletproof fashion early in Operation Iraqi Freedom. During this time while the insurgency was in its infancy, they could move freely in unarmored vehicles and with open doors. First Sergeant Koenig knew if/when things got worse, he'd need to set new conditions to maintain battlefield superiority.

An extra stamp of approval validated their proper groundwork when they assisted the marines and the 82nd lock down a coordinated U.S. effort. Brigadier General Gerritt told Jeff, "Congratulations, you have everything perfect. Now you're needed elsewhere." Jeff knew this was standard fare in the military. He was being ushered forward for a higher responsibility.

His feeling of momentary reluctance instead of joy stemmed from his sense of paternal nostalgia. He realized he had to listen to "leave the eagles in the nest you've built" and make another. He was tapped for promotion to sergeant major in the famed 173rd Airborne Brigade as a reward for a great career. And the army needed him for the upcoming deployment to Afghanistan.

Corporate folks can get stuck in a rut of not seeking enough diverse assignments within the organization or not wanting to leave after getting it "just right." Maybe that's okay in the corporate world where good people aren't typically forced to move up. But danger can arise if that "content-to-be-content" individual prevents fast-moving stars from soaking up the experience and then moving on. In addition, the organization might miss out on the benefit of fresh perspectives gleaned from rotating up, especially if some people have hit the Peter principle level and plant themselves there for life.

This scenario makes for a lively discussion from tenure loyalists in the business environment. It's easy to present a counterpoint. For sure, moving up and up is a more embraced precept in the military world, but the benefits of preventing stagnation in any organization still apply.

Overcoming Limitations

Sergeant Major (SGM) Jeffrey Koenig

A new goal to increase revenue is usually accompanied by operating limits set for you. Chances are you're given a budget and a head-count of how many folks to hire, and then it's up to you to be a creative leader.

Aside from the parameters set by the company, other constraints may include a temptation to gain the advantage by "any means possible." The businessperson with a quota to hit has to navigate overcoming limitations while still toeing the line of integrity.

Once promoted to the army's highest enlisted rank of sergeant major, SGM Jeff Koenig's 2/503 Battalion of the fabled 173rd Third Herd deployed to Afghanistan in June of 2007. There, they experienced the toughest 15 months of their lives. They set down in the adjacent Kunar and Nuristan provinces in the lawless northeast that bordered Pakistan. Their mission: to root out the lawless Taliban. Taliban fighters were terrorizing the citizens of the country from hidden perches high in the austere mountains. They were near impossible to find in the unfriendly terrain.

SGM Koenig assessed one commonality and one contrast with his previous deployment two years earlier. Both units had been well-trained with elite personas and Rangers interspersed throughout, which was common. Different (as Jeff had foreseen) was that by 2006 the Afghanistan insurgency level had grown far more insidious than in '03–'04. The Taliban were everywhere, the friendlies were frightened, and the troops couldn't tell the difference between the two. Local military forces assisting the U.S. in both areas were average at best by American standards. That assessment had remained the same or even deteriorated slightly.

Nothing about this deployment would be easy. For starters, the extended rotation time of 15 months was draconian, a burdensome amount of time to be away from young families. Husbands and fathers would all be missing a couple of kids' birthdays and anniversaries, and the stress levels of moms and young wives who heard about daily casualties was elevated from the outset.

General David Petraeus theorized that to win this kind of war, the U.S. forces needed to "be among the people." Given the decentralized nature of the bad actors, this made sense. The difficulty, though, was enacting this doctrine. The 2/503rd had 1,200 men to cover a sector the size of Connecticut, and the mountainous region made for poor commo and transportation issues due to the altitude and air density. In military parlance, that meant it would be tricky to set conditions for success in the wilderness of eastern Afghanistan.

The dilemma faced by a professional military in conflict with a guerilla force that places a low value on civilian casualties stood out as the major problem. This was the reality of the Taliban fighters. They knew they could hide in densely populated areas full of civilians. They also knew a civilized nation like the U.S. wouldn't wipe out an entire village just to get a few insurgents.

Confoundingly, the precise location of the Allies' #1 target audience for winning hearts and minds would be a safe harbor for the Taliban.

Freely able to hide in plain sight, the terrorists with a low regard for human life who blended in with the populace could thwart the U.S. effort. For example, immediately following a friendly visit to an elder in town after the Americans left, they might threaten or kill one of that elder's family members in the street with everyone watching. With no hesitation to slaughter their own people as a method of achieving loyalty, they had perfected how to "remain among the people" more effectively than the Americans could.

In previous battles from Roman times until World War II, military forces were rarely ever able to camp in towns. They knew the enemy's retort would be a carpet-bombing that would kill all the civilians, too. For millennia, this kind of collateral loss had been regarded as grossly unacceptable.

Yet, suddenly, in the past two decades of conflict was a poisonous Middle Eastern lust for martyrdom that extended to sacrificing the citizens surrounding them. Taliban, Al Qaeda, and ISIS were perfectly willing to use these citizens as human shields. Unwilling to revert to similar Medieval tactics, our forces faced their greatest challenge.

The first problem was our inability to identify insurgents around the villages; the wolves were living among the sheep.

The second problem was the lack of ability to confront them *en masse* in an urban (or dense village) environment. Walls and buildings made it impossible to engage more than a handful at a time.

The third was finding all their hiding spots for troops and weapons. Given the terrified cooperation of civilians who feared for their lives, the insurgents could hide in living rooms, public squares, or at entrances into the village.

U.S. diplomacy is simply not ready or willing to cross the line into barbarism. As a result, we may be lauded on the world stage as peacekeepers but will continue to suffer the tactical consequences on the ground.

Dime-store leaders often summarize their position in a moral leadership dilemma to respect human life or employ drastic measures—that is, "Do whatever it takes." They don't fully realize the collateral damage that could result from those drastic measures. It's easy enough to say that with flare when it's related to an athletic endeavor. The sacrifice is individual, and the stakes are solely personal. But when the sacrifice involves the lives of innocent families and the stakes are global, only barbarians have proven willing to take that step.

Similarly, we occasionally see business practices that are technically within the scope of the law but, if implemented, could cause great social harm. Examples would be pulling apart a newly acquired company to sell it off or calling in a loan that would trigger austerity in a community. The social conscience or fear of social repercussions usually prevents catastrophic things from happening, and we're tenuously lucky for it. Less extreme are the shortcuts that can be taken. Examples are making a product less safe but still within tolerance and reducing the quality of work expenditures at the office that purport to chip away at the limitations but, in reality, they chip away at morale and pride.

Walking Among Heroes

Sergeant Major (SGM) Jeffrey Koenig

> *Times may get tough when the competition's strength exceeds the predictions or a shortage of supplies becomes a factor. With no further infusion of workforce or resources and an inability to step back, the only way to face the challenge is to dig in and execute the plan with everyone's heads down. This is when heroes emerge and legends are born.*

A case in point: the furious Afghan storm ensued in 2007 with the 173rd right in its eye. There would be no additional reinforcements and no retreat from the mission. Instead, they would face the worst attacks both from the Taliban and extreme terrain. A thousand men and women performed valiantly, hundreds were decorated, and three soldiers in the Herd's 2/503 Battalion earned the Medal of Honor. This was testament to the valor of the fighting soldiers and, sadly, to the hellish conditions they faced throughout a year plus.

Operations Sergeant Major Jeff Koenig mapped out the coverage for barren jags of mountainous hell known as the Korengal Valley, Aranas, and Wanat. Teams deployed there would etch their efforts into history. His HQ assigned filmmaker Sebastian Junger to embed with the 2nd platoon of Battle company in the Korengal Valley at an austere mountaintop outpost named Restrepo. For a year Sebastian and his team covered the men and the mission, culminating in the award-winning documentary *Restrepo.*

As SGM Koenig recounted the stories of the heroes of the Herd during Operation Rock Avalanche, he reminded me that no one "wins" a Medal of Honor. It is "earned" by a soldier and "awarded" by the army and the president of the United States. In each of his three battalion battles where the medal was awarded, the recipients' messages were nearly the same—that no one man could have earned the award alone. They were respectfully accepting it on behalf of everyone on the ground and supporting from the rear.

The Medal of Honor exists as the most prestigious military award that can be awarded. Recipients must be approved by Congress. The award recognizes valor in the face of almost certain death and is so rare, only 86 of those who have earned the medal are living. In perspective, that's 1/10th the number of living Nobel Prize winners, 1/20th the number of the world's four-minute milers, and 1/60th the number of humans who have summitted Mount Everest.

Sal Giunta, Kyle White, and Ryan Pitts are the three humble humans from the Herd's 2/503 Battalion who earned the Medal of Honor. Their stories are at once spectacular and chilling, and their accounts of bravery should be read. It's easy. Just Google them if you want to experience how heroes act under fire. I feel as though I lived through the missions, listening to SGM Koenig's recollection and then researching them in moment-by-moment detail.

They all refused to call themselves anything special, but as SGM Koenig said of his brothers, "They were proud to walk among heroes."

Challenging times may produce heroic efforts that future members of the organization will remember forever as the moment that turned the tide. Not only did these individuals contribute to saving the day, but they will have added to the legacy of the organization itself.

Staying Young Enough for New Tricks

First Sergeant (1SG) John "Roses" Rowe

Have you ever seen an older worker discounted when it came to a promotion or new position generally oriented toward younger workers? It's possible that any segment, and not just the established employees, can show reluctance to grasp a new concept that replaces years of what they're used to.

In the case of new technology, though, the younger set may have a double advantage from already using tech in social settings of gaming or dating apps. Plus when it comes to physical work, Mother Nature's influence on the body makes it slowly and insidiously more challenging to maintain the stamina of previous years. But we can't leave out the older set with the wave of a hand. Like any other segment, many out there will stay young enough to learn new tricks. Don't worry. They'll be easy to spot.

My buddy Johnny Roses proves one is never too old to run the Ranger gauntlet. Thirty is not at all elderly in human years, but for Ranger candidates, it's pushing T-Rex status. In 1991, Roses had eight years in already and had just returned from our deployment in Iraq. The last thing he wanted to do that year was saddle up for Ranger School—what Roses lovingly referred to as the army's two-month emotional experience.

Only 3 percent of Rangers that make it through the course each year are over 30, and they deserve special props. My own "13–1989" class had only one "senior" citizen—a 32-year-old Green Beret named Russ. He was a human machine and happily became my Ranger buddy through the final three phases. At the time, I was also a somewhat seasoned 26-year old, and they cracked senior jokes saying we packed 58 years of experience in one sleeping bag. Seeing the gradual changes one's body has to face in the extremes of sleep loss and starvation, I gained mad respect for the older guys and their ability to survive.

Making it through to earn the Ranger tab is a young man's game—one that routinely sees aid stations full of 23-year-olds who fail out for every conceivable physical reason. Staring down the barrel of his 30th birthday in 1991, Johnny Roses had earned the name Old Man. He was a year older than the platoon leader —me. Add one more weight to his uphill climb: Roses lived hard, soldiered hard, and partied hard on Ft. Bragg's Hay Street when he was off duty with the boys. That kind of lifestyle tends to worsen the coping mechanism of the body's morph into catabolic muscle and fat loss during starvation. In other words, the drinking would hurt him from the inside out in a hellish way, considering how miserable similar body changes are for even nutritionally strict athletes.

Strictly speaking, Roses didn't have to attend Ranger School after getting back from Iraq. So why did he do it? The 82nd Scouts are required to be Ranger qualified, and he had held a class date pre–Desert Storm. Then he was successfully deployed with distinction, which meant no one would enforce the rule for another six or more months. So Johnny could have coasted.

But he was a street-smart soldier who liked to mentor the younger guys. He felt the duty to drag his three-decade-old bones to Pre-Ranger and Ranger School to live up to the image in the mirror—to never be a fraud. Competitive soldiers in other companies with their eye on making it to the Scouts gave him no chance, but Roses made them eat their words. The guys in his squad rallied around him. Two of his younger buddies, Spoony and Sanders, had just gotten their tabs too. They divined all of their "mojo" for him to make it.

Roses left for Fort Benning and came back two months later a bony ghost—but with a freaking tab! The old man had joined the brotherhood.

Score! What a great success story to have an informal leader gain formal qualifications. If company leaders are smart, they'll embrace the long-anticipated certification that an employee earns, and they'll leverage its value throughout the ranks.

Appreciating a Comeback Story

First Sergeant (1SG) John "Roses" Rowe

How many times have we seen a middle-level executive that senior management was ready to put out to pasture receive a spark of life and rise to great heights? It's wonderful when it happens. Yet maybe we haven't seen it often enough.

So, the question then becomes, shouldn't senior management have a mechanism to recognize on-the-job performance that's generously mixed with informal leadership developed over the years? In contrast to the fast movers, the seasoned line employees may have atypical demons to conquer. When they finally conquer those demons, they may be able to quickly vault ahead to become enormous assets to the organization because of those years of seasoning. They deserve a chance, and considering the upside potential, it's a promotion strategy that beats the Vegas odds more often than not.

In Roses's case, he had nailed one of the precious Ranger slots allotted to the battalion and returned with a tab—a big win. And something more happened. Johnny legitimately grew into the mentor role due to his years served as well as now being combat tested and Ranger qualified. He also stopped thinking about getting out of the army. Instead, he carried his experience into the NJ Cavalry Reserves and mentored a few hundred more over the next 20 years, his favorite being his son, Jack. Following in Pop's cavalry footsteps, SPC Jack Rowe, Cav Scout, gets to begin his own tradition, thanks to the comeback story of Johnny Roses.

Young business leaders may have a unique opportunity availed only a few times in their careers—that is, the chance to promote an older line worker to the ranks of management. They should jump on this opportunity. The loyalty given is likely to be monumental, and the senior managers who recognize the promoter's business savvy will earn them respect.

Besides, everyone loves a comeback story.

Being the Hero of Your Own Story

Staff Sergeant (SSG) Chris "Merc" Mercadante

When Matthew McConaughey accepted an acting award in 2018, he shared on stage that his father had passed on a life lesson for him—to be the hero of his own story. For college grads who have been taught to be quiet professionals, this concept adds a helpful supplement to the leadership philosophy they'll form entering the workforce. While it will eventually be a bonus to have others advocate for them, the confidence equal to the persona they desire to create needs to hatch from within. As my Aunt Lucille said, "If you got it, flaunt it . . . and if you don't speak up for yourself, nobody else will."

From the time my kids were little, I encouraged them to tell me how much money they thought they had earned from doing a side job for me. Feeling uncomfortable "monetarily" advocating for himself, my youngest, Dustin, might invariably offer a small number—probably intended not to shock Dad. But it didn't matter what amount he said. I had my response ready. I had once seen him work a booth at a tech conference with me at the age of 10, and instead of just handing out brochures to IT directors playing the role of cute kid wearing a cardigan sweater, he "leveled up" to demo SATA drives and extol the virtues of RAID 6 data protection like a techie prodigy when suddenly we got slammed with business. It was a wow moment for me, the dad.

So what was my response to his request for money he thought he'd earned?

"Sorry, that's not enough, Dusty. You're worth more than that." I believe the person doing the work should have complete confidence in buoyantly conveying their value to their managers.

SSG Chris "Merc" Mercadante embodied this concept. Even before earning his Ranger tab in '92, he had the confidence to know what he wanted. He spelled out the path to get there with himself firmly planted in the director's seat of every plan. He basically talked his way into my Scout platoon.

It's impossible to resist magnetic individuals—and the personalities of special operators are often compelling. Why? Because people like to be around doers with swagger. It lifts all the buoys in the water and makes us feel good that we are potentially all heroes of our own stories.

Merc wasn't just an empty boaster. If that were true, the concept would fall flat on his face. He had a big heart and the right motivation. When he talked about achieving the goal at hand that seemed daunting at the outset of the mission, his certainty that it would get done rubbed off on the boys. Then they figured, "Sure, why not?"

Diverse personalities with different traits from their buddies can still arrive at the same endpoint. For example, Merc disliked quitters. Other guys have a "never say die" character, and that's what drives them not to quit. Merc hated to be proven wrong. That's what propelled him to the same endpoint not to quit. It still worked the same.

At one point, Merc experienced a character-defining moment when, as a new scout readying to cross the border for a mission into Iraq, he lost the cotter pin to his M16 rifle. Why did it happen? He had tried to thoroughly clean the M16 in the desert in the dark hours before moving out. His squad leader had *explicitly* instructed them only to field strip and wipe down their weapons, *not* take them apart. Still, Merc tried to overachieve, and in doing so, he lost the cotter pin, rendering his rifle sub-optimal and essentially unusable. Fortunately, the squad completed the mission. Yet they knew one of their teammates hadn't been functioning at 100 percent had they needed to count on him. They also came back to their hide spot with the understanding that Merc would have hell to pay for the mistake.

The squad leader turned this incident into a leadership exercise and gave Merc a Ranger's choice. Option 1: Report the lost cotter pin (loss of issued equipment) and take an Article 15 written reprimand from headquarters, retrieve a new pin from the armorer, and be done with it. Option 2: Suffer the cardio smoke session of his life until he vomited in full view of the team. That would be followed by pulling every crappy extra duty the team could think of as punishment for risking the success of the mission. And the sergeant would call in a favor from a buddy at HQ to quietly retrieve another cotter pin for the M16 without anyone taking note.

Simply not wanting to "lose" in front of his squad, Merc said, "I'll take the smoke." In fairness, he held out pretty well. Approaching the four-hour mark of burpees, squat thrusts, and flutter kicks in full gear and weapon, he heaved up the prior night's chow and face-planted in the sand. Done. There was karma thrown in, though. The rest of the team went searching for the lost cotter pin, and Eggy's eagle eyes found it glinting in the sun amid MRE trash right near where Merc vomited. Ranger justice had been served, and the unit's efficiency returned to 100 percent.

Merc went on to campaigns in Afghanistan and Iraq, providing security for Vice President Joe Biden, Hillary Clinton, Donald Rumsfeld, Rush Limbaugh, Angelina Jolie, and another 30 well-known visitors.

What I particularly admire about this story is that Merc had the confidence to tell it as part of becoming a strong role model. He has been generously sharing his mentorship ever since.

As a side story, Merc's son, Steven, benefitted from a dose of can-do *en route* to becoming an all-state wrestler in Florida and then a heavyweight at Franklin & Marshall College. Merc invited me to meet his son's wrestling coach, Coach Mike Rogers, and the team in Lancaster, Pennsylvania. Coach Rogers saw enough value in learning the Ranger principles to set up a workshop. We taught his team members to promote their substantial success by hustling to become the heroes of their own stories. Go Coach, and go F&M Diplomats!

Business momentum can begin when the phone rings and the confident-sounding voice on the other end has something valuable to say. The first win turns into a second and a third—and the momentum builds. In this way, it's up to us to create our own forward motion and choose to be at the center of every one of our success stories.

CHAPTER FOUR

G

Gallantly will I show the world that I am a specially selected and well-trained soldier. My courtesy to superior officers, neatness of dress, and care for equipment shall set the example for others to follow.

Creating a Persona	SGT Panagiotis "G-Man" Giannakakos
Motivating Outrageously	SGT Panagiotis "G-Man" Giannakakos
Rewarding Those Who Shine	SGT Panagiotis "G-Man" Giannakakos
Having the Brass	SGT Panagiotis "G-Man" Giannakakos
Ushering-in Workplace Morale	SGT Panagiotis "G-Man" Giannakakos
Assuming Permission	COL Jim "Mac" McCloskey
(Not) Sneezing in the Ambush	COL Jim "Mac" McCloskey
Coming Back to Teach	COL Jim "Mac" McCloskey
Protecting the "Flock"	CSM Greg Patton
Standing Up for What You Believe	CSM Greg Patton
Rising from the Ashes	CSM Greg Patton
Being Accountable	CSM Greg Patton
Connecting	CSM Greg Patton
Improvising	CSM Greg Patton
Being a Part of Something Big	SSG Doug Quitmeyer
Guarding Your Six	SSG Doug Quitmeyer

Creating a Persona

Sergeant (SGT) Panagiotis "G-Man" Giannakakos

Lots of quality discussion over the years has been devoted to the benefits of being memorable. It's compelling. When audience members remember you, that means you stand out from the crowd. For most of us, creatively growing our talents is the route to being memorable. And a chosen few have a natural gift of a persona that is outrageously, vibrantly alive.

I once met a legend known throughout the army as G-Man. Here's what I knew about him before we met: He'd previously served in the Canadian "2 Commando" Special Forces and then had become a United States Airborne Ranger. A Greek American, at six foot three, he was as big as a Peloponnese mountain with a name that was too long and too Greek to pronounce. That's why the battalion chart simply listed him as SPC G-Man. And what most intrigued me about him? After I (or anyone else) met him, we could never possibly forget him.

I couldn't wait to meet G-Man, and it looked like I would soon get my chance. I was leaving my Charlie Company infantry platoon after just 10 months and getting bumped up to the most significant assignment an infantry lieutenant could want. It was the Scout platoon of a battalion combat team full of Rangers and the best soldiers in the battalion. Seven of them were snipers, including one Specialist 4th Class Panagiotis (Pete) Giannakakos, the infamous G-Man. He'd be in my command, and I was excited for our chemistry to develop.

G-Man was exactly as I had heard—an outrageous, larger-than-life personality, shocking in every category that a *pure* military tactician would oppose. But in fact, they didn't. No one opposed him—not sergeants major nor generals.

How in the world did G-Man pull it off: by being one of the U.S. Army's most magnetically positive personalities. He had a day job as an E-4 Ranger sniper in the middle of the Arabian desert in 1990.

At a time when there was no internet and no portable video games to buoy the men's spirits, we had G-Man. The genius of his flamboyance was providing the men with an escape. His persona consisted of more than smiling and telling GI stories. It regaled the troops and created diversions that might speak out to them in a variety of interests. He created a virtual wrestling league; he organized football games; he crafted lyrics and music for a rock band. He had an attention grabber for any taste, all to boost the morale of the men.

Pulling off a feat on this level requires a person to be pretty talented. And G-Man was already a seasoned world traveler who spoke a second language. He was a class athlete in football, wrestling, ice hockey, and boxing—those were the ones I saw—and he played some guitar and drums. He could even handle a microphone (if we had had one) for vocals.

He thought fast on his feet and was a gifted storyteller and speaker. Beyond all that, he possessed an X-factor: G-Man was genuinely likable. You'd find yourself smiling when he approached because you had no idea what was about to transpire. To relieve the pressure of deployment, his mojo was to be intentionally funny and shocking. Early on as we were overdue to receive ammo, he told our colonel he wanted to "lock and load" weapons to protect ourselves like everyone else. "But sir, don't worry. A guy with an empty weapon but high morale is more valuable to me in combat than a truckload of ammunition." No one could help but laugh and roll with the circumstances when G-Man made proclamations that poked at reality.

There's a recipe for being memorable and improving the quality of life in the workplace. The ingredients call for a blend of being eternally positive, insightful, funny, magnetic, and nonthreatening. Add in other spices to your industry's taste, and bake until the company is golden.

Motivating Outrageously

Sergeant (SGT) Panagiotis "G-Man" Giannakakos

What if a company added a new e-staff position called chief motivation officer or CMO? You would imagine the person in that role would try to buoy the spirits of all the employees to be as happy—and therefore as productive—as possible. Think about the 20 percent increase in productivity that every boardroom hopes to capture. What if that increase could happen by employees being motivated to be 20 percent more industrious? Problem solved—without machinery and additional investments.

But the solution requires more than policies or tired incentives. What's needed would be a motivator worthy of the CMO title.

After years of being in the army, G-Man confirmed that motivating soldiers had been his plan all along—and his contribution to the platoon. I wondered how many of his zany antics were shot from the hip rather than designed in advance. What I do know is that, with high-performance troops, "creativity" is sometimes just a step away from "crazy."

What exactly did G-Man do to motivate people? For one, he created a fictional football league called Romo Ball. His brother-in-law was named Tony Romo. (This was years before the charismatic Dallas quarterback Tony Romo played. Their names are purely coincidental.) It featured a legendary game played in the sand by “titans” making “monster” tackles with no equipment. There were no fans to play in front of; they played only for the honor of the warriors.

I marveled at the brilliance of G-Man’s narrative. He was a storyteller captivating his audience, and he was describing us! As a result, we couldn’t wait to get out and emulate those giants on the field of honor while blowing off steam. We just needed to wait until we got a football mailed to us from home. After one arrived, the guys figured out everything else, including an area to play and coordinated work assignments so a majority could be free at the same time. The legend was on.

Leaders regularly weigh a risk against an associated reward. Consider the concept of Romo Ball, a mammoth-sized derby of tackle football. After weeks of deployment with little physical outlet, leaders might run the risk of incapacitating the warfighters who played. But I didn’t ponder this dilemma very long. The men deserved a reward for uniting in a plan to conduct an event for fun. They had written home for a football and a few orange cones for markers. They even had fun choosing teams with absurd names. To me this was a great morale boost.

I hope every leader wants his team functioning as cohesively as this one was, and I’d never be the one to tamp down my guys’ enthusiasm.

G-Man: Sir, can we play tomorrow at 1600?

Me: Yes.

G-Man: Do you wanna play?

Me: Hell, yes.

From a leader’s perspective, this kind of event was a win even before the first pass was thrown. We trotted out to an open area and played the game where troops from the other companies could plainly see us. If they wanted to join in, they'd wander over, and we welcomed them. We had a heckuva time and usually escaped with nothing broken—only minor injuries or a couple of contusions.

Shortly after, we changed camps and set in to prepare for an eventual ground invasion into Iraq. That's when the first of many CNN news crews rolled in. The network was covering the story of the military buildup and was looking for a soldier to interview. G-Man elbowed his way over to talk to the crew who asked him for a sound bite. He looked straight at the camera, pointed, and said, "Saddam, I'm coming to get you." His image and words made it all over the network back home. G-Man looked like a desert-camouflaged Uncle Sam aiming his way to victory.

Thinking fast on your feet and having a morale-building comment about your craft always pays off. That can happen when the director pays an unexpected visit or if the manager puts you on the spot at a sales meeting. When Joey, Jake, and Dustin were growing up, I used to tease them by asking a question and setting a pretend microphone in front of them to speak into. "Always have a sound bite ready" is not nearly as far-fetched as you might think. Leaders who know what they believe in and are Johnny-on-the-spot for a timely comment appear thoughtful and results driven. More than that, they inject a shot of motivation to keep the effort moving. And in G-Man's case, ready-made comments launched his notoriety throughout the division.

In August of 1990, American troops had landed and started to mass in Saudi Arabia for Desert Shield. By Thanksgiving, we knew we'd be there through Christmas and the holidays. With 1,200 men at Camp Red, the staff got the idea for a talent show in early December to raise *esprit de corps*. So the sergeant major put out the word to drum up some acts. After all, being out in the desert meant we'd have to be our own entertainment. And we'd only have access to the materials at the camp, so for props and gear, the scrounge was on.

G-Man told me straightaway that our platoon of 30 would supply two acts. First, Britt from 1st squad was volunteered. He was a handsome, guitar-playing Ranger who went on to compete in the army's Best Ranger competition as a staff sergeant five years later. For now, he was a lock because his family had managed to mail his electric guitar from Fort Bragg all the way to Saudi Arabia without damaging it. While other soldiers were receiving gummy bears and razors, Britt had gotten his Fender and a handful of picks.

For the big act, G-Man planned to debut the outlandish wrestling federation with all the live characters they had made up. The Ultimate Warrior, North Wind, The Cop with the Green Glasses, and ridiculous names like that. Ingenuity repurposed cardboard into body armor and Coke tabs into medieval chain mail. They created an incredibly well-choreographed show, fit for the WWE. The target audience of raucous males aged 18 to 30 thunderously received the acts.

As I looked around the makeshift arena, I silently applauded G-Man for making a thousand men laugh and forget they were three continents away from home. Son of a gun.

As a civilian leader, the idea of matching the motivation to the task makes sense. Too many of us have gotten used to low-brow morale-building activities to the point where it can seem like "forced fun." I first heard that phrase from a lady cadet in ROTC. Ever since then, I vowed never to be the boss making the team sleepwalk through forced fun. It has to be genuine—as I learned from G-Man.

Bold initiatives need bold motivation that will rev up your people to get 'er dun.

Rewarding Those Who Shine

Sergeant (SGT) Panagiotis "G-Man" Giannakakos

The organization that can publicly reward high performers projects the image of the place where its employees want to go the extra mile. When people see the kind of accomplishments that garner praise, they can decide to emulate those actions too.

The new army reserves the rank of corporal for wartime—a sweet in-rank boost to give to a deserving young leader. In late 1990 Desert Shield, each infantry battalion of a thousand men got authorization for two corporal promotions. Just two. A clerk at headquarters got one of them, and Pete Giannakakos of the Scouts got the other, so he became Corporal G-Man.

As we moved out to the Saudi-Iraqi border at Phase Line Razor to establish the tip-of-the-spear location, our platoon set up an observation post (OP) even farther out in front of our line of foxholes. It was equipped with an ocular device and telephone to monitor forward activity into the vast desert of southern Iraq.

I tagged newly minted Corporal G-Man and his sniper partner Lance Helm to get this job done. A few hundred meters to our front, they found an abandoned site where pieces of a tin hut had been strewn about. Sightlines were unencumbered in all directions, so this would be a good spot. The two snipers reconstructed the flapping sides of the hut back together and fortified it with sandbags that Lance arranged in the shape of a couch inside. Then they set up the ocular device to see everything to the front and ran TA-1 telephone wire the entire distance back to battalion.

Somewhere, Pete found a piece of metal that could serve as a sign and wrote "Love Shack" on it, then hung it outside. The name came from the B52 song "Love Shack" that had just come out in 1989. *Good*, G-Man thought, but it didn't yet measure up to the level of morale booster he wanted in case roving patrols from nearby units would come.

Lance had been quite industrious while we were still at Camp Red. He loved the vacuum-sealed fruitcake that came in the MRE meals and even wrote to the company whose address was on the back. This seemed especially funny to most of the guys in the unit because most soldiers in the army (and probably most human beings) despise these awful semi-dehydrated holiday rejects.

But Lance loved fruitcakes, so he reached out to Sterling Foods of San Antonio, Texas. Five weeks later, a case of 144 individually wrapped MRE fruitcakes arrived. They were addressed to PFC Lance Helm, Red Falcon Scouts, Operation Desert Shield. We threw the case in with the gear we carried to the border and now could stock the Love Shack with cake. To go with it, they scrounged several months' worth of instant coffee to make this little outpost quite hospitable.

Patrols from other units rotated through. When they were invited in for a respite with coffee and cake, all of their reactions were remarkably the same. They'd chat about the Chicago Cubs or whatever Italian food they were craving from back home.

Surprise, relief, happiness, relaxation. Within 20 minutes, they'd be back on their way feeling a little more human than when they arrived.

The Love Shack's reputation created a buzz. On Christmas week 1990, the air war started, and by mid-January, we were dug in and conducting nightly cross-border missions to prepare for the coming ground war invasion. About then, the Red Falcon HQ got a message over the radio that the big brass would be inspecting in the area. They were on their way to the most forward Saudi outpost of the entire U.S. forces—the Red Falcon OP (aka the Love Shack).

The compound effect of promoting excellent people is that they continue to do good things for an increasingly larger audience. More colleagues catch on as the word gets out, and before you know it, you have momentum.

Having the Brass

Sergeant (SGT) Panagiotis "G-Man" Giannakakos

Consider the premise that there are three keys to carrying off a dashing plan. First—craft a viable strategy. Second—know it's worked in the past on a small scale, which gains the confidence of management. Third—energetically have the brass to carry out the strategy on the big stage.

Many a sphincter would pucker upon answering the TA-1 landline (telephone) from the commo lieutenant to hear that a pair of generals, a pair of colonels, plus the rest of the entourage were rolling toward them in minutes. However, to G-Man, this gathering became an audience to play to. He was never gun shy to speak to any crowd, and he assured the excited "louey" on the line that all was well. Yes, they would be ready to receive the command party. *Party on.*

First, Pete and Lance checked around and determined everything was squared away. To be fair, no officer above the rank of lieutenant (only me and the commo officer) had been at the outpost in the previous 25 days of operation. Not our company commander, nor battalion commander, nor any NCO above the rank of E-7. Just us. Not that it should be a problem, but I was left to ponder whether the cadre of the "old guard" closing in on the Love Shack would appreciate what G-Man had done with the place.

The *outrageous* level hadn't yet been reached—not until Pete dug into his pack and pulled out his prize possession—a bright red and gold Canadian Army ascot from *2 Commando*, one that's typically used for dress military occasions such as parades and promotions. Why he brought it for combat in Iraq and carried it in his day pack out to the edge of the U.S. Army's frontier remains a question to this day, but this ascot made G-Man unique. He neatly put on the brilliantly colored ascot around his neck, knowing it provided a farcical contrast against the sand-colored camouflage from his uniform and TA-50 equipment belt.

Their final act in preparing for the approaching motorcade was to make sure the Love Shack sign above the door was hanging straight. And then they calmly closed the hinged door of corrugated tin and waited inside.

Two *command-type* Hummers, the kind with antennas sprouting up to signal "important people are inside," pulled up less than 40 meters to the rear of the hut. That would have been about 300 meters too close under combat conditions. Still, our Scout teams had been successful in early reconnaissance, and advance U.S. bombing runs had sent their forward elements scrambling back. So it was unlikely a daylight attack across miles of visible desert would happen in the next 30 minutes.

The senior entourage nimbly jumped out of the Hummers and moved up to the sandbagged entrance to first discover a vague smell of coffee. They stepped up to the entrance and found the door surprisingly closed. Why, they wondered, would there even be a door, let alone one that was closed, in the middle of the desert? It signaled the unusual. They did know the general was coming, didn't they?

That's when they saw the sign hanging above it—*Love Shack.* Quite a surprise! As the inspecting sergeant major was processing the scene, he instinctively knocked on the door. It was promptly opened wide by CPL G-Man in full ascot and camo. He greeted them warmly with, "Good afternoon, gentlemen. Would anyone like cake and coffee?"

Their reactions were a spectacular mix of rejoinders diverse enough to be studied in a management class. They ranged from the sergeant major's "*What in THE hell, son?*" to the battalion and brigade commanders' astonished yet controlled observation that the site was secure.

Major General (MG) James Johnson, who commanded the 82nd Airborne Division, and Lieutenant General (LTG) Gary Luck, who commanded the entire 18th Airborne Corps, were standing three rows deep behind the other men eyeballing the unfolding scene. G-Man's greeting with the coffee and cake offer was so unexpected that his question hung in the air for a good three seconds. A grenade could have cooked off in the gaping silence.

Then General Luck busted through the ranks toward the door and answered emphatically, "I would." There wasn't much room inside the hut, but there was just enough for LTG Luck, MG Johnson, and our brigade commander to enter and each have a seat.

As promised, Lance handed over makeshift cups of coffee he had boiled when he heard they were on their way. "Boiled" might be an overstatement. The cups of coffee were moderately warmed and stirred up in a canteen cup under a small flame, making perfectly acceptable Ranger coffee. Accessory packets of sugar and milk powder got dumped in whether requested or not. *It really was the thought that counted.*

Right behind the coffee service, Lance produced a homemade platter cut from ripped cardboard. On it, he served broken pieces of fruitcake they likely would never have chosen to eat under normal conditions. But God bless those officers. To honor the *esprit de corps* of the fighting man, they each took a piece as G-Man stood by the ocular device and, on cue, went into his briefing.

The battalion commander and sergeant major stood at the doorway as G-Man began. "Sir, this is the Red Falcon Scout OP, the most forward position in the division." *Everyone already knew this, but it was a point of great pride to the Scouts.* "We're positioned here with an unfettered 360-degree sightline through this ocular device for three miles in any direction and a dedicated phone line we check every sixty minutes." *Unfettered?* Oh my. Just like the line from the movie *Animal House*, we didn't want to stop him when he was on a roll.

"This position is manned around the clock by members of the Scout platoon on days preceding their patrol missions. Most importantly, other elements from the left and right flanks link up at this location to check in after lengthy patrols, and we provide a little comfort with the cake and coffee to those guys rotating through."

Silence lingered for a moment while the generals digested what G-Man had presented. Then General Luck leaned forward and said, "Hmmm . . . men rotating through, giving coffee and comfort, why that's f-ing awesome."

General Luck turned to Lance, a big part of the outpost operation, and asked, "What's your name, son?" Lance replied, "Helm—like the senator, Jesse Helm, sir." *Senator* was, in fact, Helm's nickname in the platoon, and they were both from North Carolina—although Senator Helms's name had an *s* at the end. Close enough. Then Lance told the fruitcake story.

The entire engagement lasted five minutes. General Luck got up to leave, and on his way out, said directly to the battalion commander and sergeant major, "I love these guys. They understand the balance between *what Command wants* and *what troops need*."

Word travels fast. That quick one-liner praising the Ranger-style initiative to boost morale on the desert outpost immortalized the general's popularity throughout the ranks. To this day, General Luck's name has been gold to the troops. Some of that gold stuck to G-Man, too.

General Luck didn't forget about meeting Lance and G-Man. Nine months later, shortly before earning his fourth star, he needed to choose a pair of enlisted soldiers to accompany him to a military breakfast in "dress blues" for a social event. The occasion involved meeting the senior senator from North Carolina, Jesse Helms. Guess who he picked?

In and out of business, successful leaders create personas that float over the day-to-day events and influence others to follow. Having the guts to step out of one's comfort zone might turn out to lift the spirits of the common man, and a hip CEO is sure to notice.

A smart CEO welcomes a sub-persona who stands out positively within the organization. Everyone can see that the uber figure generating a buzz from the midsection of the team adds prestige. And receiving praise from the big boss reinforces that it's the right thing to do.

Ushering In Workplace Morale

Sergeant (SGT) Panagiotis "G-Man" Giannakakos

The modern workplace smartly provides snacks and a recreation area. Startups and companies of the new guard have made the work environment into a place people want to come. Workers associate it with fun and fellowship, and that's when the best in everyone comes out.

It would be a fun business school discussion to imagine what a handful of Rangers might have done knowing in 1991 their talent show/Love Shack combo would precede the kind of workplaces that Amazon, Google, and Microsoft are creating.

By stopping at this oasis in the desert, patrolling teams conducting check-ins on the outer perimeter could have a few moments of respite. To the surprise of weary long-range elements, they found comfort. The ocular glasses allowed for visibility out the front. Because their position was camouflaged, the patrollers could relax and rejuvenate, then move on feeling more productive than before.

For the old guard, the concept of creating a fun workplace didn't always compute. Perhaps it wasn't even possible to their way of thinking. Since the 2010s, though, the new guard has realized creating a fun workplace is tenable and necessary. Top companies today find the same thing G-Man's field study concluded in 1991—that is, motivation encourages one's innovative spirit.

I've seen this happen in phases: First, workers are pleasantly surprised; next, they feel appreciated for the care given by the employer; then, they feel relaxed to a point of their best work product flowing freely. Keeping the love going ensures sustainability in the workplace.

MBA discussions would likely validate the twin facets of motivation that resulted from the talent show/Love Shack combo —a haven effect. When sustained, this effect can keep employees loyal to the organization.

While the old guard considered it frivolous to insert fun into the workplace, those who have unapologetically made their environments entertaining now enjoy an enormous lead in workplace quality of life. So, does the old guard have to be *old* and the new guard *young*? The young faction discussing the topic in our class at MIT's Sloan Business School immediately nodded "yes" to the happy workplace concept. Okay, we figured that. The older faction then pointed out they've seen both during their time. Today, they would agree that having a high-morale environment boosts productivity. Score one for the mature crowd!

But did that MIT discussion settle the question of age? Flashback to the Love Shack and the young soldiers who were the innovators. Those in the middle ranks felt mostly unsure and a little wary of how the senior leaders would react. They may have even believed the older leaders would be adversely "old guard" in their mindset. But General Luck surprised everyone. He was the oldest military man present and near the army's top rank. Yet, he instantly assessed the situation and embraced the brilliance of it—quite "new guard" for an old general.

Regarding age as it correlates to an innovative mindset, this scenario revealed the bookend age groups to be instant morale builders. Those in the middle group had been unsure at first. But they were sufficiently savvy to figure out the value. Age, the MIT class concluded, does not limit a leader's ability to morph with the times; some leaders' mindsets change before long while others just need to see a success story.

Assuming Permission

Colonel (COL) Jim "Mac" McCloskey

At times, circumstances dictate that speedy action be taken in the face of ambiguity. Emergent leaders boldly step to the front. They know where they want to go and what they need.

Jim McCloskey graduated from Philadelphia's LaSalle College ROTC as a new second lieutenant in May of 1968 when the Vietnam War was raging full blast. Two months before, the North Vietnamese had launched its deadly infamous Tet Offensive under Ho Chi Minh. The draft of young soldiers was on as Americans at home grew tired of the war—the country's third conflict in 25 years. Strong military leadership was needed more than ever to solidify the ranks.

Because the U.S. Army needed every infantry-branched warfighter overseas as soon as possible, there wasn't enough time for ROTC lieutenants like Jim to go to Ranger School before deploying. With so many combat infantrymen being killed, coming back wounded, or leaving the military, the normal flow of cycling back to attend the school after a first deployment was also interrupted. This vicious cycle was depriving the army of expert warfighters who might save lives downrange if it had enough troops in reserve to hold the lines steady while others trained up.

It was during the '60s that the Ranger designation underwent discussion at the highest levels. Being a Ranger reigned as the highest mark of combat excellence. In fact, it was considered so valuable that the army's previous chief of staff proposed Ranger training be mandatory for all incoming infantry officers. However, General William Westmoreland was forced to nix this idea due to the pressing need to ship officers to Vietnam and lead units right away.

Still, Ranger School cranked out highly selective superstars in the late '60s, but it couldn't keep up with a need that had tripled overnight. The army answered by redesignating specific highly skilled Long-Range Reconnaissance units as Ranger units. This was considered perfectly valid due to the fearsome on-the-job training they were getting in the jungles of North Vietnam and the highlands of Central Vietnam. Nobody minded; these men had earned this right with their blood.

Enter Jim "Mac" McCloskey, a high dose of needed "pure-guts" leadership and someone who was fearless in the face of the Viet Cong. He was viscerally contemptuous of mediocrity or anything less than 100 percent commitment from within the ranks. This was rather quickly hailed as a positive trait when facing the enemy. However, this didn't always sit well with those in the cushy middle of his own pack.

After the gold bar that signified his promotion to lieutenant was pinned to his collar, Jim wanted to ship out. The order to do so came swiftly. It would be right after he passed the Infantry Basic course and Jump School training at Fort Benning. That would take four months max, which left no time for 59 days of Ranger School.

Vietnam HQ knew they were getting a dynamic force in Mac. When he landed outside of Saigon, he reported to a marine colonel who told him he could freelance from the firebase. That meant he was free to gather unassigned men and equipment and dial up aggressive missions as he saw fit. Within days, he had taken charge of three reasonably well-trained groups that were missing commanders. They included Navy SEALs, Marine Force Recon, and South Vietnamese Ruff Puffs (Regional Force/Protective Force).

Mac spoke some Vietnamese and had taken French in school, which gave him an enormous advantage in assimilating into the local environment. He believed in what he wanted others to do and carried off instructions so well that they fell in step behind him, ready for the missions to come.

In addition to the leadership qualities that emerge when no direction is given, consider the concept of ***amplifying vague guidance****. An executive team may simply describe a mission and allow a young leader to freelance, including deciding how best to get the job done with any unclaimed resources available. In this case, the permission to act is understood. A rising young leader like Mac could put this opportunity to good use.*

(Not) Sneezing in the Ambush

Colonel (COL) Jim "Mac" McCloskey

Every leader's style can probably be charted by tolerance to certain stimuli such as maximizing efficiency and valuing courage. If those qualities—plus moving in a forward direction and discarding detrimental assets—are high on the list, a leader will have an extremely low tolerance for inaction and fear.

Lieutenant Jim McCloskey didn't wait for guidance. He took the initiative to set up ambush sites outside the wire with his eclectic niche of experts.

Nike hadn't yet launched the slogan "Just Do It." Rogers Rangers from the colonial forces in 1755 had beat them to it by 200 years. Mac's version of "Just Do It" was a blend of his two axioms. The first was "always assume permission," which seized small unit leaders' ability to assess. In real time, they knew what was uniquely needed at the battlefront to take action. This was made possible by the supportive management philosophy of Jim's marine colonel who trusted his first-line leaders on the ground to make the right moves.

Mac's second axiom was "Don't sneeze in my ambush," which meant telling men who complained about sickness (or anything at all) to "stay the hell away." He had no use for anyone who wasn't mentally and physically 100 percent. If someone threatened the security of his ambush with a metaphoric sneeze, he would just as soon shoot that slacker himself.

Logically, a healthy disdain for mediocrity accompanies a personal drive for top performance. For Mac, his knob of intolerance was turned to high speed. Early in his command when a Vietnamese lieutenant in the Ruff Puffs showed cowardice in front of his men and refused to go on the night's ambush, Mac punched him, putting him in the field hospital. Then Mac successfully executed the ambush that night anyway. The next day, the Vietnamese lieutenant was relieved of command and sent home.

A few months later, after a blessed string of successful missions with minimal casualties, the Marine Force Recon unit was tasked to travel beyond the safety umbrella of the two 105mm Howitzers at the firebase providing fire support to them. Mac and his marine gunnery sergeant went to see the armorer. They wanted to request an 81mm mortar tube and some rounds. They found an overweight noninfantry captain in a dark underground bunker hoarding the unit's firepower. He had a spreadsheet that he didn't have the desire to update and requisition forms he took far more seriously than dispensing lifesaving equipment for missions. So Mac pulled out his .45 caliber pistol. He assured the armorer that U.S. troops were not about to die because of a shiny mortar tube sitting pretty in the armorer's cage versus thumping enemy out in the bush.

This kind of laziness was the dreaded "sneeze" that threatened to infect the rest of the platoon, so Mac stepped out to provide the cure. The marine gunnery sergeant tied him up against the cage with M550 cord sitting on the field table while Mac grabbed the 110-pound tube and base plate. Gunny grabbed rounds on the way out.

The next day's mission got hit as expected, but thanks to support from the new tube, Mac's team was able to rain down mortar fire on the VC. No marines died that day.

Setting aside any discussion of whether the ends justify the means in the business setting, leaders who confront an issue that threatens the well-being of the team and take complete responsibility for their actions have the guts to shoulder the burden. When two junior leaders see the same issue and arrive at the same atypical solution, the executive is sure to take a detailed look—especially if the junior leaders' actions saved the day.

Coming Back to Teach

Colonel (COL) Jim "Mac" McCloskey

Being present in the lives of the people you work with expands the nature of your relationship and can grow it from coworker status to work-family members. It presents in many forms like supporting folks who stumble, mentoring those in need, or returning years later in emeritus status to instruct the next generation.

Whether you agree with his combat tactics or not, Colonel Jim McCloskey developed people by demonstrating teachable moments they could carry forward after he left. None of his guys ever got left behind. During combat, that makes a big difference.

Mac had enormous respect for the South Vietnamese; they were farmers, mechanics, and rice paddy workers fighting for their land and basic freedom. By following the American lieutenant, they felt reassured they wouldn't be left facedown in a rice paddy if one of them fell in the fight. They knew Mac would get them back to their families in the village. And they knew that was true for all U.S. forces under his command.

On one of their first missions in-country, Jim's convoy got ambushed and came under heavy withering fire. The marine on point took a round under his armpit, and he went down out in front of the lead vehicle blocked off from the men and trucks behind him. Jim ordered the team to return cover fire so two men could maneuver out there and drag back the fallen marine.

As they called to him, they could hear he was alive. They tried over and over to get to him, but the fire was too heavy. Other men and equipment were getting riddled with gunfire too.

Finally, no more sound came from the wounded marine out front. His silence signaled the only move to make—to try and safely withdraw. The soldiers were able to load up and get out without anyone else getting wounded. Within 30 minutes as they pulled back into camp, the colonel personally came out to get the report. He told Jim, "You did a helluva job getting the rest of the boys back in one piece. But Mac, we can't leave my boy out there. We need to go back out and get him." That meant heading right back out to the kill zone they'd just come from.

Rangers and marines can't leave men behind. It's not in their DNA. Who knows what might have become of the marine's body if they waited. So an entire platoon mounted vehicles with heavy firepower and sped back to the front. They reached the ambush site just as night was falling and found the abandoned scene. With the ambushers gone, they quickly found their marine lying in the road. His buddies picked him up and gently laid him back on the truck to go home.

Thirty years later, Mac returned to Vietnam to help the French nuns running the Thanh Xuan Peace Village "Chicken Church" and orphanage. In fact, he made 10 more trips over the next two decades to help the same people he had once fought alongside. A combination of good work with business leaders, investment bankers, and the Catholic orphanage culminated in a 2011 meeting with General Võ Nguyên Giáp, the famed leader of the South Vietnamese Army during the war. The Vietnamese general was turning an astounding 100 years old.

General Giáp, who spoke some English, told Jim, "If Americans like you had stayed three more months, we might have defeated the North."

Giáp was impressed that Jim had returned to his country. He finished their conversation with this remarkable compliment: "You are a lot like Ho Chi Minh. You came back to teach."

The comparison to Ho Chi Minh is a mighty big statement from a world leader who knew the power of coming back to teach many lessons learned. Mac appreciated the chance to do good in a land where he had previously seen only strife. He has always tried to embody Colin Powell's 13 Rules of Leadership.[4] In Powell's 2012 book, *It Worked for Me*, the Ranger-tabbed former chairman of the joint chiefs wrote that a true leader is a leader, whether in the military or in business. The key is to adapt in every situation.

In the past 50 years, COL Jim McCloskey has fielded a variety of obstacles that included Agent Orange, Parkinson's disease, and a brain tumor in 2018. But none of those have succeeded in grounding him so far. For the last 25 years and counting, he's hit the streets of Philly to play Santa for kids with cancer at St. Chris's Hospital every Christmas Eve.

Now in his 70s, Mac continues to adapt to every situation as General Powell suggests. An entire ecosystem of goodness depends on him to keep fighting.

---

[4] "13 Rules of Leadership by Colin Powell," Center for Executive Excellence, September 18, 2013, https://executiveexcellence.com/13-rules-leadership-colin-powell/.

Some remarkable leaders never get around to retiring; they seem to shift from active to emeritus status and keep on contributing as board members or doing other community service. And like the lucky grandchildren who get to spend quality time with their grandparents, those currently in the game are lucky to benefit from their experiences. Many of them still love to "come over to the house and teach us" how to succeed in life.

Protecting the "Flock"

Command Sergeant Major (CSM) Greg Patton

Note: Greg Patton is the father of Jimmy Patton, whom you met earlier in this book.

> *The corporate world needs shepherds to watch over the flocks as they navigate their companies to the top. It's like the army that way. Imagine the CEO who shows the same level of tenacity in arming his people with professional skills as he/she does in defending the organization from attack.*
>
> *A growing number of bright stars armed to protect their people like shepherds are out there, and they're rising like cream to the top.*

"Doc, hand me your pistol."

Staff Sergeant (SSG) Greg Patton was speaking to Doc Mooney, our 19-year-old platoon medic. Greg was my second-in-command, and we had just landed in Saudi Arabia on day one of Operation Desert Shield in August 1990. Doc was a great kid from Ohio—fit and eager. Unwaveringly, he complied with Greg, saying, "Sure thing, Sergeant Patton." In one motion, he unclipped his holster snap and handed over his 9mm Beretta to the humble Ranger.

However, we all felt uneasy about the command we had just been given—to load an entire platoon of 40 well-armed troops into a dilapidated double-decker bus for transport from the airfield to our staging grounds. We had arrived only moments before knowing that, in a couple of hours, President George H. W. Bush would announce on TV that the "82nd Airborne has landed." So Greg added to his order. "Doc, give me a couple of magazines, too." His outstretched right hand reached for the mags while his left stuffed the 9mm Beretta into his cargo pants pocket.

Still, we felt uneasy. We had landed ahead of our equipment and then needed to scrounge for transportation, hence hiring the beat-up old bus. There wasn't enough room inside the bus for both men and gear. So to avoid tearing the seats into even worse condition, we had to stack all of our weapons underneath the bus in the part where the doors open upward and luggage is loaded.

However, that plan didn't sit right with either the company commander or me. But we were compelled to follow the command, "*Let's get it done quickly, and let's get there.*"

We loaded up. But doing that still didn't sit well with SSG Patton. Unlike me, though, he thought fast on his feet. He took the initiative to at least arm himself with Doc's medic pistol and a couple of mags.

Five minutes into chaotic traffic and the noisy streets of Dhahran, every young paratrooper on the bus was entranced with the happenings outside. Greg, on the other hand, focused forward. He was looking beyond the front window as we ground to a halt behind a stopped vehicle. We saw military-aged men milling around in the middle of the street. They looked back at us, and a couple of them began walking back toward the bus.

Greg had already made sure he was sitting alone on his bus seat on the window side. Then he placed the pistol next to him inside his Kevlar helmet. He reached for one of the full 15-round clips and popped it in while still pointing the Beretta downward and into the helmet.

Bang! As Greg pulled back the slide to load the weapon, somehow the pistol's safety slid into fire mode. A bullet had discharged and lodged into the Kevlar with no harm done. However, it was something that mechanically should never happen. The discovery of a rare safety flaw in the Beretta wouldn't come to light until a few years later.

Greg looked up at-the-ready as the stopped bus slowly started to move. The crowd disbanded without any further incident, but the real fallout was about to come.

The role of mentor and protector in a leader's world may come with a layer of peril. It makes sense that protecting staff from danger could be personally dangerous. When it involves quick decisions and deviating from the way the crowd seems to be going, the caretaker may be the one who's most exposed from outside influences or improbable happenings while trying to shepherd the flock.

Standing Up for What You Believe

Command Sergeant Major (CSM) Greg Patton

When a defining moment hits, it feels like time has momentarily ground to a halt. That's when we have the chance to do either what's easy or what's right.

It's often a tough decision because either option has consequences. Maybe it's a choice between the ladder or the mirror—that is, the manager who wants to climb the ladder chooses what's easy, and the leader who desires to look in the mirror decides what's right.

In all the chaos, half of the troops on the bus hadn't even heard SSG Patton's shot go off. And the rest of the men wouldn't have cared anyway. They knew their platoon daddy (the respectful nickname for the platoon sergeant even though the platoon leader lieutenant is officially in charge) was trying to keep a watchful eye. But the army held a no-tolerance position on these things. In peacetime, they even had a damning name for it: *negligent discharge.* In wartime, of course, no one would give it a second thought. What was the rub? We were only in the first few hours of Operation Desert Shield, and no shots had been fired yet. So, which status would it be?

Brigade HQ quickly decided we were still under peacetime rules and that SSG Patton's discharge would be regarded as *negligent*, even with my exculpatory statement and a few platoon members recounting the situation. No matter: an example had to be made. His punishment was a reduction in rank to Sergeant E-5 (down one rank from Staff Sergeant E-6), an Article 15 reprimand, and reassignment to another unit.

Reassigning SSG Patton to another battalion meant my men and I would lose our platoon sergeant in the first few days of Operation Desert Shield. Worse for him personally was getting a reduction in rank. Greg was close to getting a promotion from an E-6 staff sergeant to an E-7 sergeant first class, but this reprimand meant he'd go back to an E-5 sergeant. This was like losing two ranks—basically a career death sentence.

Concurrent with the punishment, I had the task to write SSG Patton's efficiency report, which is standard when an NCO changes an assignment. However, it was suggested my report should reflect the circumstances of the incident, and I'd be expected to give him a low mark for *judgment*. I knew a report like that would be another career killer. If I didn't comply, well, I risked having my own career suffer too.

So, this was it—my first big leadership moment. As a young lieutenant, I'd be forced to choose between toeing the official line versus being loyal to my best soldier. I chose the side of SSG Patton—and it wasn't even close. Even though I was his superior officer, he had taught me a lot in the previous nine months of my command. By embodying the dynamic of harmony that exists between the young commanding officer and his senior enlisted advisor, he had earned my unequivocal loyalty. He had also earned 5's across the board along with meteorically stellar praise in the comments sections.

Those were among the facts I reported as I wondered how the review board would view the combination of a glowing efficiency report stapled to a reduction-in-rank order. I hoped they would notice the ironic dichotomy.

To my company commander's credit, he took full note of what I had written, signed it, and passed it up the chain of command. I even think he agreed and applauded the defiance since it had been borne from fidelity (but due to professional decorum, he wouldn't have been permitted to say so).

Thirty years later, I'd still like to ask him.

Honorable beliefs are personal; standing up for them makes a statement that endures longer than the issue on the table. A lasting reputation of integrity will follow a loyal leader who scrupulously supports his staff. Most likely, the corollary is true for the one who doesn't.

Rising from the Ashes

Command Sergeant Major (CSM) Greg Patton

How many champions can say they stared into the abyss and didn't let it stare back at them? Knowing what it took to win the first time around means they can figure out what it takes to get back on the podium again. What's left is the willpower to gear up again and Just Do It.

Greg Patton moved to another battalion to take over an E-5's typical job as a team leader, but the cream always rises to the top. Like the phoenix of ancient Greece that rose from the ashes to greatness, Greg wasn't about to stay down for long.

After the new chain of command saw his practical expertise to go with Ranger and Jumpmaster qualifications, they bumped him up to squad leader in their Scouts. Shortly after that, they advanced him to Scout platoon sergeant to fill a needed spot. About the same time, the army came back around to see if Greg's punishment was a little harsh, given we were headed from the build-up operation of Desert Shield straight into the full assault of Desert Storm.

The three punishments were on the table for review. On the militating side was the negligent discharge. This was quickly fading from relevance since we had been in the desert for four months with more important things to worry about. On the mitigating side, though, was Greg's clutch performance. He had stepped up to fill three new roles since arriving at the new battalion.

A tiebreaker was needed, and that's where karma came in. HQ reached for the latest efficiency report to see what kind of rating he had earned from his old boss in the nine months before the incident. Had I given in out of fear to issue a lukewarm review or maybe nail him in a crucial category, it might have been "game over" for Greg Patton. But when they opened that jacket, they saw honest praise for an inspired performance from the officer in charge. Then the fates knew him as I knew him, and as a result, the army reinstated Greg to full rank and tossed the Article 15 reprimand into the trash.

Watching the way a pro rebounds from a setback in the workplace tells you everything you need to know about the resolve he or she has. It's easy to make excuses; it's a lot harder to saddle back up. But remember, the cream always rises to the top, especially in light of unfaltering efforts and successful results.

Being Accountable

Command Sergeant Major (CSM) Greg Patton

Think about applying this simple test when management sets rules in place: Are the rules intended to apply to everyone in the organization uniformly, without regard to a lofty or lowly position? When the answer is yes, everyone in the venture can be held personally accountable and also accountable to the group.

CSM Greg Patton had this rule: Any soldier of any rank in his brigade who left his locker unlocked would have to stand in his office trash can for five minutes and promise to maintain better security in the future.

Greg had one of those small gray wastebaskets next to his desk. If you got caught with an open locker and your valuables loose, you had to suffer the full five minutes of ignominy. This was a lesson observed by the lower enlisted—that is, until a lieutenant ran out of his quarters on a mission but left his padlock undone. Greg came on his morning check and, like a good caretaker, locked the padlock for the lieutenant. Later, he reminded him of the unwritten penalty—standing in the trash can. This put Greg's tradition to the test. *Would a command sergeant major enforce this rule with an officer?*

To the credit of the young lieutenant who understood the rule's purpose, he didn't have to. The butter bar lieutenant presented himself at the brigade's HQ and stood in the silly two-foot-high can for five minutes. He also made sure it was no secret he was paying up to indicate that everybody in the organization had to be accountable. *After all, if any team member with privilege could break a rule, then it really wasn't much of a rule.*

Leaving the locker unsecured posed a security issue and set a bad example for the troops. Owning up to the gaff and allowing others to enjoy a laugh sent a shiny message that the self-effacing newbie officer was committed to maintaining the famous Rakkasan (the 187th Infantry Regiment of the 101st Airborne) Ranger standard. It was a win-win-win for unit, the sergeant major, and the new lieutenant.

Exceptions can dilute any gold standard because, in the back of people's minds, it doesn't apply uniformly. If a decree mandates action for us *but not* them*, it may do more to divide the group than to improve it. A well-placed junior leader who upholds equanimity among all creates magic for the organization.*

Connecting

Command Sergeant Major (CSM) Greg Patton

> *As a senior leader, demonstrating that you're not afraid to pick up a shovel and dig with the rest of the team paints a valuable picture for the rank and file. It sends a strong message to other midlevel leaders who work with you or for you. You want them to reflect your resolve for hands-on leadership when you can't always be there. It's too comfortable to sit in the ivory tower watching from above, and if senior leaders do it, then it seems to be okay for midlevel managers to emulate. Reinforcing a peer culture is a good choice.*

On Thanksgiving morning of 2009, Brigade Sergeant Major Patton gathered his personal security detail (PSD) of three men and loaded a chopper. From Rakkasan HQ in Afghanistan, they headed to one of their most remote Afghan forward operating bases (FOBs) to celebrate the holiday with the troops. Showing command presence as often as possible was the recipe to keep morale high. That wasn't an easy task, given there were more than a dozen locations accessible by helicopter only.

The four men arrived a few hours before chow time while dinner was still cooking. The FOB's first sergeant greeted the chopper as it kicked up an early dusting of winter snow, and then he briefed Greg on recent damage to the Rakkasan base taken from enemy artillery below. Looking around, Greg could see that some of the structures and fighting positions had been dinged up pretty good. A platoon of men filling sandbags caught his eye, and he walked over to them. The first sergeant echoed that he wished the men didn't have to spend their Thanksgiving morning shoring up defenses, *but the Taliban love to attack during holidays.*

With hours to go before the turkey dinner would be ready, Greg dropped his gear by the crew with a nod to the PSD to follow suit. All four of them picked up shovels and joined the boys filling and stacking bags. Surprised, the first sergeant asked if the CSM wouldn't prefer to go inside and inspect the other buildings along with the senior staff. If the other buildings weren't damaged, then the answer was no. This was where the CSM wanted to be, even as the senior non-commissioned officer in a 3,000-man brigade. Greg preferred getting to know the working men while talking about shooting deer and smoking turkeys back in Tennessee.

Someone snapped a photo that day of the sergeant major with the guys, and it made it onto a magazine cover along with the comment, "Best CSM in the army—right out there with us."

It's impossible not to notice the senior staff who circulate through the ranks and make themselves accessible. Executives with a presence in the field seem to have a better finger on the pulse. The rank and file have long memories of great leaders who roll up their sleeves to get the job done. As a result, they generate a good deal of loyalty.

Earlier in '05 during his Iraq deployment, Greg and his crew went in an armored cavalry Humvee to investigate a mini-truck that had been reported to be out after curfew and sitting at an intersection. In the vehicle sat an older Afghani adult and a boy looking apologetic as if the vehicle were having a problem, but it was dangerous to believe that as true. Equally as chancy was to have to dismount and then walk over and examine the situation. On the other hand, the pair's mini-truck might really have been stuck, plus they needed to clear the intersection it was blocking.

By the time Greg's vehicle arrived, another Hummer had pulled up a safe distance behind the Afghani mini-truck and was approaching it. To get control of the situation, Greg plugged in his hip radio comm set to stay in communication with his vehicle's driver, then jumped out of the Hummer and went over to the scene.

The other crew checked the vehicle to get it started and verify that the grandfather was genuinely stuck and not acting as bait on the road. As they did so, Greg noticed he couldn't see forward past the intersection or around the corner. The other soldiers checking the truck were staying back safely, and Greg needed a quick set of eyes down the road. He buzzed his hip radio back to the Hummer driver as he walked forward and asked the gunner up top to cover him as best he could. He expected the old man's vehicle to be moving in a minute, but he just needed to have a look ahead.

As Greg stepped beyond the intersection, his radio transmission with the Hummer cut out four or five times in rapid succession. Pings of dirt kicked up past him from a lone rifle hitting the road near his feet. Greg's gunner up top could see the sideways angle of the shots skipping across his field of vision, but he couldn't turn his gun in the direction of the gunfire because of buildings in the way.

Calm. A CSM has to be calm, especially with young troops on the ground following his lead and listening on the radio. It looked like it was opportunistic AK-47 rifle fire from a few hundred meters away rather than a sniper ambush.

The Afghani vehicle started and, judging by his nervousness, the driver wanted to get out of there as much as they needed him gone. As he drove away, the gunner watched in awe as Greg purposefully walked a straight line back to the Humvee like a marshal in the Old West. As they pulled away, the young gunner keyed the wireless radio with a gulp. "Sergeant Major, that was the bravest thing I ever saw." Greg was slightly embarrassed with the adulation and humbly downplayed it. "Hell noooo, son. If I woulda known he was shooting at me, I woulda *ran* back."

Leaders are being watched all the time, which they want and understandably crave. People will observe the actions they take with full attention to body language, and they'll also listen to the words spoken and the leader's tone of voice. The one who quickly and calmly dispatches a tense situation becomes the stuff of legends.

Improvising

Command Sergeant Major (CSM) Greg Patton

The old phrase says, "Necessity is the mother of invention." When good leaders set a climate that rewards innovative thinking to solve issues that no one dreamed would arise, heroes emerge from within and the unit advances. That's the group we want to belong to.

Put a bunch of smart guys together, and you will usually solve the problem at hand. When the sergeant major's problem turned out to be improvised explosive devices (IEDs) that would explode under the road surface to cripple vehicles and kill passengers, we needed a solution. Rebel forces had devilishly created these IEDs with C-4 explosives, which would detonate upward into the soft undercarriage of a vehicle upon sensing overhead heat.

Our smart guys turned out to be the soldiers closest to the problem. Many were mechanically inclined and farm-raised in the video game era. Because of that, they knew how to take what was available nearby and use it. For example, Greg saw them attach a 10-foot metal pole to a small ammo can and put inside it a glow plug, which had come from the Humvee's spare kitbag. Then the pipe was welded to the front grille of the vehicle, so it stuck out in front like a Rhino's horn. Wired back to the engine battery, the glow plug heated and could set off an IED's infrared sensor just below the road surface. The bomb would then explode ferociously yet harmlessly in front of the vehicle. In some cases, the proud inventors reported that their homemade Rhino was reusable. By 2005, the military had adopted this approach and produced the first of 20,000 Rhinos.

In the case of the Rhino, field units shared their goofy-looking invention through an informal TTP network—one that passed around *tactics, techniques, and procedures* that could save lives. The army picked up on it officially and commissioned a manufacturer to mass-produce the Rhino. The first version looked like an unorthodox model the boys welded together with the equipment they borrowed.

A great case of ingenuity often starts with an unofficial workaround in the field. When it works even a little bit, the word spreads. When it works well, the news can spread like wildfire across the informal network. Smart businesses are wise to monitor the shop floor innovations that spring up by the workers closest to the problems. When they see a workaround that is gaining fast adoption, it may be wise to make it an official change.

Being a Part of Something Big

Staff Sergeant (SSG) Doug Quitmeyer

Have you ever heard of people in a company wondering if the executive team knows what the departments are doing, or if the project assigned to them makes any difference at all? When the worker bees don't feel their piece of the puzzle connects to the finished product, it's tough to get max efficiency from the team and hard to achieve high morale.

As the winter of 2006 was setting into northeastern Afghanistan, Sergeant Doug Quitmeyer and his team from Bravo Company 1/75 Rangers were briefed on an upcoming operation of substantial importance to the war effort. Navy SEALs would be joining the Rangers on this mission, and Secretary of State Donald Rumsfeld would be briefed afterward.

As the chain of command contributed each of their pieces to the plan, Doug was impressed that his small seven-man squad was included in the specifics of such a high-level mission. He immediately embraced being part of something bigger than his usual sphere of influence. While seeing the complicated pieces of the mission laid out on the map, he observed how, when, and where his team would contribute. The trust shown to the operator level was transparent.

The Pakistani border where it meets eastern Afghanistan is a harsh place, a desolate maze of barren mountains in a lawless region of the Hindu Kush range of the Himalayas. Aside from the Khyber Pass, there are no passable roads for 300 miles. The high-altitude region across the border has historically been home to religious mullahs, ethnic maliks, drug lords, tribal Pashtuns, and Taliban/Al Qaeda (they were essentially the same group within this region).

In the early 2000s, they were all eking out an existence on both sides of an indistinguishable border. Even the Pakistani government refused to enter the area. It had marked the first 50 miles over the boundary as a region called the FATA (Federally Assigned Tribal Area). Taliban terrorists concealed in the mountains would routinely come down into lower regions of Afghanistan to attack U.S. forces and then retreat. The region was also the hiding spot for some of the Taliban's most wanted, including Bin Laden's current #2, Ayman al-Zawahiri.

Doug's seven-man Ranger squad linked up with a 24-man SEAL element. The 31 soldiers geared up for a seven-day recce (reconnaissance mission) to cross into Pakistan on foot and recon a suspected enemy camp. Reportedly, the well-known Bajaur region was a hiding spot for al-Zawahiri, and it was imperative to get actual eyes on this target. Eighteen months previous, there had been insufficient intel to confirm al-Zawahiri's presence in that same spot, so Rumsfeld scrubbed the mission. And earlier in the year, a drone attack missed al-Zawahiri in Bajaur but was sadly reported to have killed 82 civilians.

War is a terrible business made worse by terrorists content to hide among innocents and children. That's why Doug knew they needed actual eyes on the target this time.

Carrying a week's worth of supplies, the 31-man patrol set forth up and down the mountains, avoiding pillboxes (small cement structures armed with lookouts, suspected Taliban locations, and even the indigenous Pashtuns). They had to stay on target and avoid detection.

In the civilized world, spending a few hours out in the snow—like a day on the ski slopes at altitude—would tire most athletes and render them ravenously hungry. At this point in their trek, Doug's patrol had carried 45 pounds of gear each for six days straight with no break from the December frost. You can imagine they were weary to the point of extreme exhaustion, focused only on putting one foot in front of the other. In the tough moments akin to snow blindness, Doug had to visualize his buddies out there just ahead and behind, each knowing they were a vital cog to accomplish a big mission.

Day seven. Having crossed into Pakistan days before, the patrol was still tracking toward the target. Night was falling fast when Doug's headset crackled a message in his ear. "Stay frosty, boys; this is the final rise before the objective, so be ready for anything."

As if he had just pounded a 16-oz can of Monster cappuccino, Doug bolted wide awake from the inside. The patrol moved up slowly online to assume its positions as the troops approached a crest they could not quite see over yet. *Almost time.* Doug self-assessed all his bodily functions: muscles, *check*; fingers and toes, *check*; breathing, *check*; heart rate (surprisingly okay), *check*. Maybe everything was the way it should be because they had rehearsed all the pieces. Immediately, he felt ownership of whatever was coming next. *Deep breath.*

Just as this tense moment threatened to be overwhelming, Doug's squad leader broke the tension with dark humor. His voice buzzed over the headset, "Harry, we're really DOING it!" The phrase referred to the movie *Dumb and Dumber* when Jim Carrey's character expressed wild exuberance for the crazy stunt they were about to pull off while in a fast-moving vehicle.

The SEALs and Rangers dropped silently to their knees and high-crawled the last few yards until they crested the ridge. They could see the lights of the village below peeking through the darkness. The presence of the targeted "bad guys" was confirmed, and the patrol owned the element of surprise. Like the Civil War's Colonel Joshua Chamberlain at Little Round Top, this overwhelming force moving downhill with the element of surprise outmaneuvered and outfired the static opposing force. But better than at the Gettysburg assault, the home team had far more than bayonets. They had trapped the Al Qaeda operatives below in a hellacious gunfight that quickly lit up the night and just as quickly retreated. In minutes, the fighting ended—the enemy neutralized and buildings cleared.

On the other end of the radio, Chinook pilots announced they were bounding in low through hostile airspace, and they exfilled the patrol via helicopters out of the danger zone. Sitting on choppers 30 minutes later, the men in Doug's patrol caught their breath, exhilarated by how their raid had proceeded with deadly precision.

Doug felt tremendous relief that the Chinook choppers were whisking them home at 17,000 feet above those same Hindu Kush mountains that had taken them seven days to cross on foot. He knew the element of surprise had been necessary. And the SEAL commander could now brief SecDef with this intel: Specifically, the terrain from here to there was navigable and the sites were locatable. Zawahiri would have to either return there and risk capture, or hide even deeper, potentially damaging his charismatic image as a leader.

In business, the elation of completing a complex operation in which the executive has incorporated all the vital cogs into the mission planning is unmistakable. The successful team members become super loyal and ready for the next mission. Seeing their passion build for the overall team encourages the leaders to find another win.

Watching Your Six

Staff Sergeant (SSG) Doug Quitmeyer

It takes a lot of guts to act when you identify a need in the workplace that simply isn't being addressed. Midlevel thinkers might say, "I'm sure someone out there must be doing it," or "If it doesn't exist, it probably won't work anyway." Those types of thinkers would probably never consider creating what they can't seem to find.

On the flip side, the high-level thinkers arrive at a gap between what they currently need and what they have available to them. If the need is current and they can't move on without it, they may decide to stop what they're working on and create a solution—as Doug's team did.

In 2011, when SSG Doug Quitmeyer left the Rangers after eight years, he was ready to transition into corporate life, and he craved success in the business world. He had piled up a wealth of skills masked in military jargon that no one had fully translated into everyday corporate terminology. This could be a problem for recruiters and HR departments in the companies he'd be working in. He was venturing into this new frontier "watching his six"[5]—military lingo for backing up a buddy or, literally, "guarding your rear end."

---

[5] The phrase "watch your six" does indeed mean "watch your back." It refers to the 6 position on the face of a clock. If you were standing in the center of a clock face facing the 12 position, the 6 position would be immediately behind you. From Wikipedia: Using this analogy, 12 o'clock means ahead or above, 3 o'clock means to the right, 6 o'clock means behind or below, and 9 o'clock means to the left.

Available to Doug was a rudimentary matching tool, essentially a paper catalog with a column on the left and the right that didn't flex or receive input. The left column listed the military's time-honored MOS (military occupational specialty) such as field artilleryman; the right column listed the civilian job that best matched the MOS. When Doug located his specialty, 11B3V (Airborne Ranger)—a role replete with management, leadership, and analytic skills—the corresponding column on the right read . . . Smoke Jumper!

What happened next? Doug turned this revelation into a call to action to form his own company that maps military jobs and skills to civilian jobs and skills. He called it Your 6, Inc.

Doug had been well qualified as a job seeker. Not finding any job he wanted led him to think outside the box. From that experience, Doug built a software tool to connect employees with employers, and a bonus emerged. Having a speedy union of workers available to a needy workforce was serendipity for employers as well as prospective employees. Doug's tool not only provided visibility for the veteran but opened it to employers. It has the potential of saving time and countless embarrassing goofs when one side of the interview has misinterpreted the job scope and shows up either over- or underqualified.

Currently, Doug's business is building a predictive analytics model for the U.S. Air Force and a new algorithm to load military qualifications into a universal database for open jobs. It's also crafting APIs (functions that let apps talk to each other) for push/pulling the info to LinkedIn (the site that has arguably become the leading marketplace for jobs).

Life isn't linear, and neither is Doug's Ranger-inspired approach to attacking problems and offering solutions.

What Doug did represents a twist on creating something from nothing. As possibly the best defensive weapon available, it could save your company from disaster and, with little tweaks, morph into a new product that generates revenue.

CHAPTER FIVE

Energetically will I meet the enemies of my country. I shall defeat them on the field of battle for I am better trained and will fight with all my might. Surrender is not a Ranger word. I will never leave a fallen comrade to fall into the hands of the enemy and under no circumstances will I ever embarrass my country.

Being Extraordinarily Creative	MSG Dave "The Mexican" Cardenas
Evaluating ROI	MSG Dave "The Mexican" Cardenas
(Not) Doing It for Money	MSG Dave "The Mexican" Cardenas
Waxing Poetic	MSG Dave "The Mexican" Cardenas
Choosing ROI over Personal Risk	The Mindset of the Ranger
Competing for What You Want	The Mindset of the Ranger
Empowering Teams	The Mindset of the Ranger - SSG Noel Cantu
Creating Mystique for Your Brand	The Mindset of the Ranger
Upholding the Ranger Creed	The Mindset of the Ranger
Keeping Them Safe	The Mindset of the Ranger
Topping the Charts	CPL Todd Williams
Thinking Fast on Your Feet	CPL Todd Williams
Nipping Problems in the Bud	CPL Todd Williams
Recognizing Expertise	CPL Dave Lafaver
Accepting That Stuff Happens	CPL Dave Lafaver
Being Authentic	MSG Joe "Trapper" Brewer
Bringing Factions Together	MSG Joe "Trapper" Brewer
Staying True to the Cause	MSG Joe "Trapper" Brewer
Creating a Higher Purpose	MSG Joe "Trapper" Brewer

Being Extraordinarily Creative

Master Sergeant (MSG) Dave "The Mexican" Cardenas

A textbook can start students off with a classical foundation to any topic. Yet inevitable variations will spring up, which could break even the best algorithms. The student who processes the intent of the classics when a new challenge hits will have the chance to get creative and figure out a hybrid solution.

Master Sergeant Dave Cardenas has a gift for imagining alternate realities with whimsical detail and nuances. He loves fantasy, and he embraces it as a living way to learn. Growing up on the Dungeons and Dragons reality board game, his ability to create complex scenarios in his head has given him the competence to build creative training for teams preparing for the unexpected.

Dave, the dungeon master, realized as an A-Team medic that he and his colleagues might be called on to do things few before them had attempted. He also knew there was a lack of textbooks to guide them through fluid situations, and that motivated him to get creative.

So he began staging reality events in which participants form teams to hunt down fictitious individuals. He calls the "full-spectrum" military training exercise he built Centurion Combat. Live OPFOR (opposition forces who play the enemy) and role players operate in civilian areas in either kinetic (in battle) or nonkinetic scenarios. They are assigned personalities and agendas that inject into the play. It's next-level training on a low budget, and it's also interagency cooperation that makes Dave's creation unique.

He first got the idea at Robin Sage, the Green Beret course's field event in North Carolina, when given the orders to blow up a guarded bridge. Conventional doctrine teaches three checkmarks are required to accomplish such a task: *security, support, and then attack*. Students like Dave were shifting skills from Ranger heavy combat to Green Beret–type unconventional situations. In this training simulation, they knew they would have to adapt to available resources when the numbers didn't allow them to set up for the holy three. With two young women assigned as "indigenous allies" for the mission, and a pickup truck, the team agreed to have both ladies drive up to the guards at the entrance to the bridge, stop their vehicle, get out, and casually approach the sandbagged position. They complained to the sentries of assailants on the road behind them who had tried to hassle or possibly rape them. A momentary relaxation by the sentries was long enough for the women to pull out pistols and shoot them. That action allowed Dave's team, hiding off the road, to wire the bridge and blow it up.

The team learned that the "holy three" milestones of *security, support, and then attack* make perfect sense but only when the resources and equipment allow. To blindly stick to the script when another option would be better is like trying to force a square peg into a round hole.

Every team that failed that night had attempted in vain to approach the problem according to conventional principles, despite lacking the human resources to execute the first principle of security properly. Engaging the two females only as additional firepower (as an example) would have been a waste of their abilities.

Brute force may fail in a fluidly moving environment that requires the finesse that gives teams who improvise a gigantic edge. For any leader, the skill is to be able to quickly process the task with the resources available in real time.

Evaluating ROI

Master Sergeant (MSG) Dave "The Mexican" Cardenas

Textbook ROI (return on investment) formulas base their recommendations on current conditions. So whenever conditions change, it means the ROI formula needs updating.

Twenty-seven years of military and contracting experience has made MSG Dave Cardenas a believer in taking a critical look at ROI. The ROI question refers to the high cost of Special Ops being worth the incremental gain. Or can well-trained regular units handle the mission?

In modern warfare, the cost of missions in terms of human lives and green dollars can be viewed with a slightly different lens, given the shift of warfare from major battles down to small campaigns. Regular army units are well trained to operate in both cities and remote areas while seeking out small yet high-value target packages. In past conflicts that often featured epic *mano a mano* battles, powerful infantry units squared off with each other by the thousands. All the delicate operations were reserved for the Special Operations Forces (SOF).

The nature of 21st-century conflict affords the benefits of leading-edge tech to large line units. That has made it possible for the regular army and marine units to shoulder much of the burden that previously needed to be done by SOF. That further shifts the types the operations for the Rangers, new Marine

MarSOC, SF, SEALs, the new specialized DEVGRU within the SEALs, and CAG (formerly Delta) to only the most sensitive, dangerous, and isolated tasks. The cost of these missions is predictably high, so the decision to offload whichever can be handled by the well-qualified line units makes sense.

For any business model that offers tiers of service, ROI consideration should be given to accomplishing the tasks with the appropriate (lowest) tier that ensures success. At the same time, it reserves the most premium (and most expensive) tiers for the hardest cases.

(Not) Doing It for Money

Master Sergeant (MSG) Dave "The Mexican" Cardenas

Incentives can come from many sources. Some may feel an inner call while others enjoy pursuing financial results. Both have a traditional role in motivating us to act, but the one that generates from deep inside is less likely to run dry.

What really drives ingenious warrior poets like Master Sergeant Dave Cardenas? It's certainly not the money since there's not much to be made in the life they've chosen. But for zealots like Dave, half of the motivation is the ability to be a contributor. And the other half is the ability to create a place where others can find satisfaction.

The environments where he has felt most professionally fulfilled have been where leaders laid the groundwork for him to establish his worth. He differentiates the value of a good leader trying to make people happy in the short term versus a great one who creates a venue for everyone to establish lasting self-worth.

In our early days together in the Scouts, for Dave, every day seemed like an adventure. He synthesized our leadership recipe: His NCO was teaching him how to be a *soldier*, and his officer was teaching him how to be a *professional*. That became his blend too, when his time came to lead and co-lead troops. His best assignments jelled when he had the latitude to get the job done, and when he, as the NCO, got to work beside energetic officers to create the ideal blend. He knew doing this would bond the teams.

"It sounds sensible," said his favorite SF battalion commander. "Now, team leaders and company commanders, go make it happen!"

Financial incentive in business is a powerful initial motivator. When deep personal commitment is added, the results are long lasting.

Waxing Poetic

Master Sergeant (MSG) Dave "The Mexican" Cardenas

The "warrior poet" is a term for the highest echelon that a medieval Scotsman in Braveheart times could achieve. It was the ultimate blend of a man who was both heroic in battle and learned in the classroom. The Urban Dictionary describes a warrior poet as a quintessential badass who has an equal love for others and the sword.

Relentlessly long work weeks and ruthless sales campaigns can wear down corporate combatants, too. To function for the long haul, they may need to manage the stress with the help of other colleagues experiencing the same stimuli.

Like other thoughtful leaders, MSG Dave Cardenas reads, learns, and then passes on what he has absorbed. His author list for fellow unconventional warriors like him features British S.A.S. Officer David Stirling, Hungarian-born U.S. tactician George Friedman, and West Point psychologist Dave Grossman. They provide a discerning need for both history and psychology lovers.

In particular, Lt. Colonel Dave Grossman is the originator of killology, which focuses on the reactions of healthy people thrust into killing situations.[6] For military operators experiencing

[6] Killology is the study of the psychological and physiological effects of killing and combat on the human psyche, and the factors that enable and restrain a combatant's killing of others in these situations. The term and field of study was invented by Lt. Col. Dave Grossman (US Army, Ret.) of the Killology Research Group and described in his 1996 book *On Killing: The Psychological Cost of Learning to Kill in War and Society* (Open Road Media).

circumstances that necessitate killing, several factors both enable and restrain the operator in life-threatening conditions. Equally important to the elite leader whose men are continually exposed to enemy contact is understanding their role as a vital cog in a machine. Beyond that, it's their ability to process it afterward without being overcome by guilt.

For Dave Cardenas, finding a way to make sense of on-demand brutality is the only way for soldiers to stave off PTSD and the hard physiological effects of taking lives. Embracing the coping mechanisms highlighted in Grossman's teaching helped Dave lead his troops during missions throughout the Iraqi Freedom and Enduring Freedom initiatives.

Imagine a moonless night in 2009 Afghanistan in pursuit of attackers who have just snuck up, opened fire on a small Marine Spec Ops outpost, and seriously wounded one of the MarSOC sentries. Sleeping with one eye open, everyone jumps up and bounds toward the hit-and-run attackers. They hit the center of the pack with grenades and rifle shots to take down nearly all of them.

Afterward, as they reach the scene to assess the damage, they see four are dead, but one Afghan who has lost both legs lies on the ground, still alive. The secrecy of the MarSOC mission depends on not being detected. Their outpost has no provision to care for prisoners, and this Afghani soldier is sure to die from his wounds within the hour.

Still, the necessary act of drawing down at close range on another human is a heavy weight. Delivering a kill shot to a mortally wounded enemy gazing blankly toward the night sky is a Herculean task—even for healthy-minded individuals. In this moment, war becomes a hell that may last long beyond the night's firefight. The smart leaders address this hell. They lovingly dialogue among their brothers and sisters about it.

Coping mechanisms such as using dark humor, snapping victory photos, and immersing themselves into video games during prolonged tours of duty may be essential even if these practices aren't widely understood or appreciated by the public. Spending time to have therapeutic discussions with trusted friends is an important salve for the soldiers as they insert themselves back into civilian life.

Disclaimer: the topic of death is one that defies any spot-on comparison to business because there is nothing in the corporate world that approximates the taking of human life. It stands alone as the single heaviest weight on the human spirit, and healing from it deserves society's most respectful approach. We need to do a better job.

What the civilian world can apply from it are any common coping mechanisms for folks who relentlessly give commendable efforts in their own arenas. Of course, no business crises can compare to the horrors of combat, but the military wants to help, and, by being a resource, speed the needed healing.

Business warriors in the big cities need their own version of coping mechanisms to stay alert for the next fight. (Disclaimer: life and death are not on the line in business, but lessons forged in fire correlate at lower amplitude for corporate life, so pay attention.) Example, my friend Tom DeLorenzo is the best New York sales guy I've ever worked with. A few years ago, he worked a nine-month sales campaign to net his young company its first-ever multimillion-dollar win.

At first, he accepted the spotlight graciously with the intent to pass along takeaways that might help the younger folks in the audience. Then he reflected more deeply on family sacrifices and missed kids' events his job required during the campaign. He realized nine months of family life had disappeared. And he empathized with the warriors in the crowd who felt as though their jobs were never finished, their efforts never good enough. But like him, they never doubted they'd win the next one for their home crew. The camaraderie of their teammates kept driving them to saddle up.

For many, reaching a horizon that's way out in the distance is possible only by focusing on the next hill in the team's path. That's what makes warrior poets a success for their companies.

Choosing ROI over Personal Risk

The Mindset of the Ranger

Another angle of the ROI discussion is defining who will benefit. Solving for individual ROI will calculate differently than solving for group ROI. If an individual's contribution results in an equal benefit for that person but also a big multiplier for the group, then it should be an easy decision. It also speaks volumes about that person's dedication.

On August 2nd, 1990, the world watched Iraqi's Republican guards roll tanks into its tiny next-door neighbor—peaceful, oil-rich Kuwait. Six days later, on August 8, President George H. W. Bush announced on TV that the 82nd Airborne Division had landed on the ground. The 2nd Brigade of the 82nd (officially called the 325th Airborne Infantry Regiment) had indeed landed in Saudi Arabia near the Kuwait border, and I was part of it. We were ready to repel those same tanks from rolling down the six-lane highway out of Kuwait into our friendly ally, Saudi Arabia.

For the first several days, everyone's body-mechanic was on high alert in the August heat. We had planted ourselves high along the sides of the highway on the Saudi side, ready to fend off the invaders. It was reminiscent of the Kasserine Pass in World War II when Allied forces had positioned themselves to repel Rommel's Afrika Corps tanks.

What the world didn't know is that we had arrived early in order to rush out and defend the critical entrance of the country. We were dug in with only the light weapons and ammo we had carried on our backs from Fort Bragg. Our tanks would take at least five to 10 more days to arrive. Our heaviest weapons were the Dragon wire-guided missile and the M60 machine gun. As the platoon leader of 40 men, I only had two of each. The Dragon was our only real weapon to take down a tank; those with rifles and grenades could do little more than annoy an Iraqi tank rolling through the pass. The M60 machine guns could fire useful 7.62 mm rounds against enemy personnel and light vehicles, but they did nothing against heavy armor. So we put them out on my edges to interlock fire—by the book.

In this situation, M60 machine guns would serve to cover my two Dragon missiles when we were prepared to fire. I kept one of the Dragon teams with me on the left third of our line closest to the direction the tanks would be coming from. The other, located by my platoon sergeant on the right side, could get off a second shot at a second target. With only two missiles per platoon and the potential of 50 tanks coming through, target acquisition certainly wouldn't be a problem!

My challenge as a leader? Scoring a hit with the one weapon we owned. PFCs Jacob Guillen and Patrick Lara were on my top Dragon team, and I set them close enough to touch on my immediate left, and aiming left. Both gritty 19-year-old Mexican Americans, they had jelled as a Dragon team in training back at Fort Bragg. They understood the need to act like one body with four arms and four legs during the seven crucial seconds needed to fire the clunky wire-guided missile. (Since the '90s, thankfully, the Dragon has been replaced with better technology.)

In 1380, the Ming Dynasty had first invented the wasp nest, which could launch fire arrows. In modern-day warfare, the idea of a similar projectile blasting out of a handheld tube and capable of destroying a tank had first been employed mid-WWII in 1943. It was called the bazooka. Then came the super-portable LAW rocket and then slightly rangier AT-4.

However, the Dragon's advantage was its ability to guide the missile into the target manually after firing. That made it both a blessing and a curse. Almost comically, a spool of wire trailing behind the flaming projectile required the gunner to keep the crosshairs trained on the mark the entire time until it hit pay dirt. In combat, that's much easier said than done.

Enemy soldiers had learned what to do when they saw a Dragon's smoky signature and its missile heading toward them. They stopped and trained all their fire right on whoever was at the end of that spool of wire. That left the gunner completely exposed. He knew the enemy would be unleashing its fire on him. Hence, it was dangerous to be a member of the Dragon team, and by extension, to be situated anywhere near them, so they often got set out on the wing.

But here on the side of this hill in Saudi Arabia overlooking the highway, we needed to ensure that everyone in the unit shared the same goal—*to protect our best chance to get two good shots at the enemy.*

The ROI calculation presented a simple answer. The leader's safety meant nothing if the mission were to fail. The same went for the resources on both flanks of the Dragon team. At whatever risk, the number-one mission was protecting the missile crew as the round headed off downrange—even if it meant placing the "wasp nest" next to them.

Adding complexity to the decision was that, in 1991, PFCs Guillen and Lara did not speak perfect English. Primarily Spanish had been spoken in the Guillen household back in San Antonio, Texas. Assistant gunner PFC Lara had left Arizona at age 18 and went straight to Basic and then Airborne training. A shy teen, he rarely said anything to senior NCOs and officers.

We solved the language problem by keeping these privates together as a team and near me. Given favorable proximity between the platoon leader and Dragon team, we could use hand signals to determine the target selection. A tap on the helmet, for instance, could be the "go" signal to fire with easy synchronization and less chance of error. With the cards we had been dealt, we could pivot the obstacle into a benefit.

The Republican Guards might do their worst, but we would hang on until the U.S. tanks arrived, and of course, we'd welcome any help from above. And we got it.

President Bush had instantly become the world's greatest poker player the moment he boldly announced to the world the 82nd Airborne had landed. Saddam Hussein decided he dared not take the bluff. That's when he changed any plans he might have had to continue the Iraqi blitz into Saudi Arabia. We held on in the 118-degree heat for four days until the Sheridans of the 3/73rd arrived and held the line that kept any early Iraqi incursion into Saudi Arabia from happening. The rush of adrenaline we got from President Bush's shout-out of support helped too.

That early bluff set the stage for eventual battlefield lines that were favorable to coalition forces while limiting the battle geography to Iraq and Kuwait.

Over time, skinny PFC Lara grew into his six-foot frame by hitting the weights. He was becoming a mountain of a fine soldier and earned the nickname Chino. After a couple of tours, he settled back in Arizona to raise a family. PFC Guillen stayed in the army and had a solid career as a staff sergeant, mentoring the next batch of young soldiers from his lessons learned in the desert. Both speak perfect English today.

Three decades later, Jacob and Chino are still pals. They met up in 2019 to drive to Oklahoma for our Desert Storm reunion where we were overcome with an unmistakable wave of nostalgic pride. While there, I finally told them the story that a general had stopped by the Dragon practice range only two weeks after they were both assigned to the 82nd. At that time, the boys simply hadn't had any training yet and, ouch, they missed a target in full view of this new general (who was the assistant division commander) and his entourage. Without any facts except what he'd seen in the first two minutes, the general said to me in front of my company commander, "Lieutenant, get yourself a new Dragon team—one that can hit the target next time."

Harsh. But I knew those boys had the right stuff to get the job done, and I stuck with them. Once they were armed with six months of training, they became my top Dragon team.

And here's my own lesson learned from the general. I grasped afterward that his words were a kickstart for *me* to kickstart *them*. That's the way the army works. Twenty-five years later, around the campfire, I finally got to share the story of a general and pair of privates who taught me about nurturing return on investment.

The coaching art requires deciding which teammates to hold on to (not replace) when you know they have the grit to succeed. In a split second, opting to stick with talented technicians and shepherding their advancement is what builds a team.

If you're a junior leader who's outranked, it's wise to quickly weigh the merits to get ready to make tough decisions.

Competing for What You Want

The Mindset of the Ranger

It's tough to get the dream assignment you want, whether you're in military or civilian life. Putting yourself in the vicinity where good things happen is the best place to be. If commanding Rangers in combat or becoming a CEO at 35 is your goal, there's sure to be a powerfully demanding and rewarding path to get there. That path is purposely narrow and reserved for the best of the best to inspire confidence in a world that deserves heroes.

If you're a young cadet in the Academy or ROTC who wants to lead Rangers, army leaders first want to see how you perform under pressure during your four college years. That way, they can evaluate your GPA (grade point average), military curriculum, and physical fitness. There are 17 branch specialties you could potentially be assigned to, so the first hurdle upon college graduation is to hopefully secure the infantry branch specialty when you commission as a 2nd lieutenant. It's also possible to secure a slot for Ranger School in one of the other combat arms specialties, but the preponderance of few available slots are reserved for infantry. So your best chance is to shoot for infantry.

A new lieutenant (abbreviated to 2LT) then attends Basic Officer Leaders Course and competes for a slot to attend Ranger School. Elite commands in the army—the 82nd, 173rd, 101st, 10th Mountain, and of course the Ranger Regiment—require/

urge all of their commanders to be Ranger qualified. This is the second big hurdle. Ranger School is lauded and vilified in the same sentences as the worst gut-wrenching, body-depleting two-month hell the military could ever devise. It's all true. If you survive, you get to keep playing the game, or else it ends there.

The 2LTs who vanquish those 61 straight 19.6-hour days of Ranger School will have distinguished themselves as choice prospects to take command of an infantry platoon. For the young leader aiming to command Rangers, the third hurdle is winning an assignment specifically to the Ranger Battalion or the 82nd Airborne.

As a single young officer in the summer of 1989, my army responsibilities filled 100 percent of the square footage in my brain. I had a singleness of purpose to "beat" Ranger School at any physical cost. I was lucky enough to nail Honor Grad along with my Ranger buddy Russ who was the class's Distinguished Honor Grad. We had made a good buddy team because he was a 32-year-old Green Beret who couldn't live without knowing he could also earn his Ranger tab. After our final patrol in some desolate region of Fort Benning, we both got our dream picks. He went on command of a Special Forces A-Team, while I got the 82nd Airborne. It has been grandly nicknamed as the "All-American Division" and "liberators of France" after they parachuted into Normandy on D-Day. As a child, I had read all about them.

Arriving at 1st Battalion of the 325th Airborne Infantry Regiment in the 82nd Airborne Division, I was assigned my 40-man platoon in Charlie Company. Eight of them were Rangers, and the other 32 reporting to them were hard-charging

Airborne infantryman. I scored a dedicated company commander to *report to* plus an experienced platoon sergeant as my second-in-command to *learn from.*

This turned out to be a priceless proving ground to hone my governance skills and learn about lives and families apart from work as well. We fused the goals of work-life balance together to resonate in moments of combat and, afterward, in the business world. And of course, we all learned to fight.

Typically, out of the 27 lieutenants in the infantry battalion, half of them wore the rank of 2LT and the other half 1LT's. 2LTs get promoted to 1LT after 18 to 24 months of doing a bang-up job. They don't salute each other, and their roles are a natural progression in combining junior command and staff duty. Each new 2LT's dream is naturally to take over a platoon and command his or her first unit. Being in command of troops is the cornerstone to moving up through the ranks in the military.

When you think of all the great generals in history, you remember them because they led troops in combat. Hannibal was atop an elephant leading his Carthaginians against the Romans in 219 BCE. Washington rejuvenated the Revolutionary forces at Valley Forge in 1777, and Patton personally directed 3rd Army tanks rolling toward Berlin in WWII in 1945. The thrill of command is a life changer and precisely the reason warriors want to serve.

Just two months into Operation Desert Shield, our battalion's Scout platoon leader got promoted to captain. To fill the position that every lieutenant wanted, our battalion commander agreed to conduct a team competition called Project 300, which tested each 40-man platoon, mortars included, to negotiate a 300-meter

Logically, a Red Falcon platoon leader who commanded well would then aspire to a second command—the all-Ranger Scout platoon. For perspective, the 82nd Airborne Division of 10,000 troops has just nine of them. There are three brigades of 3,000 each; each brigade has three battalions of 1,000 each; and each battalion (like the Red Falcons) has one specialty Scout platoon comprised of its 30 best soldiers. They're handpicked from the line companies to conduct advanced recon missions for the battalion commander. They are out alone and self-reliant. This winds up being a rare second command for a lieutenant and a chance to be with the apex of warfighters.

Some new 2LTs are also assigned to indispensable staff positions and don't ever get a shot to lead troops because there are only 15 or so platoons to command in an infantry battalion. The lucky ones definitely savor the experience.

Then comes promotion to 1LT and certain staff time, save for those couple 1LTs in the battalion who have been chosen for a specialty second command. One example is the Mortar platoon, which provides mobile artillery for the unit from four 81mm mortar teams. They give the battalion's lieutenant colonel the ability to rain down high-angle fire in front of the troops and break up enemy attacks. I'm proud to say that as of the writing of this book, my nephew Christian serves as the Mortar platoon leader for the Red Falcons, my very same unit 29 years later!

Then there is the Scout platoon, also called the Recon platoon . . . or simply "Recon." It's comprised of the battalion's rock stars operating forward of friendly lines to gather intel and conduct stealth missions. The Red Falcon's requirement for the unit was 100 percent Ranger qualified (or in the process of getting to Ranger School).

live-fire course. Real bullets! The lieutenant from the winning platoon would win the coveted Scout role.

One of the best things about the army is that performance reigns as king—it's show up or shut up. In this situation, we were given two days to practice. The colonel wasn't playing any favorites; he set the table that the highest score would be the winner, and that's how he'd choose the next Scout platoon leader.

Competitors love winning. They also want to surround themselves with other winners. That means the executive team will likely gravitate toward competitors when it's time for promotion. Better yet, they may organize a competition for individuals to go through and find a winner outright.

Empowering Teams

The Mindset of the Ranger - Staff Sergeant (SSG)

Noel Cantu

It's lucky when young leaders enjoy the opportunity to know the game and its rules from the outset. When that happens, clarity appears, and from that point, the degree of energy devoted is the only limitation.

Part of the effort is the willingness to empower team members who are crucial to the work product. Simple math tells us that many people who are in smooth control of their domains can beat just one person in control of the entire domain.

The rules of the game were clear: the execution of marksmanship, fitness, and communication (hand and radio signals) would win the competition, and they were all things we could practice. Units in the battalion were of course already good at these three core tasks. So, I presented the psychology to the platoon that, with a vigorous out-of-body effort over the next three days, we'd win over both the lesser skilled opponents *and* the equally skilled opponents who took it lightly.

We started with a vision, which was winning the Project 300 competition. We all wanted to win, and I assured them we would be holding the trophy a couple days hence. It would be our three squad leaders who would personally guide us to victory. I knew that empowering the squad leaders was key, and

I gave them the freedom to rehearse the maneuver freely with their 12 men on day one. With good first-line leaders, I could trust them to convey the tasks *en pointe.*

To let the troops know I was in the vicinity and supportively engaged but not hovering, I walked around at a respectful distance. It was fascinating to see different styles, each having a good effect. SGT Feltovic had his squad running at half speed through the maneuvers while making corrections in real time. *Nicely done.* SGT Cook had made a sand table with each team member pointing to and verbalizing his role so everyone would know and understand it. *Outstanding.* SSG Cantu had found some shade in the 105-degree heat and read slowly from the Project 300 manual to his tightly gathered team. He frequently stopped to dialogue, ensuring they all understood how they would be graded so they could maximize the points and not waste any motion. *Unbelievable.*

Real grassroots leadership had blossomed from having empowered three different leaders with three styles of instruction, each of which resonated with the dynamics of their team. I felt a cool breeze of confidence. And I believed we could ensure victory with one key linchpin move.

When it was time to gather the platoon, I praised the approach that each team had taken and the advantage we could gain as a whole by synthesizing all three. Being better to ask for buy-in than tell them, I invited the squads to share their methods followed by a live run-through. They emphatically agreed and shared, and as much to prove it to themselves as to the company leaders, they nailed the run-throughs. We added the live ammunition and the mortars component on day two and won the competition on day three.

The overwhelming feeling of pride you feel for your kids or your team after winning the "big one" is thrilling. I hope everyone gets to experience that feeling generously throughout life. Funny enough, our victory was bittersweet. Winning the Project 300 competition catapulted me right out of my assignment and into my next one. I remember leaving that first posting feeling like I was a better man than when I arrived.

Years later, I reconnected with SSG Noel Cantu. During his career, he had served the military and then Border Patrol for three decades total. I told him how much I had learned from him and how he had embodied the image of the quiet professional. I flashed back to the chemical alarm that went off in the desert when I saw Noel handing his mask over to a frightened young troop whose straps were broken. His actions always projected, "I'll go first."

At first, we might be inclined naturally toward the rousing leadership style of immediate action. Then slowly, with eyes wide open, we come to respect the studied approach.

Whichever style you choose as a business leader, comingling the varied styles from your vantage point allows you to see the benefits of collaboration and empowerment.

Creating Mystique for Your Brand

The Mindset of the Ranger

Most great teams I know have a blend of attributes that creates a mystical aura of winning. The experts may argue the exact recipe, but one mandatory ingredient is the presence of something unique that they do differently than everyone else. That "unique" thing is the X-factor they should leverage to create a mystique for their brand.

Three months into Desert Shield, the waiting game and potential for complacency inevitably took over at Camp Red. Our highly trained Scout platoon was being tasked by the sergeant major for mundane assignments: KP, guard duty, and my favorite: changing out 10-gallon drums of human waste from wooden latrines, then lighting the contents on fire with kerosene. Those were, of course, a necessary contribution to a 1,000-man battalion living in tents. But they were a dangerous no-go for forward operators who, at a moment's notice, need to be frosty and head out of the wire (aka leave the safety of camp for a mission).

I was seeing my Ranger's sharp edge, fitness, and killer instinct settling to a low simmer in that environment.

My platoon sergeant and I needed to spark some ingenuity on the way to pulling the boys away from the numbing routine and beefing up our mojo. So we devised a new schedule we called *reverse training*. It featured training at night and conducting our activities outside the confines of the camp that had gotten way too cozy.

Nomenclature reigns king in the military and in business. So rather than ask the battalion commander, "Hey, sir, could we sleep during the day and train at night to avoid crappy work details?" we crafted clever nomenclature. The tactical need to develop our "*night vision acclimatization, limited-view land navigation,* and *circadian rhythm adjustment*" is what we sought to address. We then supported the ask with an itinerary. Our goal? To stay as frosty as General Schwarzkopf expected of 82nd Recon. And the colonel and sergeant major signed off on it.

In a nutshell, we gathered at dusk to train and then slept in the daylight hours while the others were pulling maintenance,

> Word quickly spread through the camp that the Scouts were doing specialized training to keep a hard edge on their skills. The reaction was positive. The prestige of going beyond the rest of the herd resonated internally and made them once again feel invincible.
>
> It's wise to be an innovator but not a total radical. We didn't disdain ordinary training entirely because any innovative plan encounters detractors. Even with the big boss's signoff, some old-timers wouldn't like the fast pace. In business, we could call them slow adopters, so it is wise to address a portion of the methodology conventionally; say, 20 percent doesn't seem entirely outrageous. Better for the group to be regarded as innovators than radicals. For that reason, we maintained two days out of every seven for daylight functions.

eating chow, and doing "keeping busy" chores. Staying occupied, of course, is a well-respected mantra to apply for the mainstream soldier, but mindless motion without constant training can get a point man shot in the first 30 seconds of contact.

About a week after starting, the battalion commander said he wanted to begin rotating good noncombat soldiers through our Recon training. Could a handful of soldiers from the HQ join us for whatever taxing event was on the schedule the following day? Naturally, this was a real compliment to my platoon sergeant and me, so we enthusiastically agreed. In fairness, even had it been an awful idea, we would have still enthusiastically agreed, which is the smart thing to do when the "old man" asks.

We planned to exit Camp Red through the gate in full gear, rucksacks plus weapons, and proceed five clicks out until we found a flat patch of sand. We then planned to drop our packs into the shape of a football field, whereby Corporal Giannakakos (G-Man) was in charge of producing a fully inflated football and kicking tee. After that, we intended to spend the next several hours kicking the snot out of each other in a game of tackle football.

So, the next morning, four reasonably fit and willing soldiers from the motor pool joined us for training. They were probably nervous about what strenuous test of mettle awaited. Word was out that the Scouts were keeping uber fit and conducting their own PT tests plus all manner of vigorous training outside the compound. Their sergeant gave instructions for them to make the motor pool proud. They complied by following suit with the equipment list for the day: full pack (45 pounds), Kevlar helmet (four pounds), weapon (seven pounds), and 64 ounces of water (four pounds). Report time at the Recon tent was 0815 for an equipment check before 0900 departure through the wire. Get 'er dun.

We decided not to change a thing for the motor pool mechanics, and we marched toward our highly anticipated football game in the sand. In the morning, they had arrived with forlorn "before" looks on their faces, fearing the worst. All they knew was they had traded in their wrenches for rucks and a day of training in 102-degree heat.

The "after" looks of amazement that flooded into their faces were comical when they realized that, at the end of the five-kilometer march, we were setting up a gridiron. We pulled out the new leather football (from wherever it had come in the States) and broke into exaggerated football stretches. Then we divided the troops evenly and dialed them into our day of fun.

Now, if critics think that choosing to give your team an exuberant escape is a waste of time, I'd ask them to think again. Rewarding those who work hard pays off. I'm a fan of the phrase, "We work hard and play hard." To innovators at the edge, it's a key to producing high-performing teams.

I've pushed the limits over the years because, as Colonel Hackworth said back in Vietnam, "Cracking a few eggs is the only way to make a great omelet." I believe this rings true for surveillance ops in Iraq or sales calls in Manhattan.

When you tumble 30 Rangers at each other in bare feet and factor in 100-degree weather, energized with wild amounts of pent-up energy, we didn't need to fear we'd lose a day of physical training. More fittingly, I worried about injuries. After a few hours, every man had taken a small beating: scratches, welts, nasty sand abrasions, and a few sprains and bruises, but only one broken foot bone. (Actually, it was a toe on Spoony's foot, and Doc taped it to his two other toes, so we were set. We wouldn't have to report any injuries back at camp.)

On the gridiron, Sergeant Akers took a shellacking from the opposing players like I had never seen. As a kid in Cleveland, he had boxed and played organized football, so he came up smiling every time. Quarterbacking on one play behind center, he dropped back and got off the pass, but two rushers kept coming. One was a barrel-chested Native American named Gergen from Oklahoma, and the other was my trusty radioman, Onion, from Louisiana. They weren't slowing down. Just before impact, everyone heard a crazy Cajun yell out of Roberts with the flash of wickedness. They had buried him in the deep sand so completely that, for a moment, he disappeared underneath it.

SSG Akers sported a freshly shaved baldy, so his head resembled a cue ball. His bald head had been sweating heavily enough over his face that when he emerged from the sand, his body above the neck looked like an ice cream cone dipped in sprinkles. Then he opened his eyes, and for a second, two white eyes popping out from a sand-covered head looked even more alien. I held my breath to see his reaction. Slowly, he unfurled a broad smile and held it for all to see. The entire platoon broke up into unrestrained laughs. I'm betting he knew everyone was watching his "bring it on, fellas, I can laugh at myself" reaction.

When we finished the last of the drinking water we had packed, the men tidied themselves up as best they could, tucking in uniforms, and sliding torn-up feet into sandy desert boots for the 5K walk back to camp. Nearing the guard shack, some of the guys realized how beat-up they might be looking. What would the reaction be? They all had friends in the line companies who liked to stir the pot.

The guards at Camp Red gate eyeballed the double file of men, bruised and cut, as they walked through. Word was going to spread through the battalion again that LT Sacchetti and SFC Cummins were mercilessly drilling the Scouts. The vaunted reputation of the Scout platoon probably notched up a few pegs higher—a win-win.

Work hard and play hard. Every young leader should be lucky enough to have a #2 in command who is grizzled from experience yet shares forward-thinking concepts that benefit warriors on the ground. Embracing plans made jointly, feeling respected as co-leaders, and equipping workers to be psychologically prepared will create a winning mystique for your brand.

Young leaders in the process of crafting their management style might like to know that, much like army Ranger training, the high-performance environment on a sales team can be brutally challenging yet logical and supported with care.

If you'd spoken with SSG Akers back in the '90s or seen the 2013 movie *Lone Survivor* with Marcus Luttrell 20 years later, you'd hear the phrase, "My heart is full [of love]." Caring for your military buddies' welfare reaches the level of love, and in those extreme conditions, support is real and unconditional.

No one doubts that love works there *and* is appropriate on the battlefield. Back at home, if the care is genuine, it works the same for business teams. It may not reach the level of love, but by knowing the degrees of stress generated in combat that's causing it, let's hope it doesn't need to.

The thread of continuity is the word "care" for your teammates. Care can't be faked. The real business leader truly wants to nurture the people on his or her team, and the winning coach enjoys getting to know the families and interests of the players. In this case, the phrase "fake it till you make it" doesn't apply. High-performing teams can sniff out a phony boss a mile away. Likewise, they can spot a diamond from the same distance.

Upholding the Ranger Creed

The Mindset of the Ranger

> *Developing a mission statement at work has the purpose of uniting the diverse groups that make up the company. Geographies and functions may still vary within a complex organization, but one singular set of goals can guide everyone. The leader's challenge is to harness the spirit of camaraderie that exists in teams (it can still be as high in the corporate world as in the military) and light the spark in everyone that brings them together.*
>
> *Breathing life into the mission statement, through action that includes everyone, makes it viable.*

The Ranger mentality of honoring the directive to *never leave a brother behind* led to the guidance given by many Ranger leaders to outlaw (or strongly recommend against) their soldiers watching the TV show *Survivor*. Its message embodied the polar opposite of Ranger team spirit and nearly everything holy about overcoming challenges shoulder to shoulder.

"Outlawing" something is a strong concept. Of course, soldiers have the freedom to watch what they please. Still, certain aspects of leadership exist more so in the military world than the civilian world, and pervasive authority enjoyed by immediate supervisors is one of them. I have found it fascinating that good first-line bosses (in this case, squad leaders) independently arrive at the same advice absent any official position by their commanders. They quickly assess the situation, identify the ideological conflict, and then take corrective action.

For example, when *Survivor* first aired in 2000, the name of this TV show generated excitement in the Special Ops community. It was seen as an outdoor challenge for a large group to conquer hostile terrain—the kind of reality show they could have sunk their teeth into.

As it turned out, though, the show's premise was anything but teamwork for the good of the group. It prized an individual winner who had the ability to outfox teammates through clandestine alliances. "Argh," reflected military types. "What message is a program like this sending to America's youth?" *Survivor* seemed to epitomize the phrase, "It's not enough that I succeed; others must fail."

Fortunately, most smart troops realized a juicy new reality show aiming for ratings was designed for just "good TV." No American soldier could ever get behind the idea of watching contestants scheming to *aspire* to be a lone survivor.

In the corporate world, how much respect would you have for Brett at the water cooler first thing in the morning recapping the highlights of last night's reality TV and glowing about how the bearded guy tricked the girl in the bikini? If she formed an alliance with him, they could topple the teammate who had led them to win the last three challenges. Would that be the guy you'd ever trust on your next project together? If the imagery is clear enough to the Ranger sergeant to ask his men to turn the channel, it might be good advice for young businesspeople too.

My idea for TV producers would be to create a show called Impossible Challenge. In it, a dozen guys and girls would be thrown into chaos together. Then they'd be given an incredible task to accomplish on some desert island or side of a mountain. The only way to win is for every member of the team to cross the finish line. If they needed a unanimous victory to claim the prize, everyone would immediately recognize the whole team was only as strong as its weakest member. That would be a breathtaking TV show, though I can't take credit for the idea. It's called Ranger School.

I always root for the quintessential team player who's fervent about the entire squad crossing the goal line together. It includes everyone and excludes no one. They know it's the only way to win the long game, whether it's a night raid, a game show, or a sales campaign.

Keeping Them Safe

The Mindset of the Ranger

The idea of nurturing employees in the corporate world is becoming well accepted, which is a fantastic addition to a management philosophy that may not have existed 15 years ago. Today, many more connection points link the manager to the employee beyond work items. The concept of nurturing opens up a manager's eyes to acts of support and safety, and when it's business appropriate, it would make sense.

Moms and grannies have created a beautiful movement we can learn from. As we look at society nowadays, we can tell how much our nation reveres its military. Yellow ribbons wrap around trees. Flags with stars hang from kitchen windows. Travelers in airports greet military people with, "Thank you for your service." To surprise their kids, freshly returned soldiers are escorted to the 50-yard line at a football game's halftime to tears from the crowd. All around us on social media are living examples of how much our soldiers are respected.

As a young commander of troops in Iraq 8,000 miles away from home, I was committed to returning them all safely to their mothers and spouses. It felt like returning chicks to the nest. The pain of ever sitting down to pen a letter to a mom and inform her that her son had died in combat because of me was something I couldn't live with. So I made getting them all home safely my #1 mission. Just like the show *Star Trek* had its own prime directive, mine was to *bring all the troops back home to their moms.*

Placing the soldiers' welfare first made all other decisions fall into place, so no one under my watch would come to harm by a careless decision on my part. Today when asked, I pass on only this one mantra to new leaders shipping out: "*Bring your troops back safe.* You may need to sacrifice personally, but get them all back in one piece."

Safety is a message that resonates with parents all over the land. The nature of the military makes it a young person's game. Most of them have loving parents back home who wait for Facetime calls every week. They send care packages with battery-operated shavers and candied pecans, hoping to make living overseas seem a little more like home.

It sure does work. Our boys shared those packages and read their letters out loud. They could share family time for an afternoon from the Hayhurst family living room in West Virginia. Maybe Grandma was baking brownies on Sunday and hoped they'd still be still tasty by the time they arrived in Iraq. If the families only knew! Every man in the platoon got a piece of deer jerky from the one-gallon ziplock bag that Mrs. Brewer sent and savored it like it was a T-bone steak.

Each delight from home shared with the gang was like a sweet treat at a summer carnival.

When we opened my Aunt Rita's tin of homemade candied pecans, each of us ate one—just one—every day for six days until they were gone. Even now, I can taste them and remember wondering how a nut I had never paid much attention at home could be so crunchy and addicting. It took a lot of willpower to eat only one at a time. Somehow each day, when we opened the tin and savored our daily pecan, each of my buddies was magically transported back to his home in Shavano Park, Texas, or Kitts Beach, British Columbia, or fill in the blank. I wondered if Aunt Rita ever realized the effects of her baked kindness. Her reused red tin with a picture of Santa Claus on the lid was taped shut with military-grade green duct tape and buried four feet underground in my foxhole to stay safe.

When I came back home, I made sure to tell Aunt Rita how she had sweetened every day of that week for the boys and me who were living in sandy holes in the desert. Some years later, at her funeral in Pennsylvania, I shared the story about the gift I kept safe underground. Uncle Bill had been a Normandy Beach veteran. He appreciated knowing that, after we finished the pecans, I used the tin container to protect my C-4 plastic explosive and keep it dry. Truthfully, I had hoped I could refill it with more magic pecans.

I never did, but I did realize how much we enjoyed certain irreplaceable moments because mentors and family members were looking out for us. The circumstances always made the taste more special. I have a work buddy, Nico, who reminisces about a plate of Arabic pastry and coffee we enjoyed on a Middle East trip sitting at an outdoor café in Doha, Qatar. We were at the Souk Waqif at sunset. It tasted so good to sip our caffe amid the tents as we watched a local band stroll by. That combination is hard to replicate, and the memory is tucked away in a safe place.

Over the years, I've had fun crafting team events and whipping up shirts and promotional gear as giveaways to build team spirit. I love it when the high spirit that's infectious inside the team radiates to external customer events and seminars, too. Activities like grabbing the office gang to bike across the Golden Gate Bridge and organizing a Boxing Day at Kingsway Gym in NYC often sparked successful external customer events like skeet shooting and deep-sea fishing.

Once customers experienced the lift they got from fun outings, our inside team was sold on their value. It was far more effective to attract busy businesspeople out to movie premiers, top golf, and museum exhibitions than schedule a boring office webinar. We saw the joy that bubbled up from nurturing our own folks, and harnessed it out in the field.

Topping the Charts

Corporal (CPL) Todd Williams

In business today, young leaders strive to meet the standards set by their companies. It's a logical way to orient themselves for success, and executives are sure to take note of their progress.

It's simple to assess the current workers' performance using charts that compare them to their current colleagues and predecessors. But what the stats might not account for is an innovation or young leader's new niche not covered on the chart.

Today, forward-thinking companies emulate U.S. Army standards set up for the masses while still incentivizing their niche of supersizers using supplemental criteria. Both Rangers and leaders of Fortune 500 companies know that one size doesn't fit all, and when presented with extra efforts, they're smart to reward it.

When Corporal Todd Williams left active duty, he was five foot ten and weighed 195 pounds. That was 10 pounds over the army standard of 185 for his height, and a point of real pride.

Among the army's elite where strength and size are coveted, many of the best athletes power lift and fervently train with weights with their buddies in the gym—the superstuds among the regular studs. They seek to surpass the army's two-mile run, push-up, and sit-up standards. And they love to "break" the chart, which requires using measurements. A common tailor's measuring tape reportedly sits in the top desk drawer of every first sergeant. It gets pulled out for any soldiers who exceed the black-and-white chart that dictates ideal heights/weights.

Along with his lifting buddies, Todd welcomed the measures. He had already collected a pile of "300" patches that designated achieving the highest score possible on the army's physical fitness test. One look at Todd's 30-inch waist and 17-inch guns made the taping a laughable formality. It simply measured both the belly button and the neck (not the biceps, though that's a fun part of the legend). And it provided an easy check for anyone who desired to exceed the written limit.

For comparison, Department of Defense stats show the average U.S. Army Ranger is five foot ten and weighs 174 pounds. This is precisely "on the money" for the ideal balance between strength and cardio.

In 1992, Todd Williams was a living poster for the U.S. Army Rangers. For the next 24 years, he made his next fearsome impression as a SWAT team officer in Costa Mesa, California. It was impressive that Officer Williams added 20 more pounds of muscle weight, yet according to the charts, he would have still made the active-duty tape standards even at 210 pounds.

Performers in business keep performing when they know their efforts will be measured and appreciated. If statistics didn't yet exist, someone would create them. Remember when the National Basketball Association (NBA) added the "assist," and the National Football League (NFL) created the "hurry" to recognize strong players who had underappreciated skills? Statistically speaking, some of those athletes now top their sport's all-time charts.

Thinking Fast on Your Feet

Corporal (CPL) Todd Williams

Like any other activity in motion, the art of business boils down to a fluid set of actions and reactions. The operator who can process it all like a human computer gains a significant advantage over the competitors.

The kind of skills learned from intense training and honed from a tour of duty in Iraq are welcomed on a city police force. Costa Mesa would be lucky enough to snag two additional Rangers, including a lieutenant from the 101st and a sergeant from the 7th Infantry Division along with CPL Todd Williams.

The U.S. flag tattoo that Todd chose to put on his arm reminded him he had committed to continue being of service, and Costa Mesa's SWAT team quickly put those massive forearms to use. They designated Todd as the breacher responsible to wield the ram and break down doors. His new tools were the pry, Halligan, and shape charge. His Ranger ability to react quickly to a situation was also a tool ready to be used when soon needed.

One night, Todd's police team was assigned to issue a drug warrant to multiple suspects and treat the situation with extreme caution. They had to approach a rundown one-story house at four o'clock in the morning. As in combat, the best time to find the enemy disoriented is in the dead of night. In fact, military battle often commences at dawn to make use of the coming light on the open battlefield after gaining the early advantage. But daylight wasn't an issue, given the bang-smash operation and electricity inside the house. The SWAT team chose the safest possible time to take the perps by surprise.

At the lieutenant's "go" signal, Todd used the black double-handled ram—a modified six-inch-diameter pipe cut and welded to specs—to deliver a mighty blow above the doorknob. With the blow, the dilapidated house was so rickety that its entire front swayed inward and threatened to collapse. In the next surprising second, the door stayed in place as the frame and whole front wall yawed. Every window in the house broke with an explosion. In the split second that Todd assessed the house wasn't under attack but realized a glass explosion would wake up everyone in a half-mile radius, his follow-on strike blew the swaying door off the hinges and into the dark house.

All hell can break loose on a raid when it involves kicking in doors and dealing with armed suspects. This time, the element of surprise and the SWAT team's rehearsed clearing techniques worked to get them inside and gathered. Next, the team cleared the rooms for suspects and contraband. A woman screaming at the top of her lungs ran into the hallway. One of the SWAT officers frisked a suspect in the living room and went to sit him on a couch to be watched by a fellow officer. Todd stopped him. The couch itself had not yet been cleared for weapons, so the officer yanked the suspect's seat right back off the couch.

Todd thought fast. He searched the cushion and found a planted .22 caliber pistol waiting—a "piece of junk" handgun that was 60 seconds away from wounding or killing one of the officers. Ranger training once again made a difference.

Every business situation is made more successful by those who can think fast on their feet. If a technology customer states the problems during an outage, a smart engineer can diagnose the issues just by listening to the order of the symptoms. That would likely solve the disruption and get the users back online quickly.

If you believe the ability to quickly process new stimuli and then apply it to the current situation requires innate intelligence, you're right. But that brainpower can also be honed by the workers who learn detailed facets of their craft. That includes all the things that can go wrong as well as what makes them go right. With that high degree of preparation, when unexpected business problems happen, they can be readily solved.

Nipping Problems in the Bud

Corporal (CPL) Todd Williams

Wouldn't it be great if crises could be avoided before they happened? Savvy captains of industry can identify a change coming toward them before it develops. Great chess players can see several moves ahead. And meteorologists can spot storms forming days out. The ability to nip a problem early in a business allows the firm to prevent trouble from occurring. In the police department, it can save lives or (as those on the force joke among themselves) at the least it can save paperwork.

Officer Todd Williams was on patrol in Costa Mesa when he got the call about a possible jumper (someone threatening to jump off a building) downtown in Triangle Square. A female officer was already on the roof with the young man and felt timid to approach him more closely. When Todd arrived, he saw that the officer stood only 15 feet away and seemed to have relaxed the hippie jumper's wild-eyed mood. *Good.*

Todd had learned a sensible psychology in training that coached officers to relax and disarm the suspect using calming words. That instruction was based on the premise that jumpers didn't really *want* to hurl themselves over the edge. About 90 percent of the time, this was a solid premise. After all, anyone intent to leap probably wouldn't wait for the police and the cameras to show up just in time for the five o'clock news. They'd just do it. In this situation, no cameras or press had arrived. It was just the hippie, the two officers, and a growing group of onlookers leaning forward to see what would happen next.

Todd walked up to the roof and was unavoidably spotted in the jumper's peripheral vision, so he had to make himself known. He spoke as nonoffensively as his hulking frame and tatted arms could manage. "Hey, how's it going?" he asked the hippie. He then faded back a few steps as he saw the jumper become progressively more absorbed with the female officer only. Then Todd noticed the thick ledge that the hippie was awkwardly perched over and also spied a concrete column that partially obstructed his own sidelong view.

Suddenly, Todd made a spot decision to nip this problem in the bud. He casually faded backward a few more steps and even a few more behind the column. The female officer was shrewd enough to refrain looking over at Todd as she continued chatting calmly with the jumper. Nice assist.

Without warning, Todd sprang out from behind the column with a nifty leap step. Planting his right foot at the ledge wall for leverage, he lurched up and out with a snatch move, grabbing the hippie and launching him airborne backward onto the roof in one action.

Saved from the edge and not at all resisting, the jumper was taken to the hospital and treated for a drug overdose. When the young man later appeared in court to face criminal charges, he thanked Todd for saving his life.

Nipping problems in the bud can save a vast number of wasted resources when the right people are keeping an eye out for "jumpers." Todd is reminded of that whenever he looks at his final two tattoos—the SWAT eagle and his "422" badge number. They signify how much good can come from averting a disaster before it happens.

Industry veterans do well to recall their most recent poor marketing decision or financial downturn and keep an eye out for similar warning signs. If a train wreck is about to happen and can be stopped before it ever crashes, you could wind up being the biggest unsung hero no one ever hears about. Yet as President Ronald Reagan once said, "There is no limit to the amount of good you can do if you don't care who gets the credit."

Recognizing Expertise

Corporal (CPL) Dave Lafaver

"They sure have a good eye for talent." That's a dynamite compliment for managers who need to hire staff for their company. Having the ability to identify incremental additions is worth gold in today's market. Consider Brazil, where workers "rights" laws make it nearly impossible for certain employees to be replaced once hired. They make jokes about it there, but it's no laughing matter when you need to get the personnel correct the first time. It just makes good sense to choose the best people available.

For leaders, having the ability to add winners to their teams can come from using their excellent sixth sense.

Police Lieutenant Dave Lafaver learned to recognize talent from his days in the 82nd when other paratroopers surrounded him. After that, he spent 25 years in law enforcement in Northern California and continued to rely on former Rangers out on the streets when job success was on the line.

Dave says he prefers the nuts-and-bolts versus charismatic style of leadership, but a shift in the command center or riding his Harley reveals a charismatic character that's fun to be around, especially if you like to laugh at human nature. Dave has successfully carried forward an affable attitude from the infantry squad to the squad room. He's also come to lean on his Ranger brothers —especially at times when he can't afford to lose.

In 2002, the police department in his Silicon Valley city had just replaced its trusty shotgun with a brand-new AR-15 assault rifle in each squad's kit when Dave answered the call for a hostage situation. It was nine in the evening, and a 45-year-old Filipino mother had escaped from her house to inform dispatch that her 70-year-old husband was holding people hostage. That included holding her teenagers, a couple of babies, and her elderly mother at gunpoint.

Dave arrived and called for units to set up a perimeter. Nine units answered the call, including JW, his longtime friend and Ranger who had been on the force with Dave. His negotiation phone call from out in the street resulted in the perpetrator shooting his elderly mother-in-law inside. So Dave ordered the units to get ready to stack up and go in through the front door. But first, they needed to disable the porch light by the entrance. Without hesitation, Dave pointed at JW to aim a shot at taking out the lantern right as the team would batter down the door. JW's challenge would be taking out a light bulb from 75 meters without sending an errant shot through a window and accidentally striking one of the hostages.

On Dave's signal, JW nailed the porch light with a single shot. The assault team rammed the door and rushed inside before the perpetrator could react and hurt anyone else. Defeated, the perp put his revolver up to his own temple and pulled the trigger, ending the siege. His mother-in-law was rushed to the hospital with a bullet wound that had entered and exited her jaw, and she recovered.

Confidently delegating the crucial linchpin of the operation to an expert on the team can save the day and provide a valuable lesson to tuck away if the time ever comes again. Business leaders have to rely on the experts they've assembled to perform the delicate work they were hired for. By then, the leaders should have accomplished their role—to engage the specialist—and then delegate the task when the critical moment arises.

This builds loyalty also.

Accepting That Stuff Happens

Corporal (CPL) Dave Lafaver

Tension-breaking moments in the workplace remind us always to be ready to accept anything that occurs. That could be unexpected, and it might even be outrageous.

Way back in 1996 as a brand-new patrol officer on the California coast, Dave Lafaver answered a house call to find an elderly man who had died of a heart attack in his living room. When he died, he had been leashing his Yorkie before going outside for a walk. By the time his wife discovered him and called in, he had been dead for a couple of hours.

Dave hadn't prepared himself for the scene he found. The yippie dog had freaked out, possibly from seeing blood or maybe from the owner falling on top of him. It had triggered a fear reaction. Dave found the pet covered in blood and his owner's face gone—eaten off. Who knows what had happened to set off the Yorkie and result in this grisly scene?

Dave had just started on the police force, and this seemed like a cruel joke playing out. He called for backup plus advice, and his good friend JW answered the call. Having been on the force for seven years, JW surveyed the scene slowly with Ranger calm. Walking painstakingly around the room, he looked down at the victim, scanned over to Dave, and then stared at the Yorkie. Processing all of it with the deadpan acceptance that bad things happen, he tucked both thumbs into his belt and simply said, "Dog-gone it."

The silliness of the statement made them both break out in a stifled laughter. Thankfully, it wasn't so loud that the widow in the neighboring room could hear it. Stuff happens.

Often, the moments we can laugh about carry over to times when our patience is tested. It might even be that the human element wins the day as much as the actual solution. The ability to relax in tense situations enough to see the humor—whether we express it aloud or just think it to ourselves—lays an excellent foundation toward building a steady, reliable reputation.

Being Authentic

Master Sergeant (MSG) Joe "Trapper" Brewer

> *Career-minded contributors do best to discover their most genuine adaptation and hone it to a fine point. Presenting a "fault-free" version may not last long when confronted with tough times, while being yourself might allow you to invest in improving your station versus covering it up.*
>
> *Organizations are lucky to find authentic leaders. Thankfully, they're out there.*

MSG Joe Brewer served in three campaigns as an 82nd Airborne Ranger and Special Forces team sergeant in Iraq and Afghanistan. After a 20-year active career, he returned to Iraq for another four years as a contractor to assist in the training effort.

Joe was a nature type, having grown up in and near the Montana wilderness and in touch with how to survive outdoors. His idea of fun in September of 2019 was taking a biplane to a remote campsite in northern British Columbia to hunt for 30 days. He especially enjoyed the companionship of a couple of heavily armed wilderness pals, where they could exist completely cut off from society.

Joe could be called an authentic find for the U.S. Army. First, he spent a lifetime painstakingly understanding the elements, survival, and marksmanship. Then he volunteered for every specialized training he could get his hands on, and the army took over from there: Airborne, Air Assault, Sniper, Ranger, HALO, and Special Forces. I was lucky enough to have him as a squad leader in the Scouts in the 82nd in Desert Storm, and I realized how vital it was to count on a "real deal" subordinate leader. I could compare it to the Defense Department's language program that distinguishes between a Level 4 Expert and a Level 5 Native Speaker.

I love learning languages and have had the opportunity to bang around in about 12 of them. Yet even if I dedicated every waking hour to only one language and became an impressive Level 4 Expert, I could never be classified as a Level 5 native. That is reserved for people who are born into the language.

It's much the same in learning the military trade. I had the time of my life learning a variety of skills and mastering just a couple. Still, even for the ones I learned well, there's always a nanosecond that my brain takes to process a wilderness or marksmanship task rather than innately acting the instincts of a native. Joe was precisely that kind of asset, and I treasured having him on my team.

A related idea for the business world might be to scan the landscape for an authentic technician who knows the industry from having grown up in it. Equipped with at least one native expert on the team, you can build in all other ancillary skills performed by smart people who are quick learners.

For leaders lucky enough to find an industry purist, it's fundamental to continually feed their desire for niche expertise. It may not consist of activities we'd spend our Saturdays doing, but remember that the purist craves certifications and an esoteric understanding of things that make them tick.

Once you get your hands on real purists, plant your team flag around them and then protect them. Remember, they might value the method over the brand, which means that you, as the leader, may have to earn their early respect instead of the other way around.

When you work with authentic people, you'll never have to guess about the details. They'll speak up to defend the correct formula and let you know about it. So absorb the completeness of their recommendations. As long as you can balance them with the resources you possess to complete the task, then listen to what they say.

Bringing Factions Together

Master Sergeant (MSG) Joe "Trapper" Brewer

In the marketplace, mergers and new acquisitions can leave a fragmented sense of loyalty. Perhaps worse, competitive products could have placed the new allies at odds in the past, and ill feelings still remain. Or maybe the current product direction hasn't yet been set in stone by management, and a tug-of-war is still taking place.

These are the times when leadership at any level needs to bring factions together. A good start involves common ground as an icebreaker. After that, identifying your common objective or a new mutual competitor creates a momentum-building next step in forming an alliance. Maybe only a small remaining piece is causing the contention, and clear direction from the CEO will smooth the rest over. Until then, it's the midlevel manager in the field who needs to depolarize any standoffs.

In mid-2003, SFC Joe Brewer found himself just outside Mosul, Iraq, dressed as a local and living in their midst. As team sergeant for Special Forces Team ODA 375, Joe was engaged in special reconnaissance. That meant he had to blend in there—not a slam dunk for a blond-haired American who had a youthful face and not much facial hair. His buddies on the team were already sporting full beards while Joe was doing his best scruffy act after two months without shaving. Luckily, his ability to go unnoticed into the environment when necessary made up for his youthful looks.

Joe was the team sergeant for 12 diverse type-A personalities. He had become an expert at uniting a team in a common cause as ODA 375 readied themselves for their first "David versus Goliath" mission. Nearby were 200 fearless Kurds from the north as part of the allied Peshmerga forces assisting the counterinsurgency mission in Mosul. Twenty Kurds were assigned to his team for local help. Joe had warmed to the Pesh troops right away because he knew they had historically been subject to terrible oppression from Saddam Hussein. The Iraqi president had chemically attacked them in their home territory in the north 15 years before—in 1988. He saw they were committed to root out the remnants and assist in the allied hunt for the hiding Saddam Hussein who would manage to evade capture for several more months until late December of 2003. That's when he'd be found stowed in a hole near his hometown of Tikrit, and killed.

At their first meeting, Joe impressed his Pesh counterpart by knowing the term "Peshmerga," which translated to "those who face death." He communicated that he sincerely hoped to earn their respect as equals in the fight—a message the devoted Peshmerga received well.

Intel estimated as many as 50 rebels were in a complex that split a highway with a lazy W trench bisecting the road and a checkpoint. It was 25 kilometers north of Mosul Eyes. In every direction, the rebels were on the lookout for U.S. forces, which had loudly and forcefully arrived in-country a couple of months before. ODA 375's mission was to quietly get close enough to FLIR (forward-looking infrared that senses radiation) the target, marking it for a precision aircraft strike using the latest ground-air coordinated technology.

As the rebel forces were keeping a lookout for U.S. and Pesh elements in the area, Joe's team, dressed as locals, drove in a Jeep Cherokee. The car made a full lazy loop to sneak in behind the building. Minutes later, they had pulled the gear from the vehicle floor and snapped the target. Successfully acquiring it, the driver pulled away, and Joe reported, "Exfil in progress"—leaving the danger area and calling in the airstrike. U.S. fast movers owning the sky came in low and took out the target along with 40 enemy rebels.

Given there were no U.S. or Peshmerga casualties in this first coordinated mission between allied forces, the trust had begun.

When explicit instruction from the top is in place for individual teams, the same good work that brought factions together can next turn their efforts into accelerating time to trust. This trust will get them to profitability quicker.

Staying True to the Cause

Master Sergeant (MSG) Joe "Trapper" Brewer

Keeping internal teams synchronized improves their efficiency and sometimes even ensures survival, whether it be outperforming the rival or staying afloat at all. It calls for following the tested, analytical processes and confirming them with immediate after-action assessment to make sure the company ship is being steered the best way possible. Even when those waters are nearly unnavigable, it's the only option.

Not every play in the playbook will work flawlessly, even when you follow best practices. The dangerous war game has a slim margin for error. Random chance and changing intel can shift the outcome of the next mission. But if you're setting the conditions for success properly, the men will look to you to "stay frosty" (be alert, awake) and reassure them that the course is correct.

A month later, the team was on two-vehicle patrol through Mosul on a route that had been precleared. As the team rolled through an intersection, the end of the block looked suspiciously compromised. Joe was in the trail vehicle with eyes on it. The team immediately reacted, executing a brake and reverse move to back out at the highest speed possible the way they had come. In the lead, Joe's vehicle was heading directly back to the previous intersection when rebels opened fire from far down the block to their rear. It came from just where they had suspected.

One teammate in the closest vehicle took a bullet through the hip. Another in Joe's truck took one that ripped through his helmet bucket and the outer flesh of his head.

The patrol made it out of the ambush, and both operators survived, thanks to a quick audible. Even following best practices, two out of six soldiers got wounded. The after-action report confirmed intel had been good, and their swift reaction had saved lives. But sadly, yes, bad stuff unavoidably happens in combat.

A couple of months later, ODA 375 rotated out of Iraq to where it was needed—1,800 miles away at Fire Base Goresh in Afghanistan. They were added to another A-Team with the mission to galvanize the Afghan Militia Force (AMF) into action. Joe was given the same opportunity and fresh experience to bring alignment to the AMF soldiers. But he encountered a different perspective from the Afghan soldiers than he had seen in Iraq—one that required him to modify his previous approach.

The typical AMF soldier was different than a Kurd in Iraq who had been systemically persecuted. Deep motivation and a sense of community had pushed the Peshmerga in Iraq to fight ferociously. Comparatively, the allied-sponsored Afghan soldiers were volunteers with little motivation to fight the Taliban and not much cultural heritage of a professional military. Conscription wasn't an option to raise the numbers, which meant the small numbers of recruits were also more accessible for the Taliban to target for death.

Joe had to modify his approach with the Afghans, especially when he saw the equipment they had was deficient and no budget was available to replace it. For example, their AK-47s had no buttstocks on the end where the shooter would leverage the rifle into his shoulder. That meant they could only hope to hip fire the weapon at waist level and not hit much of anything over 75 meters.

At the small camp, they found wood and saws, so they carved the Afghans some crude buttstocks. They were bulky and heavy, but they worked, and the gesture spoke louder than the solution. Whether or not they loved these weapons—and whether or not there'd be an easy answer in this austere mountainous region—at least one Afghan commander named Colonel Adrease knew these allies were trying to improve the conditions. He recognized that Joe's guys had remedied the situation with the only resources they could get their hands on.

Even with the attention on best practices, ODA 375 moved out on one of the day's missions but was ambushed and pinned down by RPG fire from an elevated position. Joe's team lost a man when withering AK-47 rifle fire caught the tech sergeant in the head and killed him. Other flying shrapnel killed his interpreter. Shortly after that, the Afghan militia commander and his 2nd in command were ambushed driving down a crowded road. The ambush killed Colonel Adrease and wounded his 2nd in charge. The units regrouped, with the AMF realizing the need to stay true to the cause. It meant mutual survival. And in the months that followed, unifying the Allies was key to a measurable decrease in the violence.

Abandoning a plan when confronted with factionalism, setbacks, and loss of personnel may be an understandable initial reaction. An after-action report needs to evaluate several things: if teams can learn to operate in greater harmony, if lost staff can be replenished, and if the original course runs true. When the answers are yes, then the decision should be to forge ahead.

Creating a Higher Purpose

Master Sergeant (MSG) Joe "Trapper" Brewer

Visualizing a higher purpose elevates everyday work doldrums into a mass effort with lots of synergy and even a rewarding feeling.

Is it fair to say the difference between a manager and a leader is that the manager carries out the vision handed over, while the leader creates the vision for everyone to see, and then they carry it out together?

Joe Brewer's teams had rolled up their sleeves twice to align with both the Kurds and Afghans. During the period from '04 to '07, Joe returned with military contractor USIS as a training instructor for a volatile mixed bag of Iraqis in their newly formed Emergency Response Unit (ERU). They were a collection of Sunnis, Shias, and Kurds who were sick of internal strife and wanted a stable country to live in. So they volunteered for this hybrid government/military service akin to a SWAT team that served warrants and apprehended Iraqi war criminals. Their first step was to get training.

USIS ran a type of mini–Special Forces Selection course for them. The instructors consisting of ex–Green Berets and Navy SEALs quickly noted a new condition existed—one that they intended to encourage. There appeared to be a higher purpose for this group to aim toward—that is, a stable Iraq. They could maybe even visualize a country that could work its way toward democracy. If so, this kind of change would require solidarity that transcended all religious differences.

And the goal of solidarity worked. Everyone slept in the same barracks and ate in the same chow hall. Joe and the cadre of instructors ran the trainees through a thoroughly physical course that left them too exhausted to mass against each other. What it did provide was a sense of resolve and a chance to unify.

One candidate named Ayad who graduated to become an ERU officer particularly stood out. The instructors called him Little Ranger. He seemed imbued with the desire to influence fellow ERU officers, and within a couple of years, Little Ranger was promoted to be their first sergeant.

The trainees made progress. The ERU's main mission was to serve potentially dangerous warrants. However, at first, they had to pair up with an active duty SEAL or Green Beret team stationed in Baghdad.

As hoped, they slowly gained the ability to become independent.

It's mandatory to have a vision so everyone will show up to the same workplace every day and know why. Otherwise, the door swings open for all varieties of adverse outcomes. The savvy leader who creates a shared purpose for all can bring people in from the cold, uncertain perimeter toward the center where it's nice and warm.

CHAPTER SIX

R

Readily will I display the intestinal fortitude required to fight on to the Ranger objective and complete the mission though I be the lone survivor.

Punching Above Your Weight	Rangers with Fists CSM Aubrey Butts
Seizing the Chance for Greatness	Rangers with Fists CSM Aubrey Butts
Volunteering for a Galvanizing Event	Rangers with Fists
Getting Up When You Get Knocked Down	Rangers with Fists – Smokin' Joe
Praising It Forward	COL Brad Nelson
Highlighting Others' Success	COL Brad Nelson
Putting Your Money on the Underdog	MSG Arthur "Hard Art" Kakis
Protecting and Delivering	MSG Arthur "Hard Art" Kakis
But Nothing	MSG Dale "Onion" Roberts
Gathering from Great Sources	Desert Storm Rangers

Punching Above Your Weight

Rangers with Fists - Command Sergeant Major (CSM) Aubrey Butts

The following is a visceral message for young leaders about a coach who had a drastic plan for any motivated athletes with the guts to buy into his 12-week crash course to success. His absolute certainty that the impossible was possible served to reassure his athletes immediately. He had been a great boxer and had coached years of championship teams. When he spoke, there was absolutely no doubt that what he said could work and would work. They believed.

The 82nd Airborne takes the sport of boxing seriously. This primeval contest based on violence captures the psyche of the warfighter perfectly. Domination of one human over another can quickly be achieved and witnessed by hundreds, whose blood rises as they watch every flurry of blows thrown by the combatants. The winning fighter and his team are the ones standing at the end while the defeated suffer their loss directly at the hands of the victor. All this is primitive yet thrilling to elite troops about to go into battle.

For a high achiever, losing only means losing *today* and then returning to the heavy bag at the gym to redouble the effort and learn from mistakes. There is no time to bemoan failure and experience months of self-pity. Getting right back into the ring after getting knocked down may seem barbaric, but it's a basic formula.

The Red Falcons' boxing coach was First Sergeant (1SG) Butts, who had an easy test to determine if a soldier would make a good boxer. Fort Bragg was the boxing hub of the army, and the infantry brigades were the hub of Fort Bragg, so you get the idea—the competition was fierce to grab the coach's attention. Coach Butts wanted to win the post championship again in 1990. He'd become a local legend by then, having been the 130-pound alternate in the 1976 Montreal Olympics that featured Sugar Ray Leonard and the Spinks brothers.

Professionally, 1SG Butts, a future Ph.D was a buttoned-up paratrooper and role model to other African American troops. He had risen to be the senior enlisted man of a 250-man company. On the side, he had been given the task of bringing home another championship trophy for the brigade.

1SG Butts's test was barbarically simple: Potential boxers lined up shoulder to shoulder in a straight line facing the center of the ring. He passed in front of each one (a là Louis Gossett Jr. in the 1982 movie *An Officer and a Gentleman*) and addressed each of us directly. I was in the lineup, experiencing the same treatment as the private and sergeant on either side of me.

Coach Butts intended to make two passes.

Pass #1 commenced. "How much u weigh?" he asked. "One hundred seventy-three pounds, Sergeant Butts," was my firm response. "Then, you gonna be boxing at one-forty-nine pounds." Wow, welterweight . . . that is, if I could lose 24 pounds in 12 weeks.

He moved right down the line and assigned a weight class to each man based on the current weight he heard. It didn't take me long to figure out the algorithm—scale down two weight classes and round down one more if it was close. For 173 pounds, he went past middleweight-165 and then past junior middleweight-156, and then he landed on welterweight-149. *Do this in only twelve weeks?* I wondered silently. *Is he kidding?*

But something tickled my brain. He didn't even hesitate to assign these weights to all of us. He had certainty, and he wasn't about to let my *un*certainty slow him down for a millisecond. Walking down the line between recruits, he said, "Men, you gonna have the strength of a middleweight, but you gonna lose that weight and be punchin' lightweights instead." By the time he had moved three men away from me in the line, I already *believed* I could lose that weight.

Once Coach Butts finished with the last man, he then walked back to the first man as relaxed as if he had all day to spend with us. On the way back, he held out his hand, and his assistant from outside the ring tossed him a red 16-ounce Everlast-branded glove—right-handed. He effortlessly caught it in the air and had slipped it on his right hand by the time he'd reached the first man again.

Pass #2 commenced. 1SG Butts announced, "Men, a real boxer only has two reactions when he gets hit . . . ," and with that, he hauled off and hit the first man in line square in the face with a right cross. He continued down the line repeating the process to the shock and awe of some of the men. The coach was absolutely in no rush, relaxed as could be, connecting glove-to-flesh with every man and studiously gauging the reactions along the way.

By the time he got to me, I knew his punch was coming. Luckily, the blow didn't hurt much, plus there was the cushion of the glove, so I let go a little smile of relief. *What reaction will that get?* I wondered.

After punching the last man, he let us in on his theory. "Men, a real boxer got only two reactions to g'ttin' hit—number one: he don't even mind, or number two: he smiles 'cause it ain't nothin.'"

Had I heard the coach correctly? I felt lucky, because the blow I took hadn't been that bad. Later, I realized many people have a terrible fear of being punched in the face, which I hadn't known. Some guys had flinched, so they were out. Some guys got mad, which seemed to me like a natural reaction. But Coach Butts straightened us all out again.

"Some of you wanna get mad cause you g'ttin' hit in the face? Dumbasses, what do you think this sport is all about?" It was hard to argue with his logic.

He continued, "Men, if you wanna be the champ, you gotta be the surgeon, not the butcher. You don't ever get mad in my ring. 'Cause when you do, you lose your edge. You have to be thinking all the time." In a crazy way, that made good sense to me, and I began to think I might have found a home in this sport.

Coach Butts covered a few "musts" for achieving that level of dominance, and it worked like magic. Our team was "three for three" in post championships in the years I was there. Another half a dozen championships racked up during his tenure in the brigade. His boxers were simply better than the other guys in the division they faced. He had somehow imparted experience and savvy to new boxers who stepped into the ring. I remember he'd say this nearly daily: "Your greatest competition is going to come in this ring practicing with your fellow teammates. Forget about the competition. You're going to destroy them when they climb in the ring. They won't even deserve to be in there with you." I've been trying to emulate that same kind of confidence coaching kids ever since.

Coach's "musts" to achieve dominance:

First, be a leader who has already built credibility people can see.

Second, craft a plan that addresses the immediate obstacles, including doubt, even if drastic.

Third, breathe life into the scheme by believing it yourself.

Seizing the Chance for Greatness

Rangers with Fists - Command Sergeant Major (CSM) Aubrey Butts

It doesn't matter how we arrive there—hard work, prescient timing, or stroke of luck. If presented with the opportunity to represent the company to industry moguls, the leader seizes that moment to make a killing.

Given a groundbreaking chance to fulfill a childhood dream of being a boxer, I didn't want to blow it. The improbable path that led me to this opportunity might well lead me to be a champ.

It all began a couple of months after I arrived in the 82nd Airborne as a shiny new Louie making a good reputation by listening to NCOs and maxing PT tests. I figured those were the two best things I could do.

One day, 1SG Butts had found me in the battalion area and came over crisply with a salute.

"All the way, suhr," he began.

"Airborne," I replied with a crisp salute in return.

"Hey, sir, you eye-talian, right?"

"Yes, First Sergeant," I replied.

He was encouraged. "And you from Philly, right?"

"Why, yes, First Sergeant . . . ," I said, wondering if this was going somewhere good.

"Then, I want you on the boxing team."

"Wow, thanks, First Sergeant. You heard I'm in pretty good shape?"

"Hell no, sir. We just need an officer to sign for the equipment."

Regardless of how I had gotten the chance, I was determined to earn a place on the roster. So what if I wasn't exactly recruited for my expertise. It had still landed me in the ringside lineup on day one of practice. It was up to me to capitalize on the opportunity.

In business today, movers and shakers do a pretty good job living by the axiom "capitalize on the opportunity." They're trying to create their own breaks, but if occasionally presented with the chance to enter through the side door, they jump on it.

Volunteering for a Galvanizing Event

Rangers with Fists

Extreme training can be the kind of wake-up call that forever changes our understanding of the game we're trying to win. When our fear dissipates because we've faced the worst it can get, we can be free to focus on winning strategies regardless of how the competition may come after us.

Not everybody is lucky enough to have a mentor or a galvanizing event to vault them to the next level, but everyone ought to strive to find one. Seeking a mentor or volunteering for an event can help.

It was a month out from the 82nd Boxing Championship—nicknamed the Smoker probably because so many contestants get smoked, or maybe since a lot of people in boxing seem to like smoking cigars. Coach Butts called an optional Saturday morning practice to get in some sparring rounds. The team was down to just the 12 weight-class contenders, with everyone sweating it out and losing their assigned weight-in time for this tourney.

Coach Butts had left it that attending the Saturday session was purely voluntary. By 8:15 a.m., it was clear I was the only one showing up. Coach had planned to spar today, so he'd brought in LT Chris Townley, a former light-heavyweight division champ, to help him. But with two of them and only one of me, they were fuming mad.

We gloved up, and the two boxers alternated for six rounds as I stayed in for the duration. Boxing three rounds each, the experienced fighters gave me the beating of my life. There had always been a disciplined semblance of order to a practice, but on this day, I took a savage beating. I went down 90 seconds into the first round with 1SG Butts, and he calmly waited for me to get up to resume. Then LT Townley went to work on me with cement fists, crushing anything that wasn't covered up. As one of them got tired after a three-minute round, the next one came in. I moved, covered up, offered counterpunches that missed my targets, and generally held on for my life. During rounds five and six, I lost the ability to cover up high. Because I couldn't raise my arms any higher than my shoulders, they rained down blows to my headgear and face that blackened my right eye and cut me across the cheek and nose. The bell signaled the brutal end. Imagine that beating. But I had lived to tell the tale.

After that day, I was a new boxer, unconcerned with being hit, and free of fear to hone my offense, thanks to their extreme training.

As extra karma, former heavyweight champ of the world Muhammad Ali, on a goodwill visit, came into the boxing gym (the secret reason for the Saturday practice). We exchanged pleasantries. By 10 a.m., the room was packed with adoring fans. Ali told me, "*If you want to* ***be*** *da man, you have to* ***beat*** *da man.*" He'd probably offered that same advice to a thousand other boxers, but I like to think it was a personal message from the champ only to me. It was galvanizing.

By 1990, Muhammad Ali was firmly in the grips of Parkinson's disease and needed the help of an assistant to overcome his tremors and slurred speech during the tour. His fog momentarily cleared when he stepped up to greet the three-year-old daughter of one of our soldiers holding her on his shoulders. His entire personality returned as he kindly reached out to take the little girl's hand in his. The gym was electrified to see the "greatest of all time" back to himself for a few moments. I'm thankful I got to see that.

In the biz world, extreme training goes well beyond the norm. It's training that others are not willing to endure. "Extreme" may serve as the defibrillating shock you need to visualize your environment in a whole new way.

Partaking in that training gives you the edge. Add in a glittery moment from an industry icon, and it can be a talisman for your advance toward the top.

Getting Up When You Get Knocked Down

Rangers with Fists – Smokin' Joe

> *Preparing well beyond what's needed should make an event turn into a celebration of our great effort to get there. Confidence is high when mentors validate that we know our job and we can come out of the gate roaring.*

LT Chris Townley was that positive colleague who was good at talking things up. At a picnic a couple of weeks out from the tourney, he blurted out a nickname for me—Smokin' Joe—and it stuck. It was kind of a cool Philly-type thing *a là* Philly heavyweight champ Joe Frazier. As a kid, I had watched Frazier fight Ali all three times.

I headed into the division tourney for the pride of the Airborne and wondered what it would feel like in the ring under the lights. Once there, the referee checked our gloves, gave instructions, and signaled for the bell to ring.

At 149 pounds, my welterweight opponent came at me for a furious 45 seconds, and he wasn't connecting with anything beyond arms and gloves. Under a minute in the first round, he breathed an imperceptive letdown after throwing the kitchen sink at me. Then I went to work. Straight lefts and rights—just as the coach drilled. "Nothing wide and nothing wild, men," he said.

My opponent didn't seem to realize I'd be coming straight at him because my first shots hit him in the nose, the jaw, more to the nose, and then one smooth uppercut to the chin. All of a sudden, he was down on the mat. The ref tallied off an eight count and then waved his hands back and forth, signaling it was all over.

Was this guy already done after one minute and 45 seconds? Yes, it was a TKO. I discovered winning was magic.

Fights #2 and #3 the next day went easily. Fight #2 was a palooka I tenderized like a meat bag, and #3 rope-a-doped me until he realized I wasn't about to run out of gas in three two-minute rounds. Before long, I was in the semifinals with the Puerto Rico Golden Gloves Champ and a chance to advance to the final. 1SG Butts once called me the gas man because I never ran out of it. In this case, he said to go right at the champ and stick with what was working. So, I did exactly what had gotten me my first three wins against lesser opponents, and I carried the first round with the judges. Nice! This plan was going well.

In the second round, the champ came out probing and trying to get close, but my activity was keeping him away—at least for the moment. As I moved to the left to also jab left, he juked down and shook off the jab. Then he came up with a single right uppercut that I never saw. It landed right on "the button"—apparently, that's what was called connecting to the perfect spot on the center of the chin.

I crumpled into a heap. When I opened my eyes, the ref was looking down at me with both hands outstretched mouthing, "six . . . seven . . ." I guessed I'd been out for the first five counts and got up to make the eight count. But I wobbled backward, and that was it. Amateur fighting stresses staying safe. Unless you're 100 percent ready to go after being knocked down, it's game over.

So that was it.

As in business, we lose and then have to regroup. My boxing career had to wait another year until 1991. But during that time, I learned from early mistakes that seemed childlike over time. I was also able to add technique and defense to the raw offense and conditioning. I realized brute force had carried me through the lesser opponents, but it wouldn't get me to the next level. I had to regroup.

In '91, I sailed through the tourney with four straight wins and brought home the 82nd Welterweight Championship for the Red Falcons. I never got boxing out of my blood after that and went on to fight 75 bouts, winning 71 of them, with 49 fights by knockout. Along the way, I grabbed 12 pro fights, some Tough Man matches, and as recent as 2019, a Celebrity Boxing match for Wounded Warriors against a pro wrestler nicknamed Frankie the Saiyan. That was fun—and we raised a bunch of money.

I learned so much in life from boxing. And it certainly seems like a brilliant metaphor for rising to life's challenges, doesn't it? Mostly I learned to pick myself right after I got dropped to the canvas, then regroup and come back next time even stronger to KO the next opponent. It was anything but a fairy tale.

As the coach always loved to say, "Don't spend time on the mat; nothing good happens down there."

Praising It Forward

Colonel (COL) Brad Nelson

In a strong organization, grassroots success naturally flows upward until it reaches the top. It seems to me in the same organization that the credit ought to flow back down. Isn't this a necessary shift in thinking?

Try this: next time the boss compliments you on a job well done, simply pass on that credit. "I couldn't agree with you more about the win; it was Gina's team that had the idea and Chris's that executed it." Doing this feels fantastic. More than that, it layers in a new sense of accomplishment when you can disembogue credit beyond yourself. It's like a river sending out fresh water in every direction at the delta.

Business guru Dale Carnegie wrote that we ought to apply praise liberally and criticism only sparingly. So much can be gained by giving shout-outs to create a positive environment—especially when a business leader faces overwhelming odds.

My first company commander told me, "Never take credit for yourself when you can pass it down the line to your men." Captain Brad Nelson, the CO of Charlie Company, taught me this lesson in my first week of leading a unit under his command. He presented as extraordinarily straight and stoic to less career-minded officers. For me, he was a shining example of a great leader who never took credit for anything the team did and rarely accepted individual praise from superiors. Whenever the big boss would say, "Charlie Company performed beautifully on that mission," Captain Nelson would likely respond, "Sir, it was Sergeant X and Sergeant Y who did the work."

Brad was incredibly humble, and he was also right. It was the platoon sergeants who had trained their group of 40 men daily that knocked out a successful mission under cohesive machinery they had built. They were the third level down from the top in a company-sized mission. Brad's directions were clear and attainable for the three of us platoon leaders. We could outline our moving components, and then we, in turn, handed the prep over to our platoon sergeant, who functioned as the "big daddy" to make sure everything got done and accounted for.

Following a successful 250-man mission involving three infantry platoons spiced with heavy assets, it was the perfect time in the after-action meeting to compliment the platoon sergeants. They were midway down the line in seniority and well respected by everyone. This was not only well deserved; it was a managerially effective and appreciated maneuver by the senior leader. Well done, Captain Nelson.

I'm grateful I learned how to "praise it forward" from the selfless example Brad set for us. I figured at some point he would finally break down and say, "Gee thanks, Colonel. I sure did nail that mission," or take some kind of kudos. But I learned that, by passing on all the acclaim, his strength shined through without ever having to say a word.

In civilian life, Brad's approach hit paydirt when I was coaching high school track kids. Teen athletes had learned to run to the limits of their human ability and inevitably won their races with fantastic out-of-body efforts. Five of my teams won Pennsylvania state championships in 12 years. Incredibly, my oldest son Joey earned All-American honors in the mile and appeared on the 2009 front cover of *Penn Relays* magazine.

Thrilled parents and fans graciously complimented the coaching staff, thinking we had been "amazing" at motivating or "spectacular" at training. That praise felt lovely and a little overwhelming to hear. Yet, here were grateful folks expressing heartwarming platitudes, and I wanted to respect the joy that prompted them. And of course, I wanted to praise it forward, so I would respond, "Mrs. Mancini, those kids powered the team to victory on their own legs today. You have four champion daughters because they come from an amazing family. Today I was just a thrilled spectator cheering them on from the stands."

Praising it forward after a rational plan has been executed to perfection completes the 360-degree circle. It expresses admiration for your teammates who propelled the group to surmount the odds.

Gifted leaders know that team members who are loved will continue to be the most stunningly resilient. And when the leader passes down the praise, the team members pass it down too.

Highlighting Others' Successes

Colonel (COL) Brad Nelson

Leaders, beware: Consistently passing the credit down the line is easier said than done. Human nature makes us want to say thanks, and, well, it feels good to receive a compliment. That's just natural.

But soon enough, channeling fame toward folks who work for you feels even better, especially when they are independently bolstering the brand. The next logical step is to give them lots of latitude to keep making the right moves.

By highlighting others, in reality, we empower ourselves, and we do it with subtlety and integrity. Rangers like CPT Nelson rely on their direct reports to get the job done, and they give them the latitude to do it. A good company commander stays accessible and ready to offer guidance, but he funnels the authority out to the edge where the action takes place. Then the platoon leader entrusts each of his four squad leaders. In turn, they entrust all eight team leaders with freedom of movement. When the first shot is fired, they know they will all need to direct their resources independently and without supervision.

Responsibility always lies at the top, but authority should flow down to the end-users who hold the lightning rod in their hands. Highlighting others' successes enriches your partners positively, and then it bounces the ball right back to you.

Achieving inspiration by investing in people who work for you makes this phrase more meaningful: "If you love something, let it go, and it'll come back if it's meant to be."

Putting Your Money on the Underdog

Master Sergeant (MSG) Arthur "Hard Art" Kakis

In one of his sessions, Simon Sinek (of TED Talk fame) speaks about the phenomenon of the gifted worker versus the hard worker. He notes hundreds of cases in which a hardworking achiever with nothing to lose outperforms a naturally talented competitor. If hard workers have the endurance to keep getting up no matter how many times they get knocked down, they eventually outlast the field.

I loved what U.S. Olympic runner Steve Prefontaine used to say: "If I can narrow the race down to pure guts, then there's no way I can lose."

"Hard Art" Kakis's mother would have never guessed polite young Arthur to be the one family member who would grow up to be a Ranger in combat, and one who would save lives in the U.S. Para Rescue and as a New York State Police SWAT officer.

This "nice" boy with a kind heart always spoke softly. He wasn't physically gifted with speed, coordination, and a flair for sports like his athletic peers, but he had a healthy size and was strong as an ox. Behind his gentle eyes burned a passion for being as extraordinary as Hercules. Neither Momma nor anyone else could have known what a kindhearted difference in the world this underdog would make. It's probably because Arthur refused ever to give up. When he made up his mind to learn a skill or pass a course, he committed to whatever it took to get the job done.

No obstacle stopped Arthur from doubling down with underdog determination to return and pass the test. And then some. His plot arc reads like Abraham Lincoln's rise to the White House. Every setback only served to spur him to dig deeper—to channel his personal Hercules and come back to reach the next rung on the ladder.

In 1988 on his first U.S. Army physical fitness test, Arthur ran the timed two-mile run in a sluggish 16 minutes. That barely passed the army standard and didn't come close to the Airborne, Ranger, or scuba diving standards he later nearly killed himself to achieve. Fast forward to 2020. Arthur has run five marathons and a pile of Spartan races.

In 1991, Arthur failed his Ranger School swim test in attempt #1, and he was rated a heat casualty risk by the medical team on try #2. But he nailed attempt #3 and earned his Ranger tab with flying colors. He then went on to complete Combat Diver, Combat Survival, and HALO Free Fall schools.

Like in the movie *The Guardian* with Ashton Kutcher, Arthur needed to tread water for 40 minutes to make it into Para Rescue school. Unfortunately, on his first try, he came up a couple of minutes short and was sent home. He returned with a new resolve and vanquished the task on the next cycle. Five years of training later, he lasted the 2.4-mile open water swim and finished the Iron Man Triathlon in Lake Placid. And he was aqua-awesome enough to anchor his Para Rescue team for 19 more years.

Arthur's top three rules were:

"Building people up beats knocking them down every time."

"Consider junior team members' fresh ideas."

"Lead through example, not by fear."

These work great—whether it's for the Stokes[7] rescue basket or the office in-basket.

Whether we're talking about businesspeople, the military, or healthcare providers, the person you are at a young age—or what happens on the first try—does not limit who you might become.

Business athletes learn from their mistakes and adjust to make sure they won't make the same ones again. They focus on developing a leadership style by observing and taking notes on how to do better when their time comes.

---

[7] A Stokes basket is a metal wire or plastic litter widely used in search and rescue.

Protecting and Delivering

Master Sergeant (MSG) Arthur "Hard Art" Kakis

When it comes to extreme types of training, the hardest courses attempt to exceed realistic circumstances. True leaders who dare their trainers to "do their worst" do so because they want to eliminate the element of surprise in the field. They also want to experience the worst possible moment so they can know themselves better. In that place, they can affirm or adjust their own behavior.

Ranger School intentionally subjects candidates to the worst possible conditions they can deliver—along with deliberately little support. That way, among the surprises they may face on the frontline, self-awareness in chaos wouldn't be one of them.

As a young soldier in my platoon during Desert Storm, Arthur "Hard Art" Kakis earned his nickname because negative thoughts never seemed to penetrate his psyche. The challenging courses he sought rolled like movie credits. Already Airborne and Ranger qualified, he went after Combat Diver, Combat Survivor, HALO, and then the U.S. Air Force Para Rescue course to be eligible for an elite National Guard unit after active duty. Only Hawaii, California, and New York had Para Rescue units, so Arthur had to compete with a rich candidate pool even to get an attendance slot.

After completing the Para Rescue course, Arthur settled in New York State. There, he embarked on a dual career as Air

National Guard Para Rescue on Reserve during weekends and full-time New York State Police SWAT team.

The medical portion of the Rescue course was taxing and thorough. It included a prenatal rotation at the University of New Mexico Hospital where Arthur observed an array of high-risk pregnancies and deliveries from Albuquerque's population. He earnestly took to preparing for emergency delivery possibilities at the hospital and then returned with flying colors to a snowy upstate New York winter.

On Christmas Eve of 1999, the call came over the state police radio to respond to a pregnant woman in labor trouble. She needed to get to a hospital but was trapped in her West Chester house at 2:20 a.m. in the middle of a severe snowstorm. Roads were undrivable, and news reports warned everyone to stay in. Only emergency services were running.

That night, Arthur was covering for his married buddies like he always did on holiday shifts. He spun out to respond to the call alone. But black ice had turned the usual 10-minute drive into a treacherous 25 minutes, even driving in a powerful squad car equipped with chains.

On the way, Arthur learned from the dispatcher the pregnant woman's name was Leah, this was her second child, and her contractions had been coming every two minutes for the past hour. Three other people were in the house: baby sister, Dad, and Grandma. Thankfully, they could give her comfort as they waited for state police to rush her to the hospital. But as his cruiser skidded around the last corner a block away from the house, Arthur did the math on the contractions—the baby was coming *now*.

Arthur entered the house and was greeted at the door by three generations of a family ecstatic to see him. They took him straight up to the back bedroom. Leah was sitting semi-upright, panting, but bravely smiling for the benefit of her family. A look of relief flooded over her face when she saw the smiling state trooper walk in. Four out of the five people in the toasty house were determined to get Leah wrapped up and out the door to the hospital. But Arthur wasn't sure they'd be lucky. His "stunt driver" job could quickly turn into a "doctor" assignment that night.

First, he checked Leah's vital signs and confirmed that, yes, the contractions were coming steadily. No way could he risk a dangerously unpredictable ride with her contractions coming this fast. So Arthur announced, "There's not enough time to get you to the hospital," and then paused slightly, "so we're going to deliver the baby right here in this room."

Maybe his voice cracked a hair, maybe not. After all, state troopers, even well-trained ones, don't usually find themselves delivering babies on Christmas Eve. Leah caught her breath and understood. Grandma and Dad standing at the door were already onboard and asking what they could do.

"Folks, we're going to set the room and begin in twenty minutes," continued Arthur. At his direction, everyone ran around and pitched in to convert the bedroom into a birthing room. He mentally evaluated the danger level against the high-risk deliveries he'd seen at the Albuquerque hospital. Everything here was nearly normal—except for being trapped in at a house decorated for Christmas in the middle of a snowstorm.

Almost ready. Then they heard a knock on the door. An officer in a second patrol car had just arrived and was here to ascertain the status.

"We're delivering the baby here," answered Arthur, pulling the second patrolman into the house.

Now they were ready.

Leah looked up and asked Arthur, "Are you nervous?" It broke the tension when he contemplated the question with an embarrassed smile and answered, "Maybe a little bit." But with a house full of helpers and a state policeman leading the delivery, Leah came through like a lady Ranger. She delivered a healthy girl and named her Lucy.

Two decades later, Leah's family remains in touch with Arthur. Nineteen-year-old baby Lucy has grown up, and in August 2019, she and her mother attended Arthur's wedding in Rye, New York. Although Arthur is spending future Christmas Eves with his new wife Keylla in sunny Florida, his friends from the winter storm of 1999 were grateful he got to spend that one with them.

Who knows what kind of crazy situations leaders find themselves in, especially the ones not written in any handbook. Although the person you are when you're young doesn't define you, the way you handle an extreme situation while protecting others does. It could be delivering financial results in an economic storm or even delivering a healthy baby girl in a snowstorm.

But Nothing

Master Sergeant (MSG) Dale "Onion" Roberts

Have you noticed how enfranchising types of words like "yes" can build up your direct reports while disenfranchising words like "no" might tear them down? I have. Any "yes" answer to a question or clarification empowers the asker, whereas a "no" response tears the asker asunder.

And here's another word to consider: "but."

The three-letter word "but" is a nasty, negative-energy word that should be stricken from every leader's arsenal. The passive-aggressive insertion of "but" effectively erases all the laudatory remarks that preceded it. "Steph, you're doing a great job, ***but*** . . . ," and everything the boss said before the "but" is rendered meaningless, even disingenuous. If I were her boss, I would want Steph to know she's doing an amazing job.

In addition, that word "but" can drain the effervescence from any teammate who wants to win. I would even strike it from the business dictionary. "But" immediately earmarks the speaker as a criticizer and power grabber.

Luckily, the world is full of good people and motivators who choose to build people up and not poke holes at them. This approach builds powerful teams and sets a tone of diplomacy as well. In the best Winston Churchill voice I can muster, I say, "If someone makes a statement that's 90 percent erroneous, I shall find the words to compliment the 10 percent that is correct, and then quietly make my helpful point afterward."

Anytime students were tempted to say "but" in a sentence, our professor in a MIT marketing class suggested substituting the word "***and***." She conceded it's not an entirely accurate substitute, *yet* it's close enough. (See what I did there using "yet"?)

Imagine being a sixth-grade teacher and complimenting what a precocious pupil named Dale stated while steering him toward the right answers. The subject was rainfall in the continents. "Yes, Dale," the teacher said. "Antarctica is completely covered in ice, AND it's actually the world's driest continent." Success! Nobody trampled on little Dale's precocious nature, and he learned something. This happened to "little" Dale Roberts who grew up and became my radio telephone operator (RTO) in the Gulf.

In those years by my side, Dale remained every bit as precocious, always giving amusing answers to questions I posed, which absolutely delighted many of the younger soldiers and kept the spirit light. On our last night in Desert Storm, I threw him a trivia question when I needed to pick a squad to run to the supply area and grab a fresh set of newly arrived desert camouflage uniforms. Thankfully, the army was finally replacing the filthy unies we had been wearing for 45 days. Charcoal residue from the chemical protective gear—called MOPP suits—we wore while crossing into Iraq covered our uniforms in a filmy black soot. We looked and smelled bad.

We'd be getting a new set of desert camo uniform (DCUs) just in time to return home looking clean and professional.

The distinctive-looking DCUs were the U.S Army's original desert uniform, and were dubbed "chocolate chips" in honor of the randomly placed black dots among the sandy shades of color in the pattern that an artist must have thought existed in the Arabian desert. Chances are good he never visited. Or perhaps, in 1990, the army still believed the color black was compulsory in any camouflage silhouette, even if no black could be seen in the 3.5 million square miles of sand surrounding us. Why black was chosen is still a curiosity.

With 30 of us gathered after evening chow, I had decided to throw out a trivia question to Dale. I wanted to break a tie to determine if it would be members from 2nd squad or 3rd squad to run over and get the new duds. If my Onion gave me the correct answer, then 2nd squad would go; if his answer was wrong, then 3rd squad would get the chore.

At almost 2100 hours (9 p.m.), it was dark except for a small bonfire around which the entire platoon planted itself. Everyone had executed 32 straight successful night patrols in enemy territory and spirits were high. This evening, we had the chance to relax and reward the men for a job well done.

Here's how it went. "Dale, who wrote the U.S. Constitution?" I posed the question to him in front of the men. They were easily entertained by Dale's irreverent outlook on life and liked listening to the humor that would potentially come flying from his mouth.

Dale considered the question for a long second, and then said, "Hmmm, the guy who wrote the Constitution? Who cares? He's f-ing dead!"

The senior guys responded with thunderous laughter, and the junior soldiers were too embarrassed to laugh. I remained grave in order to egg him on further. "Yes, Roberts." (Using his last name meant I was serious.) "This famous founding father who gave us democracy did pass away a couple of hundred years ago, AND his message still lives on, which means it might be nice to remember his name." (I never liked to miss a chance to teach while having fun.) "His name was James Madison, and he was also our country's fourth president."

Nods of assent came from the crowd, still eager for more entertainment from Dale. I could see the scene had turned into a spontaneous Ranger teaching moment, so I continued. "Okay, I'll give you another chance, Dale. I know you've heard of Shakespeare who wrote lots of world-famous plays. Just name any major character from one of his plays."

"Wow," said Dale. "You're giving me a second chance after I bolo'ed the first one . . . thanks." This teachable moment was good.

"Okay, sir, I do have a response."

The boys in the platoon sat up and inched closer to listen intently to the next five words out of Dale's mouth. He broke out in a crazy grin and said, "Sir, they're f-ing dead too!"

Immediately, Chesty Cardenas from 1st squad ran up to tackle him, pinning him in 30 seconds. Everyone else cracked up. Then those in the 3rd squad got up and headed off to fetch our new uniforms. Dale, who I suspected knew the right Shakespeare answer all along, couldn't pass up the humor. He dusted himself off and joined the boys. All was well with the platoon on our final night of the war.

A year later, Dale got a promotion to sergeant. Three years after that, he became a Ranger instructor, got promoted again, and served a full career. Twenty-five years later, he resumed his education at Fayetteville State University and earned academic honors along the way. Today, he is working toward a master's degree to top off his double major in business and accounting.

A turning point in Dale's life happened when he gained the confidence to know he could be more than just a blunt instrument; he could be intelligent, too, and earn a college degree he grew up thinking was out of reach. He proved it wasn't. Maybe his "aha" moment came back in the desert when he realized his fellow Rangers encouraged his natural talents. Dale gained our admiration—no buts about it.

For business leaders wanting to encourage young bulls like Ranger Roberts, here's my best advice: Use nurturing words, put them in the spotlight when you know they can handle it, and be a safe harbor they can always trust.

Gathering from Great Sources

Desert Storm Rangers

> *Whenever I've been part of a group, I try to absorb the quality attributes that roll off the people around me. Serving in top-notch units is like spending every day in a leadership factory, and it has been splendid to soak it all in.*

Desert Storm became a proving ground for young leaders who would hatch long-lasting careers and make a real difference in the world. Many of those young leaders I'd spent seven months in the desert with, though I hadn't seen them since. It's only lately through social media that many of us have happily reconnected.

I like to think back to the leadership principles I ascribe to those leaders who made a big difference in Desert Storm. I share six of them here.

• • •

> *Your superpower can be empathy, likability, or connectability. (Call it whichever one!) If you genuinely project it, people will gravitate toward you for success.*
>
> – MG Bryan Owens

Major General (MG) Bryan Owens was a young captain in Desert Storm. He was a company commander who didn't need to show you he possessed intellect; you knew it when you spoke to him, and you liked him. He went on to earn two stars, first commanding the 82nd's Panther Brigade during the Katrina relief effort, then onto the post of Commanding General of U.S. Forces Alaska.

• • •

> *Seeking the best education possible plus always continuing to improve will swing the door to success wide open for you to step through.*
>
> – CPT John Haley

Captain (CPT) John Haley was a platoon leader and executive officer (XO) in the desert. He was a West Pointer and excellent athlete who once hit me so hard in the colonel's Frisbee football game that I didn't get up off the ground for 60 seconds. I enjoyed staring at the Saudi sky on my back until he extended a hand to pull me up.

Given his talents, John transitioned into corporate America seamlessly. A Ranger with an MBA from the University of Chicago is a deadly weapon in today's world. He now serves as the COO for a healthcare company in Texas.

• • •

> *God-given talents from one realm of the arts will always be appreciated by those in another. Share them freely, and the fates will remember you fondly.*
>
> – SSG Paul Carr

Staff Sergeant (SSG) Paul Carr grew up on the south side of Dublin, Ireland, and his "da" taught him to sing Irish ballads at the local pub. As a 19-year old dual citizen, he enlisted in the U.S. Army on a day when the only qualified official to administer the oath at the Embassy was our U.S. Ambassador to Ireland, Margaret Heckler.

Four years later, out in the desert where sounds carried far into the night air, he sang wistful renditions of "Wild Rover" and "Waltzing Matilda" while the boys in the squad cleaned their weapons or wrote letters to their sweethearts. Irish Sergeant Carr could lift men's spirits and make a "bonny" eve out of a desolate hole with no glens or mountainsides in sight.

On the last night of Desert Storm, hundreds of us had gathered outside Khobar Towers, the infamous high-rise in Saudi Arabia that would be bombed into rubble by a terrorist attack in 1996. On that peaceful night, we built a 30-foot-high bonfire to incinerate our discarded uniforms. I can still hear Sergeant Carr's voice over the blaze singing "Bonny Wood Green." He filled us with hope in great anticipation of returning home to our loved ones.

• • •

> *Embrace a leadership style that's genuine and positive. It doesn't matter if it's straitlaced or chicken-fried. If it's the real you, it'll be a hit.*
>
> – MAJ Glenn Bergeron

Major (MAJ) Glenn "Tigger" Bergeron brought home-cooked Louisiana leadership to his Delta Anti-Tank Platoon. In an Airborne light infantry battalion, you'd find an extra fourth company called D (or Delta) that had agile vehicles with rocket firepower. Delta Company platoons consisting of four TOW-mounted Humvees and a gun truck each were assigned throughout the battalion to slice out their firepower to the A, B, and C companies. We loved knowing Tigger's platoon was nearby to deliver bunker-busting rockets when we needed them in the clutch. Solid young officers led our Delta platoons and then moved on to important roles. Fifteen years later, Tigger commanded a battalion taskforce close to his heart and home recovering from Hurricane Katrina.

• • •

A three-point recipe for job success:
character that's morally straight, culturally aware, and physically fit.
A three-point recipe for job satisfaction:
a diversity of tasks, working with partners, and making life enjoyable.

– LTG John Deedrick

Lieutenant General (LTG) John Deedrick was a young six-foot-five lieutenant and already a rising star of the Delta Company officers in the desert during Desert Storm. He had done a bang-up job as a line platoon leader, Delta Company platoon leader, and then exec officer.

Returning home, he added a Green Beret tab to his Ranger tab. Over the next 20 years he commanded elite warfighters up through the ranks and successfully deployed to the Global War on Terror. He completed his command of U.S. 1st Special Forces Command and was just selected for his 3rd star to join the Afghanistan command.

LTG Deedrick's recipes for job success and job satisfaction should appeal to the piece of Special Forces Ranger in all of us.

• • •

Make an incredible first impression whenever you start running with a new pack. Strength and loyalty are rewarded by real performers, and they will accept you as one of their own.

– LTC Chris Chesney

Lieutenant Colonel (LTC) Chris Chesney wasn't even infantry but managed to be a great infantry story. Chris was our battalion chemical officer (and a Ranger!) who had done such a steadfast job on the colonel's staff that he was rewarded with a dream offer —command of an Infantry Delta Company platoon. Maybe he should have taken it, he says; we would have loved to have him.

On the other hand, it turned out that advancing his expertise in nuclear biological and chemical warfare proved superbly valuable for the U.S. Army. He was selected as commander of Pueblo Depot to dispose of 750,000 chemical munitions as the U.S. led the way in complying with the OPCW Treaty to destroy chemical warfare weapons worldwide.

Today, LTC Chesney serves as the deputy superintendent of Homeland Security/FEMA for Domestic Preparedness. Hooah, Chemical Ranger!

Grabbing bits of best practices and success philosophies here and there can give you an excellent collection of treasures to build on. Paying attention to what works and what you love about your colleagues gives you a powerful menu to choose from. From that, you can form your own unique management philosophy.

As long as you pay attention.

Guts, Smarts & Love Epilogue

Theory of Evolution

Guts, Smarts & Love chronicles the evolution of bright young men (and as of 2015, women, too) with the most incredible potential in the world. They desire to transform into machines of high performance, making themselves the strongest they can be, honed to a razor's edge in preparation for the most significant challenge of humankind—surviving combat while leading soldiers.

Trained for battlefield engagement, and with fiery success in hostile environments on their resume, Rangers and other elite soldiers are poised to lead their allies into the world of global business and adventure. The stories in this book provide a first-hand glimpse of Rangers in action and the mindset that serves them well into the future—far from the sounds of gunfire and explosions of mortar overhead.

Understanding life's most urgent needs woven into the fabric of foreign lands—then bringing it home to share—could easily spark success when developing a business team or just spreading the spiritual beauty of travel.

Surviving combat requires innovation skills and produces the ancillary benefit of learning diverse cultures. This can very well nurture the desire to lead globally minded people to achieve just about anything.

Proudly serving as a Ranger on Airborne duty, I tried to influence young lives in positive ways. At the same time, I developed a limitless curiosity about the world and its wonders. My interest in understanding different cultures then generated the spark to travel the globe and collect meaningful and poignant stories I love to share.

So what? Well, friends, the challenges we've had in the crunch of duty convey experiences that folks might find insightful or feel-good or simply entertaining. Any of those work for me. They've come with a collegial desire to spread mini-leadership experiences as far beyond the battlefield as I could find—into the everyday life of high-performance pursuits and business.

I hope this book had a similarly positive effect on the lives of curious minds who might like to know what's "out there" and add it to their personal growth. My final mission as a Ranger has been to share these stories of the guts, smarts & love of leadership—minus the hunger, suffering, and gunfire it took to figure it out.

Rangers Lead the Way.

Acknowledgments

To country music recording artist Jessie G, who was inspired to write the song "Army Ranger" because she knows firsthand what it means to wait for her man with the toughest job in the world to come back home. Thank you for your support of Rangers everywhere.

To Charlie Company and the Red Falcon Scouts of the 82nd Airborne—my lifelong friends and heroes.

I must thank the people of greatest importance and support to me throughout life, and not merely this project—my family and closest allies, who all believed there to be some spark of brilliance when I wasn't nearly as sure. To the father figures in my life who have molded me—my track coach, my Tang Soo Do instructor, my uncle Frank who taught me carpentry one measurement and one cut at a time, my first commanding officer,

. . . and of course my father—known by my family as Pop-Pop—the penultimate patriarch of wisdom, education, and integrity. Everyone should be so lucky.

To my coaching partner and idol, Coach Tom Kennedy, and the several hundred young athletes I've coached—you all know that I cherish every track meet, wrestling match, volunteer event, cool-down conversation, and every "SAT Pizza night." I would never have had the strength to run my own Masters All-American races without the reserves I drew from your grit and love over the years.

To my three best friends and world traveling buddies, my sons Dustin, Jake, and Joey, each of whom have bested 40 countries so far in their young lives, two of whom serve the USA today as army officers. It's been me who has been lucky enough to sit back and watch their unique bursting brilliance: parleying in Chinese at the Beijing markets, shark diving in Capetown while I was seasick green, or climbing Mt. Cotopaxi in Ecuador at the age of 11.

To my wife Domenica, who has been by my side during this worthy project, while I stayed up with the light on, rummaged through the fridge during late nights, was on the road to visit men of honor, and wrote for quiet days in a row. Thank you. I love you.

And lastly, for the heroes and their families in the pages of the book who shared their stories with the world.

Index

A

accepting the unexpected, 293–294
accountability
  as a core principle, 36
  importance of, 225–226
"acknowledging," in Ranger Creed, 3, 71
acquisitions, mergers and, 298
actions, fluidity of, 284–286
active leadership style, passive leadership style *vs.*, 128–131
advantage, pressing the, 44–46
advice, giving, 159–163
advisors, 159–163
after-action report, 304
Ali, Muhammad, 318
architect personality, 155–158
asymmetric challenges, solving, 143–144
authenticity, in leaders, 295–297
authority, responsibility and, 326

B

belief in your leader, importance of, 309–313
best practices
  as a core principle, 36
  documenting, 136–138
  importance of, 343
Beyond Guns and Steel: A War Termination Strategy (Caraccilo), 49
blazing the trail, 87–97
boldness, 21
The Book of Lists 2019, 153
brand, creating mystique for your, 268–274
Brazil, worker rights in, 290
bridging the gap, 47–49
brotherhood, 76
business momentum, 183

C

call, answering the, 63–64
capitalizing on opportunities, 313–314
Caraccilo, Dom
  Beyond Guns and Steel: A War Termination Strategy, 49
Carnegie, Dale, 322
celebrating life, 37–41
certifications
  importance of, 73–76
  leveraging, 177
challenging times
  avoiding, 287–289
  facing, 172–174
charts, assessing performance using, 282–283
coaching, art of, 259
cohorts, merging into established, 83–86
comeback stories, 178–179
comfort zone, stepping out of your, 203
command climate, 164
common sense, being the commandant of, 27
competing, for what you want, 260–264
connecting, with your team, 227–230
content-to-be-content, 167
continuity of care, for teammates, 274
cool heads, prevailing with, 54–58

counsel, giving, 159–163
creating
  organizations, 155–158
  personas, 187–189, 203
creativity, importance of, 243–245
credentials
  dedication to earning extra, 82
  importance of, 73–76
credibility
  earned, 14
  self-advocacy and, 154
crises
  avoiding, 287–289
  facing, 172–174
culture, units of, 27

D

debriefings, 98–100
decision-making
  applying wisdom during, 139–140
  doing what's right, 220–222
  weighing merits for, 259
dedication, to earning extra credentials, 82
delegating, 157–158, 292
disenfranchising words, 334
disruptions, solving, 286
diversification, in job roles, 132–133
doctrine, contributing to, 136–138
dominance, achieving, 309–313

E

education, importance of, 340
efficiency, maintaining in teams, 301–304
elite military forces, role of, 6
emergent leaders, 207–209
employees
  connection to finished product, 233–237
  learning from, 115–119
  motivating, 190–194
  nurturing, 278–281
  promoting, 110–114, 178–179, 197
  protecting, 217–219
  recognizing talent, 290–292
  See also teams
empowering teams, 265–267
"energetically," in Ranger Creed, 4, 241
enfranchising words, 334
evaluating
  performance using charts, 282–283
  return on investment (ROI), 246–247
events
  preparing for, 319–321
  volunteering for galvanizing, 316–318
experts/expertise
  authenticity and, 297
  recognizing, 290–292
extreme training, 316–318, 330–333

F

factionalism, confronting, 304
fallen, honoring the, 35–36
fast on your feet, thinking, 284–286
financial incentives, 248–249
finished product, employee connection to the, 233–237
first impressions, 120–122, 342–343
forward-thinking, 18
Freedom 1-3: An Army Ranger's Journey to True Freedom (Sheehan), 40

G

"gallantly," in Ranger Creed, 4, 185
gap, bridging the, 47–49
gifted workers, hard workers *vs.*, 327
go-to person, being the, 145–149
grassroots success, 322
greatness, achieving, 313–314

grit, inspiring, 22–26
grouping up, 83, 104
guidance, amplifying vague, 207–209

H

happiness, for others' successes, 61–62
hard workers, gifted workers *vs.*, 327
heroes
  emergence of, 172–174
  of your own story, 180–183
higher purpose, creating a, 305–306
high-level thinkers, 238
highlighting success of others, 325–326
honorable beliefs, 220–222
human side, 105–109

I

identifying needs, 238–240
impressions, first, 120–122, 342–343
improvisation, 231–232
incentives, 248–249
individual characters, cultivating, 27
industry purists, 297
ingenuity, 231–232
innovative mindsets, 206
inspiration, inviting, 141–142
inspiring grit, 22–26

K

killology, 250

L

ladder, mirror *vs.*, 220
leaders
  authenticity in, 295–297
  great *vs.* good, 125
  importance in having belief in your, 309–313
  low tolerance for inaction and fear by, 210–212
  managers *vs.*, 305
  protecting employees, 217–219
  as reliable sources, 125–127
  as teachers, 213–216
leadership
  bringing factions together, 298
  exercise in, 8
  transparency in, 17
leadership philosophy, 122
leadership styles
  active style, passive style *vs.*, 128–131
  combining, 267
  developing, 329
  embracing, 341–342
learning
  from great sources, 339–343
  new technologies, 175–177
  from personnel, 115–119
legacy, guaranteeing prestige of, 131
legends, birth of, 172–174
life, celebrating, 37–41
limitations, overcoming, 168–171
loyalty
  employees connected to finished product, 233–237
  from older employees, 179

M

managers
  conveying your value to, 180–183
  leader *vs.*, 305
marketing ourselves, 67–69
Meal Ready to Eat (MRE), 84
Medal of Honor, 173
mentoring, from the middle, 50–53
mergers and acquisitions, 298
Merritt, Rick, 1–2
midlevel thinkers, 238
mirror, ladder *vs.*, 220

mission statements, importance of, 275–277
moral leadership dilemmas, 171
morale, introducing workplace, 204–206
motivating employees, 190–194

N

National Basketball Association (NBA), 283
National Football League (NFL), 283
needs, identifying and addressing, 238–240
"never failing," in Ranger Creed, 3, 123
"no" answers, 334
nomenclature, 269
notoriety, 14
nurturing employees, 278–281, 338

O

Occam's razor, 139
omnipresence, 27
"on-mission," being, 28–34
opportunities, capitalizing on, 313–314
organizations, building, 155–158

P

passing down praise, 322–324
passive style, active style *vs.*, 128–131
path, knowing the right one to take, 77–82
pearls of advice, 101–104
peers, relating to your, 15–17
performance
  assessing using charts, 282–283
  rewarding high, 195–197
permission, assuming, 207–209
personal risk, choosing ROI over, 254–259
personas, creating, 187–189, 203
personnel. *See* employees
Pinto, Joe, 158
poking fun at yourself, 105–109
praise, passing it forward, 322–324
preferences, recognizing, 157
Prefontaine, Steve, 327
preparation, importance of, 319–321
pressing the advantage, 44–46
problems, avoiding, 287–289
promotions
  competition and, 264
  of personnel, 110–114, 178–179, 197
  preventing, 165–167
protecting
  in extreme situations, 330–333
  others, 21
public speaking, 153

R

Ranger Creed, 3–4
reactions, fluidity of, 284–286
"readily," in Ranger Creed, 4, 307
Reagan, Ronald, 289
realism, extreme training and, 330–333
rebuilding, 42–43
"recognizing," in Ranger Creed, 3, 9
relatability, 15–17
Renaissance man, 65–66
responsibility, authority and, 326
return on investment (ROI)
  choosing over personal risk, 254–259
  evaluating, 246–247
rewarding high performers, 195–197
right, doing what's, 220–222

S

sales channel leaders, 157
schadenfreude, 62
seizing the moment, 313–314
self-advocacy, importance of, 150–154
self-effacing approach, 17

setbacks, recovering from, 223–224
sharing talents, 340–341
Sheehan, Andy
  Freedom 1-3: An Army Ranger's Journey to True Freedom, 40
shout-outs, 322–324
Sinek, Simon, 327
social conscience, 171
social repercussions, fear of, 171
sources, learning from great, 339–343
Stokes basket, 329
strategies, having the brass to carry out, 198–203
subject matter experts, 115–119
sub-personas, 203
success
  highlighting of others, 325–326
  importance of philosophies of, 343
  marketing ourselves for, 67–69
  recipe for, 342
superpowers, 339
survival, positioning your team for, 18–21
synchronizing teams, 301–304

T

talents, sharing, 340–341
teaching, expanding relationships by, 213–216
team activities, 281
team identity, as a core principle, 36
team spirit, 281
teams
  connecting with your, 227–230
  continuity of care for, 274
  empowering, 265–267
  members poking fun at themselves, 105–109
  synchronizing, 301–304
  trust on, 135
technology
  learning new, 175–177
  using up-to-date, 69
thinking fast on your feet, 284–286
thinking outside the box, 143–144
trailblazing, 87–97
training, extreme, 316–318, 330–333
Tri-Deca, 158
trust, value of, 134–135
"turn it around," 43

U

unconventional, being, 143–144
underdogs, betting on the, 327–329
unexpected, accepting the, 293–294
uniqueness, of your brand, 268–274

V

value, conveying your, 180–183
vision, importance of having a, 306
volunteering, for galvanizing events, 316–318

W

walking the walk, 11–14
warning signs, for crises, 287–289
warrior mentality, 59–60, 250–253
warrior poets, 250–253
watching your six/back, 238–240
wisdom
  applying to problems, 139–140
  words of, 101–104
words of wisdom, 101–104
workers, gifted *vs.* hard, 327
workplace morale, introducing, 204–206

Y

"yes" answers, 334

Captain Joe Sacchetti

Captain Joe Sacchetti is a U.S. Army Ranger-qualified Paratrooper who served in Operations Desert Shield and Desert Storm in Iraq and was awarded the Bronze Star for actions in combat. After leading troops, he successfully transitioned to the business world. His 30+ years in sales and management have spanned the pharma and tech industries. A graduate of the MIT Sloan School of Business Executive Education program, Joe currently runs global channel sales for a California software startup.

A two-time USA Masters Track & Field All-American in the half mile, Joe escorted the Olympic torch as a teenager through his Pennsylvania hometown in 1980 on its way to Lake Placid, and he coached the 2014 Indoor Track High School National Champions at Cardinal O'Hara High School.

His website, www.ArmyRangeratMIT.com, and YouTube channel, ArmyRangeratMIT, highlight global business, travel, and leadership experiences from visiting 130 countries and learning to communicate in half a dozen languages. Joe is a proud father and family man.

Connect with Joe online at:

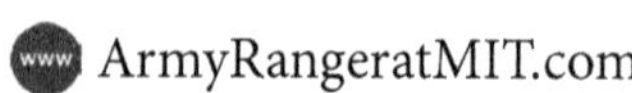

@ArmyRangeratMIT

ArmyRangeratMIT